Shapeshifters

BLACK GIRLS AND
THE CHOREOGRAPHY
OF CITIZENSHIP

Aimee Meredith Cox

DUKE UNIVERSITY PRESS   DURHAM AND LONDON   2015

© 2015 Duke University Press
All rights reserved
Printed in the United States of America on acid-free paper ∞
Typeset in Chaparral Pro by Westchester Publishing Services

Library of Congress Cataloging-in-Publication Data

Cox, Aimee Meredith, [date]
  Shapeshifters : Black girls and the choreography of citizen-
ship / Aimee Meredith Cox.
    pages cm
  Includes bibliographical references and index.
  ISBN 978-0-8223-5943-2 (hardcover : alk. paper)
  ISBN 978-0-8223-5931-9 (pbk. : alk. paper)
  ISBN 978-0-8223-7537-1 (e-book)
  1. African American girls—Michigan—Detroit. 2. Homeless
girls—Michigan—Detroit. 3. African American homeless
persons—Michigan—Detroit. I. Title.
  E185.86.C5898 2015
  305.23082'896073077434—dc23   2015005598

Cover art: Jamea Richmond-Edwards, *Power, as in Actualization*
(detail). Ink, charcoal, and mixed-media collage on board.
Image courtesy the artist, Jamea Richmond-Edwards, and
Galerie Myrtis.

This book received a publication subsidy from Duke University
Press's First Book Fund, a fund established by Press authors who
donated their book royalties to help support innovative work by
junior scholars.

Shapeshifters

Contents

Preface

Black youth are under siege in the United States, especially those living in and near poverty. When most people hear that my research focuses on the experiences of Black youth, they assume I am talking about boys and young men. The same people, regardless of their political affiliations, can rattle off the realms in which Black boys appear to be underperforming or failing to live up to the ideals of citizenship. These usually include references to police brutality and racial profiling, incarceration, the crisis in public education, absentee fathers, and, tangentially, sagging pants. Girls and young women,[1] if they are mentioned at all, are cited as either victims of the actions taken by Black men and boys or one of the primary reasons why Black men and boys have it so hard. Our failure to understand and, therefore, address the interlocking systems and entrenched policies that affect the entire diverse community of Black people in the United States has disastrous life-or-death consequences for the community's most vulnerable members: children and adolescents. Research in the social sciences on Black men and boys, media attention, and even the initiatives taken by our president have provided the general public with at least a language to talk about young Black men. Black girls, however, remain illegible. Don't get me wrong. I don't confuse visibility or sound-bite language with social value or even protection. But being held in a discursive frame, however misinformed, minimally establishes a place from which histories can be revised and stories told from the perspective of those whose lives are actually on the line. Being talked about at least means that you have a chance to speak back.

Shapeshifters: Black Girls and the Choreography of Citizenship is an attempt to find a way into the lives of contemporary young Black women in the United States, a language to talk about the factors that circumscribe their realities. This book is based on eight years of engagement with young women in Detroit, most of whom were residents of the Fresh Start Homeless Shelter (a pseudonym) for young women. Although the narratives here are embedded in the particular place of Detroit and the particular time period of 2000 to 2008, the themes that emerge and the events that resonate travel beyond spatial and temporal boundaries. *Shapeshifters* is an ethnography; it is not a chronological historical account of Black girlhood or a study of the impact of all the socioeconomic elements that affect contemporary young Black women. Ethnography's thick description allows Black girls to address the fullness of their lives, not just those aspects that could be defined as putting them at some ill-defined risk or as responsible for preventing their success.[2] Black girls, like all of us, create beautiful and fulfilling lifeworlds that are far more than reactions to the challenges they face. Yet *Shapeshifters* is set in a homeless shelter in arguably one of the most beleaguered U.S. cities. When I chose Fresh Start as a site, my aim was to understand how individuals positioned on the losing end of power differentials rooted in age, gender, sexual identity, social status, access to financial capital, city of residence, and race experience social citizenship in the United States. What I found was that the Black girls at Fresh Start shift the terms through which they are categorized as worthy or unworthy or as acceptable or disrespectable citizens through their own definitions of family, care, love, success, and labor, which reflect a belief that the ability to experience a creatively self-determined life is a basic human right—an entitlement.

The young women and I use *entitlement* here and throughout the book intentionally. *Entitlement* typically connotes greed and undeserved favor when used in conversations that mention Black or poor members of society. This is especially true when talking about low-income young Black women. We need only to refer to the Reagan-era discourse that continues to unjustly haunt welfare recipients who happen to be young, female, and Black. Entitlement as theorized by Janice—the central figure in this ethnography—and the other young Black women in this book, however, is an empowered statement that disputes the idea that only certain people are worthy of the rights of citizenship and the ability to direct the course of their lives.

This book covers a lot of thematic ground but is by no means all-inclusive. I organized the chapters based on the events that the young women at Fresh Start identified as most salient to their experience and most in need of further discussion. These are how Black girls theorize the struggles experienced by their mothers and other older women in their families; the problem of low-wage work; their bodies as the primary sites through which they experience social degradation, but also where they enact potentially socially transformative responses; the limited social scripts they are allowed to live within and speak from; the fluidity of love, sexual identity, and family as critical to how they establish networks of care; and the importance of performance and creativity to health and well-being.

Along with others who write about and work in organizations dedicated to supporting young Black women, I am stunned by the void in information and research on Black girls.[3] *Shapeshifters* adds to the small body of literature on Black girls that we do have while suggesting possible road maps for future research. The central theme of each chapter could warrant an entire book-length response or some concerted effort at further investigation. The experiences of the young women in this book beg qualitative and quantitative researchers, policy makers, educators, elected officials, creative artists, and Black girls themselves to latch onto even a single thread in these stories that they may pull out and weave into inquiries that afford Black girls the full rights, freedoms, and protections of citizenship.

Acknowledgments

This book has been in process since I was in fourth grade, when I wrote short stories and used images from *Essence* magazine to tell a familiar story of what it feels like to be a Black girl in the United States. *Shapeshifters* would have never come to be, however, if it weren't for the overwhelming generosity and fearless honesty of Janice and the other young women at the Fresh Start shelter. I owe this work to all of the young women in Detroit, and particularly the women and girls in the Brown family, who agreed to share their lives with me. I am also grateful to the staff and administration of the Fresh Start shelter. They worked tirelessly with the best intentions to make a space where none had existed for Black girls in Detroit. We loved, soared, failed, and tried our best together.

The first version of the manuscript took shape while I was a graduate student in the Anthropology Department at the University of Michigan. The Rackham Merit Fellowship and support from the Culture and Cognition joint program in anthropology and psychology allowed me to complete extended years of fieldwork in Detroit. I thank Larry Hirshfeld for believing in me and this research in my first year of graduate study. My dissertation chair, Andrew Shryock, encouraged me to trust the truth of the stories as they were revealed and was never anything less than enthusiastic about the importance of the work. As members of my dissertation committee, Kelly Askew, Ruth Behar, and Alford Young offered critical insights and were central to helping reshape my graduate research into this book. Rosemary Saari was and continues to be one of the most challenging and honest mentors I have ever had. She prodded me to remember that my relationships with the young women in this book were first and foremost about the interactions we had outside of the text and the theoretical frame. I would have been lost were it not for the sound advice that Rosemary gave me while I was the director of the Fresh Start shelter. Michael Baran, Jill Constantino, Karen Hebert, and Patricia Moonsammy kept me sane through all phases of my graduate study. In the weeks before my dissertation defense, Karen repeatedly drove the forty miles between Ann Arbor and Detroit to deliver by hand the hard copies of the chapters she so graciously helped edit.

I feel unusually lucky to have benefited from inclusion in a community of brilliant and compassionate scholar activists. I am indebted to the groundbreaking work and models of bold feminist ethnography of A. Lynn Bolles, Elizabeth Chin, Arlene Davila, Dana-Ain Davis, Faye Venetia Harrison, Joyce Ladner, Leith Mullings, and Gina Ulysse. John L. Jackson and Deborah A. Thomas played the multiple roles of sounding board, counselor, mentor, cheerleader, "real talk" critic, editor, and friend from the moment I entered the academy. Their practical wisdom always came from a place of thoughtful attention and love. My aim in work and life is to extend their generosity to my students and peers. They remind us all of the importance of the work we do and how it gets passed on to the next generation of curious minds. Dana-Ain Davis pulled me and this book through the most difficult times. Guthrie Ramsey always answered my frantic calls with the patience and sage reflections of a saint. Jafari Allen and Tukufu Zuberi frequently appeared at just the right moment with exactly what I needed to hear to remind me of my responsibility to tell these stories with love and grace.

The work of Jackie Brown, Cathy J. Cohen, Patricia Hill Collins, Dwight Conquergood, Angela Y. Davis, Michelle Fine, Nicole Fleetwood, Kyra Gaunt, Ruthie Wilson Gilmore, Brenda Dixon Gottschild, Steven Gregory, Farah Jasmine Griffin, dream hampton, Richard Iton, E. Patrick Johnson, Robin D. G. Kelley, Setha Low, D. Soyini Madison, Alondra Nelson, Imani Perry, Rebecca Wanzo, and Kevin Young was especially fortifying as I read and reread their words for inspiration during the latter stages of revision of this book.

I also belong to a community of artists, starting with but by no means limited to my friends and family at the Alvin Ailey American Dance Theater, some of whom knew this book was necessary before I did. I thank Vernard Gilmore, Lakey Evans Pena, and Wendy White Sasser for being my steadfast friends on and off stage. My writing was additionally invigorated by the creative work of Camille A. Brown, Rashida Bumbray, Invincible (Ill Weaver), Simone Leigh, Paloma McGregor, and Nina Angela Mercer.

Other scholars working in the field of girlhood studies as both practitioners and theorists offered consistent camaraderie. We are all indebted to their commitment to improving the lives of Black girls and enriching our understanding of their realities. I am immensely grateful for the sisterhood of Ruth Nicole Brown, Dana Edell, Alexis Pauline Gumbs, Carla Stokes, Salamishah Tillet, and Scheherazade Tillet, and I thank Kyra Gaunt, Zenzele Isoke, Nikki Jones, and Oneka LaBennett for writing about Black women and girls with great rigor and love.

The Department of African American and African Studies at Rutgers University-Newark gave me my first tenure-track job. Sterling Bland, Sherri-Ann Butterfield, Belinda Edmondson, Wendell Holbrook, Laura Lomas, and Beryl Satter were wonderful colleagues whom I continue to learn from in various ways.

My friends and colleagues at Fordham University understood this project and offered their unwavering support from my first day as a new faculty member at Fordham. Bentley Anderson, Jane Edwards, and Claude Magnum showed me the ropes and enriched my teaching and scholarship through example. Amir Idris and Irma Watkins-Owens used their compassionate leadership to guide me through the tenure process and the various last phases of *Shapeshifters*, all while indulging me in my endlessly annoying fears and concerns. Mark Naison read and commented on multiple drafts, often sending me texts that were longer than the passages he read. Mark Chapman invited me to speak about my work at his church in Hollis, Queens in New York. This event helped me rethink critical parts of the introduction and gave me hope that the book might have a hungry and receptive audience. Hugo Benavides and Aseel Sawalha in the Sociology and Anthropology Department, as well as Daniel Alexander Jones and Matthew Maguire in the Theatre Program, have also supported this project and found innovative ways to offer friendship and mentoring.

Multiple grants gave me the time, money, and/or immersion in intellectual communities necessary to write a book. The sources of these grants were the Rutgers Institute for Research on Women and Gender, the National Council for Black Studies (a Cutting Edge Gender Research Award), the School for Advanced Research, and Fordham University (the First Year Faculty Funding and Dean's Funding Awards). Receiving the Ford Foundation Postdoctoral Fellowship in my last year of revisions allowed me to complete the book and gave me access to a wide community of scholars working across disciplines. The Association of Black Anthropologists folded me into its network and gave me a platform for my work through my appointment as co-editor of *Transforming Anthropology* and through the Vera Green Publishing Award for my article on the Black-Light Project. The association will always be my academic family.

John Collins, Setha Low, and Jeff Maskovsky invited me to speak at the Graduate Center of the City University of New York as part of the anthropology talks series. The feedback I received helped me substantially revise chapters 2 and 4. Conversations I had after talks I gave at Eastern Illinois's Women and Gender Studies Conference and the Feminist Futures Conference at the University of Illinois at Urbana-Champaign were also fruitful in helping me give the book greater clarity. My students at Fordham in my Black Feminisms, Black Popular Culture, and The Poetics and Politics of Youth Performance courses inspired my approach to writing about the Move Experiment and the BlackLight project in the final chapter. I am honored to teach and learn from such brave young thinkers.

Ken Wissoker at Duke University Press is as kind as he is brilliant. It is impossible to imagine moving through this process without having him as a guide. Our communications emboldened my writing and invigorated me for the work yet to come as I write these acknowledgments. He and Jade Brooks seemed to care about *Shapeshifters* just as much as I did. For this, I am eternally grateful. The press's two anonymous reviewers pushed me to write with more force and authority while encouraging me to let the voices of the young women sing. Their comments were the perfect blueprint for revision.

Wherever I have landed, no matter how long or hard the fall, I have been uniquely blessed with a loving and forgiving family of friends to pad the descent and offer cover when I most needed it. In Detroit, Greg Hawkins and Zackary Brandt met me just as I was starting my fieldwork and attended my dissertation defense. In between, they cooked dinner for me almost every night and read the beginning of each new chapter. Courtney Dempsey Burkett and Adam Burkett and their families always made sure I felt at home no matter where I found myself. Petra Kuppers and Robin Wilson reminded me to dance as much as possible and write from the same place of joy and confidence that moved my physical body. Dimitri Mugianis, my dear friend and brother, has been a constant beacon in this work and in my life. His passion for justice and love of humanity are unparalleled.

My closest friends shared every defeat and triumph with me as I tried to bring the lives of the young women in *Shapeshifters* into print. Monica Barra and Tynesha McHarris, my sister in spirit and action, read drafts and offered invaluable insight. In too many ways to name, Tynesha kept the heartbeat of the stories alive while reminding me that truth telling is the most loving political work in which we can engage. In the very last days of copy editing, Philip McHarris provided much needed resources and encouragement to support the final push. I will always be grateful for their generosity. Bryan Epps and Daliah Heller were especially supportive and encouraging and offered levity and necessary distraction at just the right times; their friendship is revelatory. Nicole Fleetwood, my sister from Ohio, reminds me that our work is not separate from our lives—and if it is, we are doing the wrong work. Her presence allows me to know that it is possible to be in the academy but not of it; that we can be both compassionate and critical, and that we must chart ways of being in this space that honor the place from whence we came. Darnell L. Moore redefined friendship for me as he crossed what often appeared to be insurmountable mountains in search of new ways to offer unconditional love. I thank the universe every day that he lived only four doors down from me in Bedford-Stuyvesant, Brooklyn, so that he could literally come running if necessary.

My sister, Jennifer, to whom this work is dedicated, heard every story before it hit the page and read every word of this book. She demanded that I write better, smarter, and more courageously. My cousin, Jana Perry, grew up alongside me and was the first shapeshifter I knew. Her daughter, Joanna, portends what twenty-second-century shapeshifting has in store for us. We ain't ready. But we need to be. My aunts, the Wallace sisters, followed a trajectory of love, loss, pain, and self-proclaimed (the most important kind) victories, evolving from indefatigable girls in West Virginia to grown women who organized labor strikes, educated hundreds of people, raised strong children, and fought to keep laughter and celebration at the center of their experience. I only wish they had known earlier that the secrets they sought to protect us from were the fuel we needed to follow in and extend their footsteps.

Baye Wilson always provided comfort and space. His measured silences and rousing words, and his attention and strategic disregard, were orchestrated to create the optimum conditions for me to dream and create in the pages of *Shapeshifters* and the world beyond the work. I thank my parents, Larry and Mary Cox, for planting gardens and for encouraging us to be brave and kind above all else. I write because they made me believe that words are transformative and stories heal. I only hope they believe that all they gave and sacrificed was not in vain. We heard you. We hear you. We live by your grace.

Last of all, to my grandmothers, Bessie Cox and Mary Bethune Wallace—your lives are written here. Every word bears your light and ferocity.

PART I Terrain

Introduction

Blackout

If there had ever been another time that was this dark, this hot, I could not remember it. The itchiness of the sweaty fabric on the couches sent most of us to the floor. We sprawled out on our backs, faces to the ceiling we could not see. The sticky carpet hardly offered more relief, but it felt good, I think, to take up more space. From the battery-powered boom box, the news commentator told us we were in the middle of what would become known as the Great Northeast Blackout of 2003. It had spread from the East Coast to parts of Ohio and Michigan, he reported, and Detroit was just one of several major urban centers covered in darkness.

"Who's that? Y'all heard him before." I could make out Janice's[1] silhouette as she propped herself up on her elbows and sent her question in my direction. Her generally clear, deep voice was shaky.

I imagined the newscaster from the AM radio station sounded caught in time to these young women, who were between sixteen and twenty years old. His tone was official, uninflected, more standardized than an automated recording. The unfamiliarity of his voice added to the sense that we were in the middle of something we would be wrong to assume we understood, an event whose outcome we could not necessarily predict, even when the lights came back on.

"Yeah, he sound real old. Like he just creaked his ass out a coffin." Danielle's remark won a few uneasy laughs.

I knew this was my cue and that I was expected to say something ex-
planatory, since we were in the middle of playing out our usual script:
someone expressed a veiled fear, someone else made a joke, and I offered
information that the group either pretended to find comforting or tore
apart, depending on the circumstances. But I was too hot and too tired
from spending all day figuring out an emergency blackout plan with the
agency's new executive director (a plan that appeared to be failing) to step
into my role. I suspected that my silence, my lounging on the floor, and
my hiked-up skirt were inappropriate for the director of the Fresh Start
Homeless Shelter (a pseudonym) for girls especially during a crisis. But
for now I hoped that we could just be content to not know together.

It was already past 2:00 in the morning. Some birds were chirping,
which made it feel even more like a temporally suspended dark day. Someone asked for a story, a scary one to fit the current mood. Clearing my
throat, I sat up and turned the flashlight on under my chin to illuminate
my face, the way it's been done in countless campfire dramas, and began
a meandering tale. Midway into a story that included mysterious woods
and alien abductions, Janice stopped me.

"If aliens dropped down here, this be the last place anybody would be
checking for," she said. The choir fell in line behind her.

"Shit!

"A homeless shelter?"

"What? Detroit?"

"What?"

"You know that's right."

"Anyway," Janice continued, "the aliens would come in and be like,
'They should have told us this is where they keep all the Black girls. Never
mind, let's go back to planet Zeptron,' or whatever."

With that, my story was over. Our bubbling anxiety and fantasy talk
of alien abductions had at least kept us buoyant. Now the possibility of
our intergalactic undesirability deflated us back to the mundane logistics
of Black girl reality. I turned the flashlight back on and scanned the room
to see who was still awake. The remaining girls who were uninterested
in making the walk back to their hot rooms by flashlight whispered to
one another as they stretched out on the floor. Restless and no longer
afraid, Janice shifted from position to position on the carpet. Tina's fingers played in her hair, making long shadows on the wall that looked like
alien tentacles preparing to snatch Janice's brain. I kept that thought to
myself, though.

This brief dialogue, seemingly unremarkable at first, had taken a turn that was not unusual among the residents of the Fresh Start Homeless Shelter and its independent living program. When Janice and the other residents considered the meaning of events, their commentary was regularly informed by what it feels like to live in bodies that are given multiple unstable identifications. These include, as I had just heard, blackness, femaleness, youth, nationality, and poverty. But these categories are less important than what they signify about discrepancies in the value of human life. As girls who were also Black and homeless, the residents of the Fresh Start shelter were constantly reminded of where they did and did not belong, how they should and should not be seen, and the consequences for stepping outside of the boundaries meant to define and contain them as poor Black girls. How they experience their lives is thus "inherently political,"[2] even while their politics are inaccessible in the narratives that situate them in various, often competing, discourses. Despite these factors, the Fresh Start residents see themselves as more than either examples of resiliency or social casualties.

I write this introduction to the chapters that follow with a renewed urgency, as citizenship and the nature of the rights that it is grounded on are fiercely fought over in legislative battles and court decisions with life-or-death consequences for young Black women like the ones who appear in this book. On the public stage of mainstream and social media and in the private spaces of intimate conversations, inclusion in the U.S. collective—with the attendant protections, resources, and access that constitute social citizenship—accrues multiple and conflicting meanings. It is midsummer 2013, and the diverse U.S. population at large is debating the immediate and long-term significance of acts such as draconian laws restricting women's reproductive rights, suppression of voters' protections, drastic cuts to unemployment assistance, gun laws that favor perpetrators and create victims, and neoliberal processes involved in public education reform. Black girls and young women living in or close to poverty are the population most adversely affected by the implementation of these laws and reforms. Their vulnerabilities, however, are concealed by their displacement from the dialogues that swirl around them, even as these dialogues are grounded (on all sides of the debate) on intractable assumptions about Blackness, youth, gender, sexuality, and class.

Our contemporary concerns are not unprecedented, but they are unique in that they aggressively belie the belief that racism has been in decline since the election of Barack Obama to the presidency. The nation-state known as the United States of America was built on the labor and exploitation of descendants of Africans and has been continuously legitimized through citizenship defined primarily by the racist and misogynistic exclusion of all but wealthy white male landowners. The more recent regressions represent only the latest innovations in ways to perpetuate inequalities in and through the state. The setting of this ethnography is the Fresh Start Homeless Shelter and its transitional living program in Detroit, Michigan, between 2000 and 2008.[3] Yet the larger dynamics of interlocking privileges, visibilities, powers, and inchoate resistance signal consequences that extend beyond the city of Detroit and the first eight years of the twenty-first century.

The young women from Fresh Start had yet to experience Barack Obama's presidency, but they had an intuitive inkling of what the aftermath of such an event might be, given the ravages of Hurricane Katrina and the stories that disaster made plain. The early twenty-first century anxieties that pulsate around the residents of Fresh Start like a song's rhythmic refrain echo the tensions that catalyzed the shelter's emergence in 1987, late in the presidency of Ronald Reagan. Contemporary characterizations of young Black women take shape within narratives about educational reform, urban renewal, social service policy, and the academy that are generally invested in identifying the source of urban ills and contemplating their possible solutions. In all of these cases, the stories that attract mainstream attention are those that characterize the lives of Black girls as dysfunctional sites on which reform and improvement strategies should focus. Yet even these narratives are few and far between, as our national consciousness around what it may mean to be Black, young, and exceptionally vulnerable is narrowly focused on Black boys.

I want to stay attuned to both the danger and the futility of placing Black youth in discursive predicaments where they must compete for space at the bottom.[4] The bleak statistics about both Black girls and boys reflect the material outcomes of an encompassing devaluation of blackness and the ravages of capitalism as they play out through the nexus of age, race, and gender.[5] Black girls and boys experience these social consequences differently. But in identifying methods for protecting and improving their lives, establishing hierarchies of inequity between them obscures the broad white supremacist terrain that inflects their shared social worlds. However, the stories of young Black women that I present in this book demand that we consider why a sympathetic liberal public will readily mobilize to protest the death or threat to life of Black boys, while the plight of Black girls fails to garner a comparable response.[6] There is a history here. There is a historical project of recovering the pathologized Black community and the shamed Black family through the reclaiming of a fictionalized, normative Black masculinity inscribed on the bodies of Black boys—alive and, therefore, dangerous, slowly dying, or efficiently killed.

President Obama's My Brother's Keeper initiative is an example of the self-consciously anxious political moves that use a rhetoric of failed Black masculinity, primarily evinced by tropes of absentee fathers, to demonstrate the federal commitment to rescue the Black community from itself while effacing the state policies that devastate Black life.[7] In a critique of this initiative to "build ladders of opportunity and unlock the full potential of boys and young men of color," Mary Anne Case points out that girls and women are not only excluded from the capital investment in their futures but receive "less attention and encouragement" as they continue to primarily "be defined by their relationship to men."[8] The Black girls in this ethnography are aware of the statistics and the policies that prevent them from being seen as more than minor accomplices in the at- and high-risk construction of Black boyhood, and even they often demonstrate a worrisomely greater concern about the well-being of boys and men than about their own.

Shapeshifters: Black Girls and the Choreography of Citizenship is unapologetically many things, just like the young women who appear in its pages. Ultimately, however, it is a book that presents an analysis of the contradictions and failures of twenty-first-century U.S. citizenship through the critical perspective of Black girls. *Shapeshifting* describes how young Black women living in the United States engage with, confront, challenge, invert, unsettle, and expose the material impact of systemic oppression. Shapeshifting is an act, a theory, and, in this sense, a form of praxis that—although uniquely definitive of and defined by Black girls—reveals our collective vulnerabilities. In the context of a homeless shelter in postindustrial Detroit, *shapeshifting* most often means shifting the terms through which educational, training, and social service institutions attempt to shape young Black women into manageable and respectable members of society whose social citizenship is always questionable and never guaranteed, even as these same institutions ostensibly encourage social belonging.

In the pages of *Shapeshifters*, Black girls speak the truth of their lives, opening up much-needed theoretical space for interrogating how power, value, and protection are conferred and refused based on corporeal readings of individual behaviors, and how those processes are enacted on the bodies of young Black women. The experiences of the residents of Fresh Start both inside and outside of the shelter establish the narrative arc of this book. Their reflections on why their lives unfold in the ways they do, as well as the decisions they make and the actions they do and do not take because of this, are the basis of my theoretical frame. Yet, although I center Black girls in *Shapeshifters*, I do not consider Black girls units of analysis I need to romanticize to counter negative representations. Black girls are not the problem. Their lives do not need sanitizing, normalizing, rectifying, or translating so they can be deemed worthy of care and serious consideration. I ask that instead of approaching their stories as narrative puzzles to be solved by superficially affixing them to the theoretical perspectives developed through Black feminism, queer theory, youth cultural, and girlhood studies, for example, we explore their potential to inform and transform theory and, thereby, its ripple effect on policy and material realities. I ask that instead of a one-sided reading of Black girls, we open ourselves up to a conversation with them with the full expectation that we will, at least, be changed. Ultimately, through these individual shifts, perhaps we can develop collective strategies for living fuller, self-defined lives without the threats of extinction that attempts at living in this way generally incur when you are young and Black.

The interlocutors I call into the conversation with the Fresh Start residents cover and cross various disciplines, genres, locations, and time periods and fall into the messy, overlapping categories of scholar, activist, and artist. I employ them to talk with and about young Black women because their work helps formulate a liberatory politics that begins but does not end with Black girls. Although I have confidence in this dialogue, I am humbled by the limits of the work and am grateful for the reminder of the anthropologist Jafari Allen that "scholarly work does not create everyday resistance within and survival by the most multiply vulnerable among us, but it can give light to it—helping expand recognition of those sites as legitimate political expression" (2012, 221). Allen's words also point to the charge that Cathy Cohen persuasively presents in her game-changing article, "Deviance as Resistance." Addressing interdisciplinary African American studies scholars, Cohen advocates for research agendas that focus on the everyday politics of the most marginalized members of the African American community to determine "how the normalizing influences of the dominant society have been challenged, or at least countered, often by those most visible as its targets" (2004, 30). A centering of infrapolitics (Scott 1985) or politics from below (Kelley 1994) as taken up and refined by Cohen is what I intend to be the heart of *Shapeshifters*, as well as its theoretical entree, method of investigation, and ethical core. Working from this starting point, I situate both the mundane and seemingly spectacular occurrences in the lives of the Fresh Start residents as a challenge to the myths that construct and uphold social citizenship in the United States. Thus, the focus on young Black women here stems from the imperative to interrogate how categories of race, gender, and age are created and re-created to undergird systems of power and establish the social construction of Black girls and Black girlhood.[9]

Cohen's directive summons significant interlocutors to this ethnography. Interrogating structures of power as a part of developing new ways of identifying and mobilizing Black politics is work that has been undertaken by Black feminist scholars and activists (Giddings 1984; hooks 1990 and 1999; Collins 2000), particularly Black feminist anthropologists (Bolles 1996; Harrison 1997 and 2008; Mullings 1997; D. Davis 2006; Ulysse 2007) and queer theorists (Muñoz 1997; Allen 2011; R. Ferguson and Hong 2011; Judith Halberstam 2011; J. Jack Halberstam 2013). The rigor of their analyses matters most in the context of *Shapeshifters* for the book's potential to conceptualize and enact oppositional politics that redefine "the rules of normality that limit the dreams, emotions, and acts of most people." (Cohen 2004, 12). Janice and her peers present alternatives and possibilities for living in ways that honor individual humanity and, like these radical scholars, long for the vital link that can transform living on the fringe and working outside of normative ways of life to the center of a transformative politics. These shapeshifting young women reveal the destructive nature of normative ways of life that valorize white supremacy, patriarchy, and modes of production that render young Black women at best superfluous and at worst valueless. Yet, when it seems too easy to write their actions off as failures or ineffective reactions to failure is precisely when an oppositional lens is most necessary. In other words, Black girls should not be objects of critique and/or worry but should be seen as the vanguard of a political movement capable of building and creating what neoliberalism dehumanizes and destroys.

Missing the Middle

Although there are many narratives in *Shapeshifters*, Janice's is the hub from which most events and stories originate and where they intersect. It is Janice's analysis of the "missing middle" that also lays the foundation for the concept of shapeshifting that is developed across settings and enacted at various moments in the text. Janice uses the term *missing the middle* to describe the tendency on the part of the adults she encounters in her daily life (including the Fresh Start program coordinators, teachers in her public school and training program, and caseworkers) to view her and the other young Black women in the shelter as stagnant statistics instead of human beings. In this case, as Janice explained to me, the middle includes:

> The way we always have to think about how other people see us and compare it to how we see ourselves. I mean it is really who we are and what we need to do on a daily basis to survive being Black and female in this world. But, I mean, not just surviving like getting a job and getting a degree, but surviving by holding onto our truth. The truth you don't see on TV or in the papers like you should. They miss the middle because they are always focused on the outside and making assumptions about who we are. There's a lot in the middle, but who's trying to hear that?

For Janice, the missing middle is the thick, complex, richly textured, and uncategorizable aspects of the lives of young low-income Black women, and that is what constitutes their "truth," or their legibility as fully human. Her words convey a double consciousness that is both aware of external assumptions made about Black girls and attuned to the fact that Black girls create their own measures of success, health, and happiness. One of the key analytic gains of Black feminism has been what Janice calls missing the middle—or, in other words, compelling representations and theorizations of the lives of Black girls to place Black girls experiences "at the center of analysis" (Collins 2000, 44). Missing the middle is a statement about intersectionality, multiple jeopardy,[10] and the peculiar position of Black girls in the United States. Missing the middle speaks to Black girls' understandings of their rights as citizens and how other people abuse these rights. The missing middle is grounded in Black girls' identification of the complicated interplay of external and self-evaluations fueled by the representational work of labels and tropes hurled at them from multiple points of origin. One of these points is the nexus of intersecting discourses erected around youth culture, girlhood, low-income black communities, and social mobility in the United States.

Janice is the central figure in *Shapeshifters* for several reasons. She was one of the first young women I met when I came as a volunteer to the larger social service organization, Give Girls a Chance, that housed the Fresh Start Shelter, and we quickly developed an intimate bond. At the time, she was a participant in the Community Outreach Program, but she would eventually participate in all three Give Girls a Chance programs, which gave her an experiential overview of the entire organization.[11] In addition, Janice's family included her younger sister Crystal and an extended network of female cousins who provided an accessible and willing group of young Black women who were surprisingly diverse in terms of aspirations and life philosophies although they were from the same biological family. As I became closer to Janice and her teenage sister and cousins, I also got to know her grandmother, her mother, and her aunts. The adult women in the Brown family provide a historical grounding for the stories of the girls.

The Problem with Youth: Youth Culture and Girlhood Studies

Popular social commentary and academic research on children; youth; adolescents; teenagers; the Me Generation; and Generations X, Y, and now Z[12] reflect the relationship between the ideas and images used to categorize young people and larger social trends, economic anxieties, and political agendas. The concepts of *children* and *childhood* as an identity and a period of time distinct from adulthood emerged as early as the fifteenth century. According to Tracey Skelton and Gill Valentine, the "mythical condition" of childhood grew and became part of the collective consciousness in the nineteenth and twentieth centuries, as mass schooling was introduced in society (1998, 3). With the rise of industrial capitalism and the expansion of the time thought necessary for children to be engaged in schooling, the transitional period of adolescence was born. Adolescence, as a purely distinct and conceptually loaded period apart from childhood that is similar to other social categories, has been variously called imaginary, made-up, and invented due to the diverse ways in which definitions of adulthood[13] have been manipulated to fit the interests of dominant ideology and the prevailing economic structure.

Childhood—encompassing a younger age range than adulthood and connected to the ideas of domesticity, motherhood, and safety—has been crafted as a time for growth and development, for innocence and dependence. In this vein, children are perceived as being in need of care and attention that are grounded in the intentions of guiding and protecting. Adolescence, in contrast, "was invented to create the space between the innocence of childhood and the realities of adulthood" (Skelton and Valentine 1998, 4). During the early twentieth century, adolescence as a monolithic and slippery category of unidentified youths started to cleave into different subcultures, according to the work of researchers concerned with tracking and ensuring what they saw as proper transitions into adulthood. Stanley Hall (1904) demonstrates the early concern with defining the differences among young people, so that the differences are correlated to perceived threats posed by nonwhite youth to the social order.

It is fair to say that research on adolescence has largely been written from the perspective of fear. Hall's work betrays the tension of straining to protect middle-class values by controlling and containing the working and lower classes, with the delineated boundaries of adolescence a critical part of how value is attributed and social responsibility assigned or abdicated. Throughout the history of academic work on youth, the idea of control and containment is a recurring theme. Youth increasingly represent middle-class anxieties, and the particular subpopulation of youth in need of systematic subjugation changes to meet the prevailing embodiment of racialized fears and the concern with enforcing class- and gender-based boundaries. Thus, the category of adolescence, like those of race and gender, is essential to defining and limiting citizenship. Black girls are, therefore, forced to confront their supposed inferiority and deviance on multiple intersecting and continually shifting social planes—adolescence being one of the critical places of intersection. There are overlapping and mutually reinforcing similarities between the ideologies surrounding young people and the practices enacted to control them and the ideologies used to monitor and contain the lives of Blacks (especially Black women) through codes of respectability and boundaries of exclusion. These intersections complicate the ways in which young Black women mediate experiences in the public and private spheres.

The field of girlhood studies has questioned the changing nature of citizenship for young women who are defined primarily by their status as both female and adults in the making. Scholars across disciplinary orientations writing in this field have addressed the historical absenting of the experiences of girls in the context of youth cultural discourses, both in the academy and in popular culture. Part of their work has been to document the evolution of the idea of girlhood as a specific period of time in the life cycle of women, and to present the evolution of girlhood studies as an academic intervention that questions the privileging of boyhood and masculinity in youth studies (see, for example, Ward and Benjamin 2004; Caron 2011). Although youth in general are seen as "scapegoats for social unrest, social change, and civic disintegration" (Harris 2004, 65), in more recent scholarship on young women, the modern girl emerges as a contemporary problem, and the discourse on girls and their cultural spaces as a commentary on modern life. As Caroline Caron states, "the spectacular modes of girl culture which, then and now, raise concerns about girls today are in this sense always part of debates about citizenship and culture" (2011, 77).

The range of concerns addressed through girlhood studies in the late twentieth and early twenty-first centuries includes interrogating the idea of a universal girl conceived as white, American, and middle class and burdened with the baggage of internalizing the negative connotations of her marginalized gender status. The link between girls and women has received much less attention than the study of girls as a unique and "separate entity" (Ward and Benjamin 2004, 23). Bullying between girls and "mean girl" culture, girls' navigation of institutions from family to school and religion, girls as consumers and producers of popular culture, girls' embodiment and the disciplining of their bodies, and sexuality are the social arenas that are most frequently under investigation. For many of these subjects, ethnography has become the preferred methodology to use in investigating the particularities of girls' lives. Although revealing the texture and complexity of girls' experiences is the underlying goal of girlhood research across these topics, we can still discern a dichotomy for young women that Anita Harris defines as the "can-do" or "at-risk" girls (2004, 9). Through this binary comes the rise of the über-productive self-made girl of the twenty-first century and the continuation of the trope of the perpetually at-risk girl rendered unproductive and, ultimately, surplus by a combination of factors such as her race, class, geographic location, and sexuality. These are generally discussed in terms of another dichotomy: either her bad choices or external structural failures. Harris illuminates the ways in which funding efforts support initiatives that capitalize on the leadership capacities and civic engagement of girls rather than addressing the circumstances many young women face, such as concerns for their bodily safety, physical and emotional health, and overall ability to be cared for and care for themselves. State support for the ideological and material construction of this self-made girl additionally valorizes the previously at-risk girl who becomes a success through her own fortitude and hard work, despite the array of obstacles she might face.

Shapeshifters is concerned with populating the space around the illegible Black girl in youth, cultural, and girlhood studies. I find Harris's dichotomy useful for thinking about how the Black girls in this text occupy both categories without necessarily receiving the benefits of valorization (the can-do girl) or protection (the at-risk girl) implied through the binary. The Fresh Start residents are officially defined as embodying and managing dangers that make them risky, at risk, and high risk. At the same time, social institutions charge them with transforming their circumstances, so they exemplify Harris's can-do girls. Their at-risk status is a baseline requirement for inclusion in the Fresh Start shelter and other social service institutions. Yet their actions in these institutions reflect the fact that their "can-do girl" behavior is, in many ways, part of the actions they must perform to insure their livelihood. The self-made can-do girl Harris describes is both supported by and supports the state through her leadership skills, advocacy for the state and community, and ability to act as a good consumer citizen.[14] However, the labor of the Black girls in *Shapeshifters* is not legitimized by the state and is, in fact, categorized as detrimental to the normative practices that constitute the state.

Urban Ethnography and the Missing Black Girl

For over half a century, Black girls have been the absent referent in urban ethnographies in the social sciences, which instead have been chiefly invested in explaining the life patterns of poor young and adult Black males. During the height of the civil rights movement and continuing into the following decades, both federal agencies and individual sociologists and anthropologists (often working in tandem) studied Black men living in poverty in rapidly deindustrializing inner cities as the main characters in the story of urban decline and social disorder. The concerns about urban poverty, migration, and the resulting shifts in neighborhood composition were also concerns about the stability within and reproduction of the male-headed nuclear family and middle-class status.

St. Clair Drake and Horace Cayton's *Black Metropolis* (1945) marked the beginning of a social science tradition that continues into the present of studying the Black inhabitants of the Bronzeville area in Chicago's South Side (Wilson 1987). The migration of southern Blacks to Chicago illuminated the internal ruptures in the Bronzeville Black community as Blacks from the lower, middle, and upper classes lived in fairly close geographic proximity. The chapter titles in *Black Metropolis* ("Style of Living—Upper

Class," "Lower Class: Sex and Family," "The World of the Lower Class," "The Middle-Class Way of Life," and finally "Advancing the Race") reveal the assumption that bridging the gaps between the classes in the Black community, made visible through lifestyles and behaviors, could lead to the "advancement of the race." In one of the text's most compelling passages, Drake and Cayton recount the internal monologue of an upper-middle-class physician responding to a house call in a lower-class community where a woman has stabbed a man in a tenement building:

> For a moment, Dr. Macguire felt sick at his stomach. "Are those my people?" he thought. "What in the hell do I have in common with them? This is 'The Race' we're always spouting about being proud of." He had a little trick for getting back on an even keel when such doubts assailed him. He just let his mind run back over the "Uncle Tomming" he had to do when he was a Pullman porter; the turndown he got when he wanted to interne [sic] at the University of Chicago hospital; the letter from the American Medical Association rejecting his application for membership; the paper he wrote for a white doctor to read at a Mississippi medical conference which no Negroes could attend. Such thoughts restored his sense of solidarity with "The Race." "Yeah, I'm just a nigger, too," he mumbled bitterly. (1945, 566)

After Dr. Macguire has finished assisting the injured man, he finds himself in conversation with the small crowd that has gathered: "'I'm gonna be a doctor, I am,' a small, self-confident urchin spoke up. The crowd tittered and a young woman said, 'That's real cute, ain't it? You be a good one too, just like Doc Macguire.' Dr. Macguire smiled pleasantly. An elderly crone mumbled, 'Doctor? Humph! Wid a hophead daddy and a booze houn' mammy, how he ever gonna be any doctah? He bettah get his min' on a WPA shovel.' Everybody laughed" (ibid., 566–67). I quote from *Black Metropolis* at length because *Shapeshifters* wrestles with questions regarding race, social mobility, and social reproduction similar to the ones indicated here. The event described here also shows the key themes of culture and community transformation that appear in urban ethnography from the time of Drake and Cayton's study to more contemporary research on U.S. cities. Although Dr. Macguire expresses frustrated disdain for lower-class Blacks whose behavior he finds not just crass but potentially harmful to all Blacks, he quickly reminds himself that his credentials and elevated educational status do not protect him from being Black in the context of white supremacy. He is, in his own words, still "just a nigger, too." A young boy, watching

Macguire work, confidently proclaims that he will be a doctor one day. A cynical woman from the small crowd that's gathered doesn't hesitate to remind the boy, and everyone else in earshot, that his class status and, perhaps more importantly for her, the behavior of his parents will insure that his dream goes unfulfilled. Her comment about a more realistic choice being employment through the WPA is made even more relevant by the fact the Works Progress Administration, a product of New Deal legislation that employed out-of-work men, funded Drake and Cayton's research for *Black Metropolis*.

For the most part, the second half of the narrative, which addresses the question of what is likely to happen to the lower-class Black boy who dreams of becoming a doctor, has received a great deal of attention from social scientists, policy makers, educators, social service workers, and journalists— who have remained concerned with this question since the 1940s. Whether invested in maintaining hierarchies that make it nearly impossible for low-income Black youth to achieve educational goals that lead to economic stability, or concerned with disrupting interlocking systems of inequity that prevent social mobility, people in these fields share an underlying assumption: that normative markers of success and respectability should be the desired outcome. The identifiable problem is painted as the elusive nature of success and mobility in the lives of poor Blacks and has resulted in what Robin D. G. Kelley calls a "cultural and ideological warfare that continues to rage over black people in the inner city as social problems" (1997, 4). Thus, the task becomes determining either how to fix the Black community or how to challenge persistent inequalities so that Black children's dreams can be realized.

What has received far less critical attention in ethnographies about urban Black communities is Dr. Macguire's ambivalence toward the utility of normative markers of success for Black Americans in the first place. The doctor sees himself as distinct and separate from the lower-class Blacks in Bronzeville until he reminds himself that regardless of their material differences, he and they are united by their status as only contingent and partial citizens because they are Black. In *Shapeshifters*, I am interested in using the lens of contemporary Black girls living in Detroit to take up the contradictions of American dreaming and social mobility expressed in Drake and Cayton's narrative. The young women of Fresh Start are charged with believing in meritocracy, in thinking that despite the realities of homelessness and undereducation, a disciplined can-do attitude can transform their lives and put them on the road to economic independence and productive citizenship. Yet they recognize that no matter what they achieve in education and employment, their viability as worthy citizens hinges primarily on their Blackness and gender. They understand that being at risk is a characterization that cannot be easily erased by their efforts and good intentions.

It is also important to pay attention to gender in the *Black Metropolis* story and to ask how the notion of success in low-income Black communities is gendered. The doctor and his hopeful imitator are both male. The perpetrator of the stabbing attack is a woman, and her victim a man. Although this incident occurred two decades before Daniel Patrick Moynihan published *The Negro Family* (1965), we can imagine this incident as a classic example that he would have found useful for condemning Black families and, in particular, Black women. The poor Black woman, enraged and apparently inebriated, slashes a man who is not her husband but her lover. The Black doctor hesitates to make a house call because he is in no mood for the chaos he predicts he will encounter and the overwhelming likelihood that the woman will not be able to pay him for his services. The doctor represents upper-middle-class ascendancy not just through his title and occupation, but also because of his gender. And the community's hopes for the future are embodied in a boy who articulates his desires, only to be mocked by a cynical older woman.

Drake and Cayton pull this narrative out of their extensive, rigorous research and nonfictional ethnographic analysis. I am not interested in a critique of their work as much as I am intrigued by how this scene brilliantly represents the hopes and fears of state investments in constructing the Black family as the dysfunctional root of Black poverty. A man has been stabbed and a young boy publicly humiliated. The Black women's actions here are dangerous, even life threatening, and also mean-spirited and malicious.[15] Without knowing the subtext and rich histories of the people involved in this scene, we find the women taking shape as the embodiment of the hysterical and sexually promiscuous Jezebel and the sharp-tongued, insensitive Sapphire. The men and boys here are allowed internal turmoil, conflicted compassion, and the ability to envision and desire a life beyond the ghetto. It appears that Black boys can dream of becoming successful Black men only if they can survive Black women.[16]

As the tropes of Jezebel and Sapphire, the sharp-tongued, rude, and malicious Black woman, expanded to make room for the controlling images of the bad Black mother of the 1960s and 1970s and, eventually, the 1980s welfare queen, social anxieties remained firmly entrenched in concerns about Black men's viability as economic providers and Black boys' ability to safely navigate schools, homes, and the street. During the social unrest of the mid- to late 1960s and rebellions in cities like Detroit, Newark, and the Watts neighborhood of Los Angeles, poor Blacks living in inner-city neighborhoods were now fully visible as active oppositional actors willing to lose their lives for the rights of citizenship. The Du Boisian query, "How does it feel to be a problem?" (1903, 1), took on an even weightier meaning as federal and local elected officials, aided by the work of social scientists, anxiously clamored to define and ultimately constrain a Black population perceived as an undisciplined and a particularly dangerous strand of the civil rights movement.

Elliot Liebow (1967) conducted fieldwork during this historical period among underemployed Black men whom he called street corner men, living in the Washington, D.C., area. This demographic group of underskilled and undereducated men would later be defined as the underclass, a term marking them as stagnant and intractably gripped by poverty. As Liebow explores his interlocutors' relationship to work and family, he finds that Black women form the backdrop in Black men's lives. In keeping with the tradition of the "historiography of race in America," Black men are presented "as the central characters in a history of exclusion" (R. Ferguson 2004, vi). The overwhelming focus on Black men and boys in urban ethnographic research beyond Liebow's study is clear across fields covering topics that range from managing street behavior in a gentrifying community (Anderson 1990) to understanding underground illegal economies (Bourgois 1995; Bergmann 2008) and exploring the criminalization of Black youth in school systems (A. Ferguson 2001). Much of this work has transformed the way we talk about race and community change as well as our understanding of how critical the complexities of identity and identification are to everyday acts of survival. Yet aside from the pioneering work of Joyce Ladner (1972) and Carol Stack (1970), young Black women were virtually left out of the equation until very recently, when research in what can be categorized as Black girlhood studies began to appear.

Shapeshifters, as well as all other ethnographic work that centers on Black girls, owes a debt to the work of Ladner and Stack. In particular, Ladner's research in St. Louis with young women living in the Pruitt-Igoe housing projects informs the methodological spirit and underlying theoretical intent of my work. Black girls are nascent dangerous Black women. They emerge as the partially hidden fulcrum at the center of spectacular Black urban tragedies, and their failures are corporeally located and inscribed.

Whether in judgments that they are unproductive and their sexuality is abhorrent or in their placement in homes and neighborhoods where their inability to conform to norms of mainstream domesticity and an aesthetic of white femininity becomes the crux of family and community demise, low-income young Black women are always already defined as the problematic given. Ladner was primarily committed to providing an analysis of low-income Blacks' lives that served as an intervention in discussions about young Black women that were based on the deviancy model. The Black girls in her work are not measured against a white girl norm. In addition, Ladner conscientiously positions herself in the text and is transparent about her own experiences growing up Black and female. One of her central goals was to present the complex humanity of Black girlhood that was missing in previous ethnographic accounts of Black urban life.

It is interesting to note that more recent ethnographies in the area of Black girlhood studies narrow the focus by concentrating on particular concerns in Black girls' lives. The various foci of these works testify to the generative groundwork laid by Ladner and Stack (even if these authors are unacknowledged in the texts) and also reflect what the researchers identify as the most urgent and compelling issues for Black girls. The most prominent ethnographies about Black girls address the following two major areas of concern: negotiating violence, from domestic and street violence to involvement in gangs (J. Miller 2008; N. Jones 2010; Ness 2010); and Black girls as consumers and producers of culture (Chin 2001; LaBennett 2011), with their relationship to hip hop a significant subcategory of study (Sharpley-Whiting 2007; B. Love 2012). *Shapeshifters* is clearly in conversation with these works on Black girlhood. However, I broaden my focus with the understanding that these and other significant areas in the lives of Black girls can be subsumed under the work of exploring Black girls' navigation and practice of citizenship. In other words, citizenship and everyday acts of political engagement undergird all aspects of Black girlhood.[17]

The theoretical lines that I follow, extend, and diverge from are largely located in Black feminist anthropology and women of color feminism. These epistemologies have always trafficked in the unknown and the unworthy as a way to identify possibilities for living better and more fully. Thus, they have always interrogated the nature of citizenship and the terms of inclusion that devalue the lives of people who are identified as nonwhite, nonmale, nonheterosexual, or poor. In *Shapeshifters*, I am interested in how partial and conditional citizenship both shapes and is manipulated by the agency of low-income young Black women in the United States, as well as in the ways in which young Black women construct theoretical frameworks that are echoed by but not always recognizable in women of color feminism.

The Site: Give Girls a Chance and the Fresh Start Shelter

Give Girls a Chance (GGC) helps homeless and high-risk girls and young women avoid violence, teen pregnancy, and exploitation and helps them explore and access the support, resources, and opportunities necessary to be safe, to grow strong, and to make positive choices in their lives. The Fresh Start shelter is part of this larger social service organization. GGC is a nonprofit, private, community-based social service agency located in southwest Detroit. Its gender-specific services are designed to meet the developmental needs of girls, young women, and women, and it achieves this goal through three core programs: the Fresh Start shelter and Transition to Independent Living (TIL) Program, the Early Start Program, and the Community Outreach Program. The Fresh Start shelter was the first program that GGC established. In fact, Fresh Start and GGC were synonymous in the years before the two other programs were implemented. Even now, most people in the community think only of the shelter when they hear the name Give Girls a Chance. Fresh Start, however, is much more than a warming center for a temporary reprieve from the streets. The goal of the shelter is to provide support, training, and guidance to young women aged fifteen to twenty-two who are homeless and labeled "high risk," with the goal of helping them transition out of homelessness and into what the organization called "independent living situations." When I started volunteering at GGC in 2000, the shelter capacity was twelve beds. The shelter moved to a new building in December 2002, when I became its director, and the capacity increased to nineteen beds. At the same time, young women with children in their care became eligible for housing in the shelter. By the time I had been the director of the shelter for nine months, its capacity had reached twenty-nine beds, including five for women with children, and it was raising funds to realize the capacity goal for the new building that had been outlined in a capital campaign, to forty beds.

In addition to the increase in resident capacity, which necessitated an increase in staff to meet the state licensing requirements for staff-to-resident ratio, the biggest change for the shelter with the move to the new building was the addition of infants and young children. Young women who came to Fresh Start were initially tracked into the shelter component of the program, meaning that they were considered residents only for emergency stays of two weeks, while staff members assessed their individual circumstances and worked with them to set immediate goals. Some of those who stayed for two weeks or less decided that they did not want to participate in a long-term program or were in need of only temporary support. A majority of these short-term residents were minors who, with the intervention of Child Protective Services, were reunited with their parents or primary caregivers. The TIL Program was designed to train young women in employment readiness, help them acquire life skills, and guide them in educational planning so that they could live on their own and avoid future homelessness. Two program coordinators implemented the curriculum by facilitating group workshops and working one-on-one with each resident to provide academic tutoring and job search support. The program also employed four caseworkers, one to work with each of the following resident populations: minors (those younger than eighteen), pregnant and parenting young women, emergency-stay residents, and adult participants in the TIL Program. The day-to-day operations of the shelter—which involved the chore schedule, meal times, curfew adherence, group attendance, house meetings, and so forth—were all monitored by the resident advisors.

Although there was no enforced time limit for stay in the shelter, the average stay while I was there was six to eight weeks, with the shortest time being a few hours and the longest recorded uninterrupted stay being seventeen months.[18] When you consider what this means on a practical level, it is a miraculously brief amount of time for an adolescent young woman (or any individual, for that matter) living in one of the most economically depressed cities in the United States to transition from homelessness and unemployment to stable housing, a job that pays enough to live on, and substantial progress toward educational goals. There was, undoubtedly, something powerfully effective at work here for young women to succeed in these transitions on such a regular basis. Part of my interest in Fresh Start was rooted in figuring out what was working in these young women's lives and how they defined a successful transition.

Who Seeks Shelter?

The Fresh Start shelter is a productive site for charting how racialized self-improvement mandates gain credence from the historical construction of Black femininity in the United States, and how they are sustained through contemporary attempts to fix low-income young Black women as part of an eternal underclass. More than 92 percent of the young women who sought shelter and other services at Fresh Start were African American—the majority of them defined themselves as Black. Young women come to Fresh Start because of a variety of overlapping circumstances that threaten their ability to find safety and protection in the broadest sense of the words.

The typical Fresh Start resident was a young woman who identified herself as Black or African American, was between nineteen and twenty-one years old, and had a child younger than three years old. She called the shelter hotline or showed up in person to talk to an intake caseworker about gaining admittance into the shelter. Typically, she had become homeless in one of the following ways: being put out of her home by her mother, who believed the daughter to be the cause of tension with a new man entering the home, such as the mother's live-in boyfriend; having to leave home when it became too crowded with various relatives and friends; having exhausted her extended network of friends whose homes were available for couch surfing; leaving an abusive relationship with no other options for making a home; and having no family to turn to after leaving foster care or the juvenile justice system. Although some young women came to Fresh Start after aging out of foster care, young women who were current wards of the state via either foster care or the juvenile justice system could not be admitted to the shelter.

In terms of employment and education, the typical Fresh Start resident dropped out of high school in tenth grade and was working on her General Equivalency Diploma (GED). Her employment record was brief and spotty, and most of her work experience was in the service industry.[19] Although she may have entered Fresh Start with hostile feelings toward her parents and other relatives, throughout her stay one of her goals was to reunite and build a more sustainable relationship with her family. Her other goals included earning her GED and entering a program in which she could attain a certificate in the health care field prior to pursuing a college education,[20] finding an apartment that she could afford to live in on her own, and eventually starting her own business. After five or six months, she had either found a job and affordable housing, reconnected and moved back in with family members, or become frustrated with the program's structure and discharged herself—usually returning to the shelter within less than a month.

There have, of course, been people in the shelter who differed from this typical resident. Some young women identified themselves as Caucasian, Arab American, Mexican American, or Puerto Rican. Some young women entered the shelter after having earned a bachelor's degree; others hadn't advanced beyond the fourth grade and had difficulty writing their name. While I was the director, there was a marked increase in the number of functionally illiterate women in the shelter. There was also a growing population of young women who were diagnosed as manic depressive. The program struggled to provide appropriate care for these young women, since staff members were not adequately trained in severe remedial adult education or in the type of clinical psychiatric care that many of these residents required. In addition, many of Fresh Start's partnering community health centers that traditionally worked with these populations closed their doors due to cuts in state and federal funding.

As much as the girls talked about "getting out" and "moving on," they often returned to the shelter to visit, check in, report on their progress, and get the material assistance and counseling many of them still required for months after their official departure. The Fresh Start shelter both mimicked and redefined home for these young women, as evinced by the complicated emotions that they and staff members had for each another and the ambiguity surrounding both groups' perceptions of the shelter as a place of safety, stability, and love.

The Early Start and Community Outreach Programs

As noted above, the other two programs that were a part of the GGC organization were the Early Start Program and the Community Outreach Program. The Early Start Program resembled traditional after-school programs in that it provided academic tutoring, recreational and physical fitness activities, performing and visual art opportunities, workshops on topics ranging from sex and dating to making papier-mâché masks, and counseling and case management to girls and young women between the ages of five and twenty. Participants in this program were identified as at risk.

The Community Outreach Program hired high-risk young women as peer educators to work on street outreach teams and trained them to educate other high-risk young women about a range of behaviors considered unhealthy, in addition to encouraging these young women—in a version of the self-made can-do girl—to be leaders in their school, home, and community. As many as five street outreach teams were in operation at one time, with four to seven peer educators on each team. These teams included the Care project, which focused on issues related to alcohol, tobacco, and other drugs; the Community Justice project, whose audience was young women transitioning out of the juvenile justice system; the Move Experiment,[21] which used dance, poetry, music, and other modes of creative self-production by the peer educators to reach out to other young women; the Free Project, which focused outreach efforts on young people identifying themselves as lesbian, gay, transgender, bisexual, or questioning; and the first peer educator outreach team to be established, which was simply known as street outreach. All of the outreach teams planned and facilitated trainings, events, and workshops that took place in institutions like schools, recreational centers, churches, and other social service agencies.

Unlike the other outreach program employees, the street outreach workers rode around with their staff coordinator in an agency van, searching the streets of Detroit for teen girls to provide information on where to access community resources if they needed support or assistance, how to avoid dangerous or high-risk situations, and what services they might be eligible for through GGC. Watching the street outreach teens at work was always exciting. Their education and instruction of other young women happened on sidewalks, at bus stops, and at the entrances of parks where boys and girls mingled after school. With only a few critical seconds to make a positive impression and establish trust and rapport, these peer educators had to develop a unique demeanor that combined boldness and sensitivity. Their work was a more formalized version of the street education that young women engage in everyday—sharing wisdom, passing along warnings and opinions tempered by experience, and showing loving care to other young people whose faces reflected their own.

Although Fresh Start, Early Start, and Community Outreach were different programs, they were all housed under the larger GGC organizational banner. The administrative staff of all programs held weekly leadership team meetings to make plans and solve problems across programs and to chart the organization's overall trajectory. Girls and young women had the option of participating in all three programs if they met the age criteria. For example, Fresh Start residents could be hired as peer educators if that work did not interfere with their school or other training obligations. Peer educators from the Community Outreach Program often attended employment and wellness workshops facilitated by the shelter staff. It was common for two or even all three of the programs to share grants and to collectively report on their progress toward grant goals. When GGC moved into one large building, the lines between the programs were further blurred as staff members and young women from all programs shared classroom space and meeting rooms. Once a month, an agencywide meeting was held, at which each program director reported on the program's successes and challenges, the finance director reviewed the budget, and staff members were led in a team-building exercise. The site for this book is the Fresh Start shelter and its location in the GGC organization, in the city of Detroit—which in turn was entrenched in the spatial and ideological structure of the U.S. political economy. These nested sites overlap in *Shapeshifters*.

Traditions and Genealogies

> To be without documentation is too unsustaining, too spontaneously
> ahistorical, too dangerously malleable in the hands of those who would
> rewrite not merely the past but my future as well. So I have been picking
> through the ruins for my roots.
> —*Patricia J. Williams (1998, 5)*

Noliwe Rooks states that "concerns for the dynamics of space and power are a common thread" (2005, 2) in the academic and artistic work by and about Black women since the nineteenth century. From Hazel Carby's (1992) pioneering research on the moral panic in northern cities inspired by the inclusion of Black women migrants, to Gloria Anzaldúa's (1996) poetic discussion of the ways in which women of color enact and imagine space without deferring to the restrictions of boundaries and borders so that they become adept jugglers, the act of shifting spaces is a critical grounding concept (see Davis and Craven 2013a). Black women are, out of necessity, inherently shapeshifters. Thus, understanding the ways in which everyday Black women make sense of their lives by theorizing the present and imagining the future is essential for supporting ways of living that resist the dehumanization implied in normative scripts, that shapeshift, and that offer us opportunities to interrogate the texture of citizenship for Black girls. Moving from this standpoint as an anthropologist in the context of this ethnography means paying close and generous attention to the quotidian spaces of meaning making that Black girls enliven and invent.[22] Black girls' presence changes the possibilities for what can occur in public and private spaces while also requiring us to see and understand these spaces differently. I am interested in the theories and methods Black girls use to shift the shape of spaces that restrict and punish them as well as those that offer care and support.

There are guides along this shapeshifting journey. Black feminists and radical women of color theorists across disciplines, genres, and time periods cleared the way for these theoretical travels. In addition, and more specifically, Black feminist anthropologists such as Leith Mullings, A. Lynn Bolles, and Dána-Ain Davis who take seriously the lives of Black women as resources for new theoretical currents in anthropology, critical race, and feminist theory provide not only theoretical frames of reference but also models for methodology predicated fundamentally, and most importantly, on care.[23] It is this type of careful work and paying this deep attention that allows for the sorts of transformation in anthropology that constitutes what Faye Harrison (2008) calls "reworking" the field. I agree with Kelley (1997) and others who assert that the terrain of culture is an important site of struggle across the Black community. However, the culture work and cultural remapping produced by Black girls is a space of possibility that has yet to be fully investigated. Anthropologists working in the 1960s and 1970s in the United States (Hannerz 1969; Lewis 1970) approached the relationship between culture and social inequality in cities in ways that were expanded and refined in research by urban anthropologists (Gregory 1998; Low 2002; Davila 2004 and 2012; Susser 2012) who were more centrally concerned with how people work within and through culture to reshape city spaces. *Shapeshifters* positions Black girls in the context of these anthropological inquiries into the dynamics of place making.

Shapeshifting

In writing that "the material world is a house that is only as safe as flesh" (2006, ix), Katherine McKittrick acknowledges the interconnectedness of geography and humanness, space and bodies, cities and people, and their practices of mutual constitution. Neither the theoretical link between place and personhood nor the attention paid to Black women's different experiences within and reordering of space are new subjects of analysis. What is uncharted territory are the theoretical frame and embodied methodologies that low-income young Black women use to read and respond to the evaluations of their social value—evaluations having implications that unsettle the notion of unified and knowable identities and the presumed stability of geographic spaces. The history of Detroit tells a complicated story of displacement within urban deindustrialization and contemporary attempts to revitalize the city. In the discourse that surrounds the rebuilding of inner cities, the predominantly Black and low-income populace is often constructed as an undifferentiated mass with little or no productive agency. For example, in Detroit, political leaders—whether corrupt and self-interested or well-intentioned but fatally flawed[24]—are situated against a backdrop of alternately drone-like or mindlessly hostile Black residents who are presumed to have the political representation they deserve.

It is essential that efforts to counter and complicate the representation of Black inner-city residents, and Black youth in particular, take seriously not only how the category of Black girl takes shape within the larger context of national politics but also, and more important, how Black girls develop their own rhetorical performances and creative strategies—essentially, how Black girls establish their own politics of the body. The context of urban space continually emerged as a primary organizer of the ways young women in Detroit considered who they were as individuals and how they were seen and treated as a collective under the banner of Black girl. Because of this perception of individual and collective identity as inextricable in many ways from space (in terms of both the tangible and geographic as well as the rhetorical and representational), the relationship between Detroit and the making of Black girls across and within class differentials was a significant dynamic to explore in *Shapeshifters*.

Black girls suggest that we take up the challenge posed to all of us by M. Jacqui Alexander to think of ourselves as "refugees of a world on fire" (2005, 264). This is an acknowledgment of the dynamics of social processes and the potential held in our capacity to embrace, rather than fight against, our inevitable and perpetual displacement. We should, in fact, allow ourselves—like the young women at Fresh Start—to use our displacement as a starting point for regeneration and the creation of new lifeworlds and spaces that affirm our collective humanity. As such refugees, committed not to inclusion but to creation, we get closer to Cohen's transformational politics, which is a "politics that does not search for opportunities to integrate into dominant institutions or normative social relationships but instead pursues a political agenda that seeks to change values, definitions, and laws that make these institutions and relationships oppressive" (2009, 29).

Shapeshifting is a term that appears in science fiction when beings shift form—most often from human to animal or extraterrestrial entity.[25] *Shapeshifting* is also a term used to talk about the mutable nature of molecules and genes, the transformations of self and spirit that occur during rituals, changing energy fields during hypnosis, and computer coding. The meaning of *shapeshifting* that I find to be most usefully aligned with the cultural work of Black girls, oddly enough, comes from an introduction to a series of logic puzzles that explains how to cognitively approach resolving the puzzles. Here *shapeshifting* is defined as a method used to "find solutions, master concentration, recall, recontextualize ideas, and map out plans" (Schreiber 2012). The emphasis on memory and mapping is significant because they reflect the ways in which young Black women mobilize history, whether officially documented or bricolaged through recall and desire, to give new meaning to social contexts that engender cartographic capacities beyond particular physical or ideological sites. The shapeshifting practices of young Black women compel us to move from where we are and how we see and talk about our globalized neocolonial realities to a "society whose outcomes cannot be fully known" (Purcell 2014, 145).[26] I have chosen not to hyphenate *shapeshifters* as an aesthetic nod to the mutually constructing and mutually disruptive relationship between the contexts and the shifts within them that are catalyzed by Black girls. They touch and reciprocate.

Choreography

Perhaps because I trained for most of my young adult life as a professional ballet and contemporary dancer, the term *choreography* seems to me to be the most apt descriptor of young Black women's interactions with the institutions and practices of the state. Choreography is concerned in a very fundamental sense with the ordering of bodies in space. Choreography is shapeshifting made visible. Choreography is embodied meaning making, physical story telling, affective physicality, and an intellectualized response to the question of how movement might narrate texts that are not otherwise legible. Social choreography, as performed by the young Black women in this book, privileges and celebrates the instability and flexibility of identity in variously configured locations that are more than "merely containers for human complexities and social relations" (McKittrick 2006, xi). Choreography, in its most radical sense, can disrupt and discredit normative reading practices that assess young Black women's bodies as undesirable, dangerous, captive, or out of place.

Choreography suggests that there is a map of movement or plan for how the body interacts with its environment, but it also suggests that by the body's placement in a space, the nature of that space changes. In the world of concert dance, choreography was something that, as paid dancers, we had to learn and master, using our bodies to express the intent and feeling a choreographer embedded in a sequence of steps. Being able to pull this off required a combination of virtuosity in physical technique and affective manipulation—or, in other words, the ability to execute the steps and infuse them with feeling. While I was dancing with Ailey II,[27] I would often hear the mandate "Stay in your body!" hurled at dancers during rehearsals. Until my recent analysis of young Black women's relationship to their bodies and space, I did not understand what the imperative to stay in the body could fully convey. Staying in the body asks that the dancer move from a place of intuitive knowing that allows movement to both feel and look organic. It also means moving from the center of your body and extending outward rather than allowing your extremities or the technical demands of the movement to finally dictate your body's journey in space. Exceptional dancers are able to give the impression that they are deeply in their bodies as they transcend it—carving stories, meanings, memories, and images in space that surely emanate from the physical being, but somehow appear to make the body irrelevant, despite its virtuosity.

The young women in *Shapeshifters* stay in their bodies to rewrite the socially constructed meanings shackled to them. The body, like the notion of home for these young women, can be by turns a space of safety and protection or one of instability and expulsion. In the body as well as in home spaces, the ways of establishing inclusion are inherently unpredictable for young Black women. They are aware that if they rely on socially determined assessments to define their self-worth, they would be exiled from their own bodies and any home spaces they might establish for themselves—a state of eternal homelessness. Young Black women propose the possibility that the body may be the space to which we may finally come home, or where we make a new one. Staying in the body, therefore, may very well mean moving in and, most importantly, beyond it to locate new ways of imagining oneself and of remaking one's surroundings. Choreography, as I use it in the context of this ethnography, shows how young Black women read their location in social contexts with consequences that may lead to shifts in those spaces, themselves, and the processes through which they are seen and assessed.

I apply choreography to the theoretical project of Black feminism that is interested in dislocating Black women's "entrenched fixity" (P. Collins 1998, 4) at the bottom of social hierarchies throughout historical changes in economic and political processes at the local and global level. Tropes of Black girls' marginalization, isolation, victimization, and absence are so pervasive that they conceal Black girls' centrality in the social spaces they inhabit as well as how girls nurture connections, relationships, and community in these spaces. These creative and strategic efforts are missed when we look through the lens of binaries that reinforce individual attainment over relationships and community.[28] Paying attention to shapeshifting and choreography thus forces theorizing to move "away from analyses of injustice that re-isolate the dispossessed" (McKittrick 2011, 958).[29]

Janice, her sister, and her cousins—and Janice's fellow residents of Fresh Start—represent a generation of young Black women who are the granddaughters of women who came to northern cities like Detroit in search of more flexibility in and ownership over their lives. The economic, social, and familial disappointments this generation of late Great Migration women encountered in northern cities was largely due to racism and gender and class biases that confined them in positions scarcely better than those they had abandoned in the South. Members of Janice's generation, however, read disappointment and thwarted plans differently than their mothers and grandmothers. The younger women read social inequities as they gain traction and demand legitimacy on Black women's bodies. They read the ways they are captured in the white and adult gaze and respond with their own self-possessed, and often politically informed, choreography. Thus, choreography, like culture, is a process of meaning making. And like other cultural productions, choreography integrates practices of improvisation, borrowing, and sampling to disassemble and reconstruct current social realities.

Undoubtedly, the strategies young Black women employ to narrate themselves frequently do nothing more than strengthen the systems of containment in their lives. Nonetheless, if we learn to pay a different type of attention to the ways young Black women move through and write their own worlds, failures and unfortunate outcomes may still offer blueprints for mapping a different world. I take up Judith Halberstam's definition of failures as "the spaces in between the superhighway of capital" and take seriously the call for intellectuals to aspire to work "that revels in alternative ways of living and moving through the world that are not readily legible, known, visible and, thus, valued" (2012, 19). Black girls' practices of reading, choreographing, and shapeshifting provide directions on these new roads. Ultimately, although young Black women are undoubtedly the focus of this book, *Shapeshifters* is concerned with locating the radical potential in all efforts—intentional, accidental, and otherwise—that move toward living outside of normatively scripted models of self-improvement and social mobility.

Observing Participant

I worked at GGC in all three service areas in the roles of volunteer dance teacher and program coordinator in the Community Outreach Program, director of both the Fresh Start Shelter and the Early Start Program, and as a worker under contract to implement the Move Experiment. In all of these roles I had direct and sustained contact with the shelter residents and girls in the other programs, and I interacted with direct service staff members as both co-worker and supervisor. As I moved up the agency ranks, I also developed complicated relationships with upper-level administrators and board members. In these relationships it was often made clear that my education, background, and ability to present myself in certain respectable ways was a form of cultural capital that could benefit the agency staff and clients. In my role as shelter director I had a unique view into the various ways cultural capital was performed and resisted at GGC. My physical presence as a relatively young Black woman collided with my role as program director and my position as a doctoral student to produce an identity within Fresh Start that in many instances served as the mutable screen on which ideas of race, class, and gender authenticity were projected. The ways in which the young women and the staff chose to interact with me were related to the roles I played and the wide-ranging situational contexts in which we found ourselves, but they were mostly about who others believed me to be despite these external considerations.

Although I am fully and inevitably present in this text, this ethnography is not about me. I am here throughout, though, as a reflection of the process of paying attention to what Soyini Madison calls the "being with in body-to-body presence with Others that makes the present realizably present" (2006, 323). My relationships with both the young women and the staff were shaped through eight years of daily contact that often challenged the boundaries between the social and professional, intimate and public, work and home. I have watched shy fourteen-year-olds grow into self-possessed twenty-seven-year-old women and pregnant young women develop into mothers of beautiful thirteen-year-old sons and daughters. Several of the young women, like Janice and Sharita, whose stories will be traced throughout this book, were in my company for at least four hours a day, three or four times a week, for over eight years. We traveled together on week-long camping trips, choreographed dances and wrote poetry, protested and spoke out, and just hung out together: running errands, visiting relatives, shopping, attending outdoor festivals and slam poetry readings, and sitting in parks in the summer and coffee shops in the winter talking about the things that bring this ethnography to life—our families, ambitions, fears, desires, and images of ourselves in the world.

Currently we trade weekly texts and photos and find time once a month for catch-up phone calls that last two or three hours. "In order to collect 'accurate data,'" Philippe Bourgois has written, "ethnographers violate the canons of positivist research; we become intimately involved with the people we study" (1996, 13). Madison uses Dwight Conquergood's concept of "co-performative witnessing" to expand on the nature of the connections and commitments that emerge in the ethnographic process within methodologies typically captured under the term *participant observation*. Madison defines *co-performative witnessing* as "shared temporality, bodies on the line, soundscapes of power, dialogic interanimation, political action, and matters of the heart" (2007, 827). The point about political action is central here, as co-performative witnessing also requires us to do "what others do *with* them inside the politics of their locations, the economies of their desires and their constraints, and most importantly inside the materiality of their struggles and consequences" (ibid., 829). Both Bourgois's and Madison's articulations are helpful for explaining the intention with which I approached this project and continue to think about and enact the relationships that made this book possible.

Anthropologists' claims to deep and enduring relationships with their interlocutors are both expected and easily dismissed as the disingenuous musings of self-congratulatory ethnographers. The fact that I developed close and complicated relationships with the girls whose stories I present in *Shapeshifters*, their families, and the Fresh Start shelter staff was not exceptional but required by the nature of the research and intensified by the fact of my employment with GGC. We shared time and space and jointly constructed "soundscapes of power" that were animated by our hearts, with all their expansiveness and limitations. Though we may have struggled in the same temporal and geographic boundaries, the shape of our struggles and the consequences for the actions we took to move through them were not the same. The social spaces that we created together were rife with power differentials. There were many things I was not. I was not homeless, not a girl, not born and raised in Detroit, not an hourly staff member, and not a parent. There were other things that I was. I was a PhD student, a program director with the power to hire and fire, and a middle-class Black woman. The things that I was and was not, the labels that preceded me, and the ways in which these labels were attached to privilege mattered in every context for how I was both seen and able to see. It also mattered that I was often able to witness and write about struggles that did not necessarily affect me outside of my own political investments and commitments to these girls and women.

Through each stage of the process of producing *Shapeshifters* (entering the site, conducting fieldwork, writing, revising, writing and revising again, and reentering the site, and conducting more fieldwork), I was confronted with my own collusion with the structural, institutional, and ideological forces that constrain the possibilities for Black girls. I was also confronted with opportunities for taking productive actions as responses to these constraints. I write with as much love and honesty as my facility with language will allow about our individual and collective maneuverings through constraint and opportunity as they differently presented themselves to us—Black girls and a Black woman with the privilege of witnessing, living with, and renarrating their stories.

In my countless informal conversations with the Fresh Start residents, I have always been impressed with their candor and fearlessness in talking to me about issues that are not only revealing and sensitive but also often critical of the agency and me in my role as the shelter director. I was grateful for the opportunity, through the gift of these young women's honesty and critical insight, to learn more about myself, especially my blindness to my own presumptions and biases. I undoubtedly used the myth of my exceptionalism to my advantage and, I hope, to the advantage of the young women in this ethnography and those like them who will be affected by their truths. Thus, it is important that I am transparent about my less academically motivated intentions in taking on the boundary-crossing roles that inflected many of the events in this book. The idea of being the director of a homeless shelter was appealing to me for several reasons. Having been in graduate school for nearly four years and witnessing the passing of normative milestones such as the birth of babies, job promotions, and marriages in the lives of my nonacademic peers, I craved a concrete, discernible example of forward movement in my life. The position of shelter director was a way for me to project a shift in my life that I believed would be read as an appropriate adult achievement by my friends and family.

While I was working in the outreach program, more graduate students than I could count from the social science, education, and social work programs at the University of Michigan received clearances to conduct research at GGC. Young researchers with notepad and pen in hand would sit at the back of the room during our workshops or call young women into small rooms for interviews. I believe the majority of the scholarship was well-intentioned and intended to raise important questions. Yet I always wondered while running a workshop or participating in a meeting how different the agency looked from the perspective of the back of the room and distanced from the very real stakes that held all of us so tightly in their grasp.

From all I heard and saw about Fresh Start during my first year at GGC, the shelter was at the vital heart of the agency's tensions and was a microcosm for many of the challenges that confronted Detroit. The prospect of directing the shelter was immediately terrifying to me: it was clearly a difficult job that had substantial consequences for the young woman who depended on the shelter's institutional support and care. Directing the shelter was also immediately appealing: it was an embedded position from which I would be unable to deny the invisible tensions that made the shelter more than just a site housing interesting interlocutors. In this role, I believed, it would be impossible to write about Black girls without also including the imprint adult professional caregivers provide in simultaneously constructing and resisting the practices of exclusion that constrict Black girls' access to resources and opportunities that enable them to live self-directed lives. I suspected that acting as the shelter director would produce a more complicated narrative than one that centers on a faceless neoliberal institution that either subjugated Black girls or romanticized their resiliency. I also believed that working as an employee of the agency would reveal the multiple perspectives and competing interests that frustrate young Black women's attempts to transition out of homelessness and define success for them.

I was never surprised, but often disappointed, by just how much I was a product of the very norms I set out to disrupt through my research. On my first day as a volunteer I told the residents that I was an anthropologist. My description of my research at that time included references to the lifeworlds of Black girls and processes of identity formation. The three residents who came to my first class laughed in response. The one who appeared to be the oldest said: "You can write what you want, but don't get it twisted. You are Black just like us. We are going to want you to do more than write while you're here."

I am not suggesting that this young woman sanctioned my appointment as a program coordinator and then shelter director. I do know, however, that the residents and the resident advisors did not consider me a typical researcher, making comments about how I would have to "help out" and "wouldn't be allowed to just sit there and take notes," and I was more than receptive to this reading of my positionality. With my own complicated relationship to the various ways capital was inscribed in and through my body, I imagined Fresh Start as a space where the narration of Black girlhood would require cross-cutting orientations to "help out." We were all in this beautiful mess together. And only together could we craft models for different, more life-honoring ways of living.

Chapter Descriptions

The first chapter in this book tells the stories of three generations of women in the Brown family. It begins with Janice's grandmother, Bessie, who came to Detroit from Alabama in the mid-1960s as part of the late Great Migration, and also includes Janice's mother and aunts. The story of the Brown family charts a map of Detroit and tells a narrative of Detroit history from the perspective of low-income Black women who came to the city as processes of deindustrialization began to leave a visible mark on the lives of Black Detroiters. Bessie and her daughters had to earn their livelihood through backbreaking work in the low-paying service sector and care industries. I use the experiences of Janice and her sister and cousins, who are the third generation of Brown women in Detroit, to reconsider a politics of care as defined by Black girls. *Shapeshifters* is about Black girls, but Black girls do not fall from the sky or mysteriously emerge from state institutions. Their stories matter but do not exist in a vacuum. Janice and her cousins theorize their lives in relationship to the life stories of the adults to which they have been exposed, the experiences of their family members, histories that have been passed down to or hidden from them, and their own understanding of these intersecting trajectories.

In chapter 2, I introduce the period in the shelter known as the shelter renovations or takeover when Camille, a former automotive industry executive, became the interim executive director of GGC. The renovations, makeovers, and improvements that Camille and the GGC board mandated for the shelter encompassed more than the physical structure of the building and, in fact, were primarily concerned with remaking the shelter residents through a specific focus on the discursive and embodied practices that construct the idea of successful Black girlhood. Chapter 2 addresses protest as it relates to the class politics, read through culture, that undermine Fresh Start's mission of "empowered positive choices" often repeated by the shelter staff.

Chapter 3 opens with the retelling of the story of a week-long camping trip and visit to a dude ranch in Ohio. It then moves to an analysis of the narrative—part urban myth and part oral history—surrounding a protest staged by the shelter residents and staff in the early days of Fresh Start's opening. These events and, most importantly, the ways they are retold and performed illustrate how Black girls respond to the ways they are misread by creatively narrating themselves and locating spaces of play in and through protest.

Chapter 4 focuses on how sexuality and gender organize the lives of young Black women by investigating the way ideas regarding normative and deviant sexuality as well as appropriate and dysfunctional gendered expressions circulated in the Fresh Start shelter. I introduce this chapter with the spoken word performance of a shelter resident named LaTonya whose words, and the intention behind them, force us to acknowledge the implications of perceptions of young Black women's sexuality as read through class. This chapter also tells Dominique's story. Dominique is an out lesbian who identified herself alternately as a "thug" and "mack" in the shelter and proceeded to charm the residents and shelter staff members with her compelling bravado. Through the accounts of those whom Dominique calls the "wannabes" (the other young women in the shelter who start dressing and comporting themselves in imitation of Dominique's machismo style), the staff members who are simultaneously repelled and seduced by Dominique's confident sexuality, and Dominique herself, we witness specific examples of how social benefits are offered to and sanctions leveled against Black girls depending on their perceived sexual orientation, gendered performances, and assumed sexual practices.

The Move Experiment and the BlackLight project are the focus of chapter 5. The Move Experiment was a project in the shelter through which residents were hired, trained, and paid to develop and lead movement, self-care, and creative writing workshops for other GGC participants. This chapter shows how the young women hired as peer educators moved the work of the Move Experiment outside of the shelter by using performance as a form of community engagement and political commentary in the city. This chapter also takes up the connection between health and well-being, creative expression, and political engagement in communities. The young women in the Move Experiment demonstrate the limits of re-presenting the self through staged performance, while the young women in the BlackLight project establish self-knowledge and self-care as the starting point for broader transformative politics in the city of Detroit. Ultimately, the stories in this chapter provide real-life, practical examples of how performances of self in everyday life and in the formal performing arts are mutually definitive, embodied responses to the fundamental need to be seen and heard on one's own terms.

1 | "We Came Here to Be Different"

The Brown Family and Remapping Detroit

WHERE I'M FROM
I'm from a big family.
Deep as the ocean, close as twins.
I'm from the Dirty D
You know it's the place to be
I'm from originality x2
Great Grandma's legend leaves us blue.
Eyes that see kids skating ghetto kids
Fighting.
Still a place of love.
Where I keep my head up high
'Cause I know I can make it.
—*a seventeen-year-old Fresh Start resident*

WHERE I BE FROM
I be from a place
Where shelters used to be
An option.
I moved to a place
Where not many houses were built
But many ghetto kids stay.
I moved again to a place
That I hate where hos stroll

And tricks pay.
The school is a disgrace
Feels like it is erasing
The images of my face.
—*a sixteen-year-old Fresh Start resident*

What she wanted for her girls was more than that. She wanted
happiness, however they could get it. Whatever it was. Whoever
brought it.
—*Ntozake Shange,* Sassafrass, Cypress, and Indigo

Getting Lost and Coming Home

"Stop! Turn here!" Janice hustled her older cousin, Karlyn, out of the
right to sit in the front seat and was making the most of the coveted spot
by screaming directives in my ear.

It was only my second time driving the monster fourteen-seater
white van that transported girls home after the Give Girls a Chance (GGC)
program activities ended for the evening. What I had read as lethargy
among the group during the hour-long dance class I taught now felt
like an intentional, almost meditative, stillness. The quiet was nice, and
I was happy to accept it without question. The dance classes were open
to participants in all of the GGC programs, so the van carried a mix of
middle-school girls who were a part of the Early Start Program, high-
school young women in training to become peer educators and street
outreach workers, and a few of the Fresh Start residents who felt like
coming along for the ride on this unseasonably warm early October evening. We were lost. Or at least I was, and it was getting darker as the
shadowy dusk transitioned into night. We left the Corktown neighborhood where GGC was located, almost directly across the street from what
was then the historic Old Tiger Stadium, a half hour earlier. The van was
making slow and hesitant progress down the wide expanse of West Grand
Boulevard. We passed homes with wooden front porches that wrapped
around their large brick frames like shaky, fragile arms. Houses boasting
recently mowed lawns whose edges were dotted with planted flowers sat
next to structures that were barely whole, boarded up and leaning to one
side. As we approached the Dexter Davidson intersection, there were
more pedestrians on the sidewalk, and the streets appeared brighter,
better lit.

"What you doin' out here, boy? Where's your brother? Get back home."
Janice leaned over me, nearly turning the steering wheel, to holler at a
young man who looked to be about fifteen and who was just coming out
of a corner store. He smiled, looking both shocked and pleased to see her,
and then turned down a side street with a quick wave.

"You know him from school?" With my right hand, I tried to gently
persuade her back into her seat.

"No, that's Troy. He just be around the streets. He used to hang out
with my cousin, Davey, but now he's out here on his own. Doing whatever. Worry about him. I know how people can watch you. Nobody really
wants to see us out here. He'll get picked up for nothing. Might come back
tomorrow and see if I can find him." Janice craned her neck to look back
at the spot Troy vacated, then turned to face the passenger window and
was silent for the rest of the ride.

A few of the older girls from the shelter talked in low tones in the row of
seats directly behind us, apparently charting the next day's route through
job interviews, uncertain child-care arrangements, visits with friends,
and their nightly chores at Fresh Start. As it became clearer that I was lost,
it also became clearer that no one was interested in telling me the way home
or cutting short the meandering tour of the city and their conversations—
which were, finally, safely out of judgmental and authoritative earshot. So
I settled in, too. With one eye on the gas gauge and both ears wide open,
I paid close attention to the young women as they used their own stories
and fragments of historical anecdotes about the streets and neighborhoods we passed to narrate a Detroit different from the one I was coming to know through urban legends and social science texts (which were
not mutually exclusive). This van ride was just the beginning of a nearly
decades-long project grounded in a deep listening that compelled me to experience Detroit through a cartography of the city mapped by the young
Black women who both form and are formed within its geography.

In this chapter, the process of getting lost and the repeated act of coming home form the basis for understanding a past, present, and possible
future Detroit through the experiences and speculations of Black girls
and the women in their extended families. Traveling along unknown
paths, with both the limited freedom of mobility and potential dangers in
the unexpected this implies, accurately describes the shapeshifting movements I explore here.[1] Janice, her younger sister Crystal, and their cousins
were the third generation of women in the Brown family currently residing in Detroit. The first generation was Janice, Crystal and their cousins'

grandmother, Bessie Brown, who moved to Detroit from Alabama in 1964 during the latter part of the Great Migration. The second generation, which included Janice and Crystal's mother and aunts, made lives for themselves in Detroit as young women during the 1970s and 1980s. Each generation of the Brown family tells historical and contemporary versions of a Detroit story that disputes the constructed normativities on which much of the canonical social science literature on urban poverty and race is based. The rapid deindustrialization Bessie Brown encountered almost immediately after arriving in the city meant that she, her children, and her grandchildren would have a very different relationship to work, stability, success, and comfort than she had anticipated when she left the South. The disconnect between her expectations and the reality with which she was faced can be traced in large part to contested meanings of home and family.

The impact of deindustrialization on Detroit and the consequences of related factors such as depopulation and disinvestment in the center city, high unemployment, suspect city and state legislative practices, and the erosion of public services has been covered extensively in several rigorous works from various disciplines. The so-called Moynihan Report (Moynihan 1965), the pivotal social text that has left us with the enduring trope of the emasculating Black matriarch, has also been discussed extensively in other work, particularly by theorists interested in the social construction of Black women and the ways in which the Black family has been pathologized.[2] Although this background is essential for contextualizing the Brown family and the experiences of Black girls in the twenty-first century, what is most needed now is a situating of this historical narrative and a remapping of urban geographies like that of Detroit by the girls and women at the center of these interwoven discourses of urban ruin and dysfunction. A critical aspect of this reimagining is located at the intersection of space and the body and takes shape from the prospects that Black girls' place making allows for identifying new physical and psychic sites of empowerment.

The fears and anxieties of the nation-state are projected onto Black women and actualized through the discursive and material control of their bodies. In *Troubling Vision*, Nicole Fleetwood attends to how "human value is assessed based on visual blackness" (2011, 71). Largely through a detailed exploration of the work of visual and performing artists and representations found in popular culture, she demonstrates the ways in which "blackness and black womanhood are coded historically and geographically" (ibid., 119). The concern with the relationship between black women, value, and citizenship that is embedded in Fleetwood's analysis plays out in real time in the lives of the Brown family. Normative codes of white femininity mark the boundary between valued and devalued that determine how the Brown women and girls experience the multiple political and economic variables tied to their partial social citizenship. The three generations of Brown women confront several layers of corporal containment in their daily lives, including the reading and categorizing of their bodies, the regulation of their bodies legislated by the state, and the use of their bodies as surplus labor.

You Really Live in Detroit?

"Your mayor was voted worst mayor of the year. How fitting for the worst city in America," commented an acquaintance of mine who lived in Ann Arbor, Michigan, some forty miles west of Detroit. She was referring to Kwame Kilpatrick, who became Detroit's youngest mayor in 2002. Kilpatrick was just at the beginning of a decades-long scandal that included a felony conviction and his resignation as mayor in 2008. Across various media, smug amateur pundits implied that Kilpatrick was the embodiment of the character of the city and its residents. I traveled the stretch of highways that connects Detroit to its suburban and outlying neighbors at least three times a week. Although the drive could be mind-numbingly boring, the contrast between living and working in Detroit and functioning primarily as a student in Ann Arbor was quite dramatic. As a Black woman who grew up learning how to mediate predominantly white institutions, I found a great sense of comfort in Detroit, a so-called chocolate city.[3]

To the youngish, professional middle-class Blacks who worked and made their living in the heart of the city, the "in your face" Blackness of Detroit was a source of both pride and frustration. This segment of the population, in which I somewhat reluctantly included myself, was happy to be a part of the revitalization of the city but confounded by the daily reminders of the failures of the economic and social turnaround of Detroit that always seemed to be just on the horizon. Over the eight years that I lived in Detroit, I became an invested resident of the city—a Detroiter. This was an identity that people felt, believed in, and claimed in ways that could never be accurately represented through an official marker of citizenship like a certificate declaring that someone had been born within the city limits. To many native and self-proclaimed adopted Detroiters, an authentic Detroiter was identified according to intentions and actions in the present—the conscious choices people made. You might be authentic, or at least an authentic ally, if—like being Black in America—being a Detroiter was a badge you polished every morning and wore with pride despite (or often because of) its implications. Just as complicated and uncontainable as Blackness, Detroitness is an identity and a way of being in the world that has generated its own policed boundaries and criteria for inclusion. And, like Blackness, it is defined by the continual transgression of these boundaries. Thus, history becomes another measuring stick for legitimacy and belonging.

Beyond just living in Detroit, a Detroiter had to become familiar with misrepresentation, dismissal, disrespect, and hostility. Being a Detroiter meant digesting the things other people thought and said about you, while holding onto the truth of who you know yourself to be. In many ways, this game of identity defending and self-conscious self-protection is not unlike the one Black girls are forced to play. Detroiters' double consciousness involves simultaneously reading themselves and others through the emotionally colored implications of race, class, and place. Detroiters seemed to understand the deeper meaning beyond all of the disrespect and cultural clowning, whether it was being the butt of jokes on late-night television shows or having images of crack houses in the city broadcast during a nationally televised NBA game to depict the character of the city's basketball team, the Pistons.[4] The national dissing of Detroit, which continues in the present with more aggressive undertones following the city's bankruptcy, reflects a nation struggling with its own discomfort about and fears of the poverty and Blackness that Detroit seems to embody. Thus, Detroit—dark and dangerous—can be stripped of its gritty, urban powers to intimidate and inspire guilt and become a laughable enigma in the narrative of the United States as a nation with accessible wealth and limitless opportunity. In light of these contemporary images of Detroit, the importance placed on history (both personal and collective) in the lives of many Detroiters can be better understood. Detroit's history is like its shadow—always close by and moving like a darker version of the present.

The history of Detroit as understood through that of the Brown family is cast in relation to cars, music, and creative self-making and is punctuated by the relations of power that make race, gender, and class coherent as experiential categories. The life experiences of the three generations of women in the Brown family represent a challenge to the history of Detroit that is taken for granted and retold in popular culture and the academy. The Browns' experiences also raise new questions about the relationship

Black women and girls have to notions of respectability that are deemed so central to their ability to succeed. Janice and the other members of the third generation of Browns are influenced by their family history of migration from the South and the subsequent problems their grandmother and mothers faced living in Detroit, but the younger women are not solely defined by these narrative precursors. Although the Browns could be seen as a casebook example of the many families of different races who face challenges living in underresourced urban areas, including generations of households headed by single women, early pregnancies, low-wage work, absentee fathers, inadequate housing, and minimal education, these labels do not tell the full story. The work that these labels primarily accomplish is to mark young Black women, like Detroit, as sites of perpetual devastation and pathology. This mutually reinforcing bodily and geographic devaluation influences how Black girls move through and carve out space for themselves in the city and create communities of care.

Home Is a Verb

The van hummed along a wide avenue whose name I tried to confirm as we passed one headless street sign after another, the empty posts erupting from the ground and triumphantly signaling nothing. At this point, I didn't even bother to ask my passengers for directions. Two of the older girls from the shelter had fallen asleep, and as their snores rose and fell in volume, the younger girls alternately lowered and raised their voices. I recognized the large white wooden frame house on my left and realized that we were just a block away from Janice's grandmother's address. I had made a full circle almost back to where we started at GGC. I looked out of the corner of my eye to see if Janice had noticed and then, sheepishly, glanced in the review mirror to see who would be the first to call me out. No one said a word until I started to turn back toward Bessie's house.

"We can keep riding, right? I can tell you the shortcut to drop the Morris girls off but then we can keep riding, right? The rest of us?" Karlyn asked. I met her eyes in the review mirror and nodded yes.

"Just don't take us past Wesson," Janice said. "I don't feel like seeing nobody tonight." Wesson was the street where Bessie Brown and, at any given moment, at least four of her six children and seven of her nineteen grandchildren resided. The rented two-story house was always filled beyond capacity. I thought of the house as literally bursting at the seams whenever the younger children pulled back the thin window treatment on the second floor and poked their heads out of the window. This happened every time I picked up or dropped off one of the Brown girls. The loud idling of the van's engine gave me away before I could honk. Eyes glued to the van, the children would melodically yell out of the window in unison, "Cryssssstaaaal!" or "Geeeeeenah!" even though Crystal or Gina was usually sitting right beside them.

I knew why Janice did not want to pass by her grandmother's house but was not sure of Karlyn's reason for wanting to linger in the van. Karlyn was arguably the coolest of the Brown girls and, I was told by other staff members, frequently refused to ride in the van unless the driver agreed to remove the magnetic decal with GGC's logo from the side of the vehicle. On this night, she sank down low in the seat until we had safely ridden out of her neighborhood. Karlyn lived with her mother, Donna, and her three younger brothers and sisters on 7 Mile Road near Dexter Road on the west side of the city. Janice and Crystal lived with their mother, Gwen, and their two younger brothers with Bessie on Wesson Street, just a ten-minute walk from GGC. Bessie's oldest daughter, JoJo, lived less than three miles away on Fourteenth Street with her boyfriend. Ruby, the daughter born between Gwen and Donna, lived with Bessie on and off, when she wasn't staying in the homes of friends or other family members.

Janice hadn't been home in over two weeks. She had been staying with her aunts and friends since her uncles, Phillip and Bip, moved in with Bessie. "It's always packed. But enough is enough," Janice had said after coming home from school to find out her two uncles would be staying indefinitely. Janice did not want to ride by the Wesson Street house and risk being spotted in the van by one of her younger cousins. She was also in no rush to get back to the house of her friend, whose mother was strict about bedtimes and chores. It was 2001 and Janice was fifteen, but she appeared much older. It was difficult to imagine anyone making her wash dishes or turn in early. Karlyn finally admitted that she had her own things and people to avoid. Her mother, she hoped, would be asleep by the time she got home or at least too tired to ask her about school. The street lights had been on for over two hours now so it was likely, she thought, that the boys at the corner who relentlessly harassed her would have moved on to the more serious and covert activities that required their presence on the street.

The Brown girls crisscrossed the city to make their homes in houses that included their grandmothers, mothers, aunts, and friends and sometimes Fresh Start. As crowded or uncomfortable as a house could get with adults and their children, it always seemed to be the teenage young women who were displaced. Another body moved in, and the first one pushed out and made to figure things out in another place was one of the girls. It wasn't clear every time this happened if Janice, Crystal, Gina, Anita, Davina, or Karlyn was asked to move or if they moved on their own. According to the girls, the distinction was murky with innuendo and all that was felt in the tense silence of adult frustration. Essentially, they always knew when "it was time to keep it moving" or to "switch it up." For Janice this time was really about her feelings about Bessie. She would grow tired of watching her grandmother's increasing exhaustion and would know that the domestic help Janice offered did not outweigh her hostile attitude toward the other family members in the house. But it was clear that it was Bessie the girls missed on that night, as we continued to make wide circles around the homes no one wanted to enter.

Bessie Brown

The front porch of the house on Wesson Street was long and deep, but I never saw anyone use it for standing, sitting, entering, or exiting. "The porch don't work," was the warning that greeted me when I approached the front of the house. Eight-year-old Daryl blocked my way before I could climb the three concrete steps leading to the porch. I peered beyond his narrow, shirtless shoulder and saw that the porch had no floor. I could see clear through to the dark, moist ground. Daryl reached for my hand, a gesture that was unexpected and sweet, and walked me to the end of the driveway, where Bessie was leaning against the railing of the much smaller back porch. It was stifling hot, and the glass of ice water in her hand looked like the answer to just about anyone's prayers. The back porch was more of a landing and had just enough space for us both to sit down near the steps and still allow people to pass. When the door opened, it barely grazed my leg, and the hot air from the kitchen hit me in the face like a sucker punch.

"You want some water?" Bessie laughed. "Daryl, go get a glass of water and another sweat rag." Bessie pulled Daryl's arm to put more urgency into his labored steps. The temperature of just over 90 degrees seemed tolerable to Bessie and, I imagined, was nothing compared to summer temperatures in Florence, Alabama. Bessie never said much about her time in Florence, although she hadn't left for Detroit with her mother, Mary, and newborn baby, JoJo, until 1964 at the age of nineteen. This was just one year after her father, Johnny "Doc" Brown, a renowned blues musician in Florence, had passed away.

"There was always music in the house, and it was always clean, clean, clean. Do you hear me? Like a whistle. That was the way." Bessie knew I understood her to be talking not just about her father's music but about that made by her twin brothers as well. The melodies, the rhythms, and the almost obsessive work ethic her mother brought to their home were at least a few of the things that carried over from Florence to Detroit.

Samuel and Simon were consummate blues men—unabashedly emotional and full of tricks—like their father. The twins made a name for themselves in the South, having formed a band by the age of fourteen and traveling from small town to small town performing their authentic Delta blues.[5] Samuel played the harmonica and sang, and Simon was a master of the rhythm guitar. Their modest but loyal following was testimony to their talent, but performing music wasn't lucrative enough for the twins to ignore the possibility of making real money—"home-owning type money," as Bessie put it—up North. Coming to Detroit in the pursuit of economic gain, the Brown Twins (as they soon came to be known) had to put their blues playing to one side in exchange for work in the Ford Rouge River and Chevrolet plants where Samuel and Simon, respectively, found jobs. Yet they were never more than "a holla away from down-home type blues," as Bessie put it, since they always managed to find a way to play in clubs on the east side of Detroit in the evenings and on weekends when they were not too spent from their day jobs.

The twins had not finished high school before they left Alabama at the age of eighteen, and they had minimal work experience. Although they were confined to low-skill service jobs in the automobile plants, they were still able to do much better financially than would have been the case had they stayed in Florence. Bessie made it through her sophomore year of high school before JoJo was born, and the only work she had known in Alabama was helping her mother, Mary, cook, clean, and take care of the laundry for the only slightly more financially secure white families in and near Florence. By the time their younger sister and mother made their way to Detroit, Samuel and Simon were in a fairly good position to help them get settled, even though it was unclear what prosperity, or even just getting by, might look like for Black women like Mary and Bessie. Their main priority, Bessie told me, was to "make sure Mary didn't have to be dealin' all day breakin' her back working under white folk." Bessie said that this was the work their mother left in the South, and it would have been shameful for her to return to it in her new northern home. Even though Mary told her children that she ultimately came to Detroit because "she had a sign from God in her dream," they knew that this was just her way of letting them know she was tired of the South.

"I was nervous to come and leave Alabama, but I was excited 'bout what could be here for me," Bessie talked about migrating to Detroit as she took a measured sip from the small amount of now-warm water that was left in her glass. In Florence, she had taken on odd jobs primarily as an assistant to her mother in other families' homes. In Detroit, the work Bessie found was similar except for the fact that she was providing services to working-class Blacks as opposed to working-class whites. The initial employment she found included waiting tables, providing kitchen help, bussing tables, and cleaning up after hours in various restaurants and clubs, primarily in the all-Black area known as Paradise Valley. Bessie stayed with these jobs throughout her twenties and into her early thirties.[6] When she talked to me about the distinctions between Alabama and Detroit and found herself at a loss for words, Bessie would often simply say by way of explanation for her migration north, "We came here to be different."

In Detroit's history, 1967 is a landmark year. What has been called the rebellion, civil disturbance, riot, and resistance of 1967 began on July 23 of that year and continued for almost a week, leaving forty-three people dead, over one thousand injured, and over seven thousand arrested after a police raid on an after-hours club on 12th Street and West Grand Boulevard, less than a ten-minute drive from the Wesson house. The after-hours spot—or blind pig, as such places were known at the time—was not much different from any of the half-dozen clubs and lounges Bessie worked in during her mid- and late twenties. However, the connection she felt and the memories she tied to the late 1960s, and 1967 in particular, had much less to do with the social science and urban policy fascination with this specific date than with the circumstances that led to the five days of unrest. For Bessie, 1967 was the year when she turned twenty-two and her second daughter, Gwen, was born, to be followed a year later by Ruby, and a year after that by Donna. It was also the year when she realized she would be largely responsible for providing for her mother and taking care of her own children. It is not that Bessie had no memory of that long, hot and pivotal week in the summer of 1967. What was imprinted on her consciousness and lived out, still, every day in 2004, however, were the precursors and aftermath of the rebellion, not the enduring symbolism of the act itself. Failing to feed her children and maintain a livable home were constant fears fueled by the precariousness of her employment and the unreliability of relational ties. The rebellion punctuated but did not define this time for Bessie.

At this point in our conversation, we both stood up to stretch our legs, and I asked Bessie if she felt like taking a walk. I could sense that she was about to decline when her oldest son, Phillip, flew through the screen door.

"Slow down," Bessie said with a smirk. "You can go right back in that house and make sure nothing is getting tore up more than it already is. I'll be back soon." Phillip, lanky and full of restless energy, raised and then dropped his hands as if he was dismissing us. Bessie and I made our way to the end of the dusty pebbled driveway before we heard an unconvincing, "Well, all right then. Damn. Just leave. But I got somewhere to be in an hour."

"Somewhere to be. . . ." Bessie turned her face to the sky and laughed. "My ass."

She spoke with a combination of affection and resignation. It was the same tone I heard her use when talking about her other children, her brothers, the fathers of her children, and her mother. In contrast, her grandchildren seemed to provoke less of a mixture of the two emotions.

Starting in the late 1960s and continuing into the early to mid-1970s, Bessie moved into the role of primary caretaker and income provider for her children and her mother. By the late 1970s all of her children had been born, and Samuel and Simon were engrossed in juggling their shrinking hours at the plants with their increasing popularity as musicians overseas. They were traveling more and couldn't be counted on to offer Bessie more than intermittent support: "They tried and they cared. They just had music in them." Bessie did not talk about the twins' inability or unwillingness to provide for their mother, even though they had promised to do so when they left Florence, as representing malice or even neglect. I imagined this was due to the fact that Samuel had passed away in December of the previous year and Simon just three months later. Their lives and deaths were still fresh in her mind and may have made her more accepting of what they had done. But when I suggested that to Bessie, she denied it and claimed that once you "know who people are and what they can and can't do, the rest is on you. You can't ask for something people can't give." I laughed at this because I was thinking of a time when Bessie didn't ask but demanded what she needed. She was twenty-four and raising four children while taking care of her mother. Frustrated, depressed, and propelled by a deep fear that actually made her act fearlessly, Bessie caught a Greyhound bus bound for Columbus, Ohio, to confront Donna's father: "One day I just got on the Greyhound, took it straight to Ohio and dropped off Donna. He opened the door and I put that child in his hands with nothing on but a diaper. No bags, no clothes, no bottle, no food, no money, nothing. I said 'take care a her' and left. I came back three months later, and for sure that baby had everything she needed. I said 'thank you,' took her right on back to Detroit. There times you don't ask, you make."

Just a few weeks before our impromptu walk, Bessie had told me this story when I asked her how she managed to take care of everybody in her home on the meager wages she was earning at the time. She also told me that she went on public assistance even though that was a hard decision for her to make. Her mother, Mary, was against any form of "government aid" and called welfare "shameful." Bessie said her response had been, "Is it shameful to eat?"

The three men who fathered Bessie's six children and who were for varying amounts of time her lovers, friends, and partners worked inconsistently at jobs that included janitorial and maintenance work and "hustling," which Bessie defines as "runnin' numbers, sellin' junk to get more junk, and things of the street." Bessie understood that without an education she was even more limited than other poor Black women and southern transplants. The jobs she was able to land would always provide low wages and no benefits and would earn her very little respect or legibility outside of her low-income and predominantly Black neighborhood. Service sector work, in spite of its meager economic and social benefits, was the only way for Bessie to provide for her family. This usually meant that she was forced to work more than one full-time job at a time. By the late 1970's, when Bessie was thirty-one, she transitioned out of the restaurant industry and into home-based health care. Since she did not have a degree and was not certified, Bessie cared for working-class elderly individuals in their homes, where she primarily fulfilled the responsibilities of being a sitter and domestic worker. She worked for one client, an older woman who was suffering with dementia, for over fifteen years. The woman's grown children owned the two-story building where she lived and allowed Bessie and her family to stay on the second floor rent-free, in exchange for her care of the woman. Bessie was also paid for her time at the minimum wage. Without this limited opportunity, Bessie wonders how she would have been able to manage through the 1970s and early 1980s. Despite this change, she was still among the ranks of low-skilled, low-wage service sector workers in Detroit who tried to piece together a living outside of the automotive industry. In 1976, Bessie had her first son, Phillip. She had her last child, a boy she named Robert (but whom everyone took to calling Bip), at the age of thirty-five.

In her relationships with her brothers, lovers, and mother, Bessie defined what it meant to care and be cared for as context driven, a basic right to life and livelihood that necessarily shifts depending on circumstances. Her assessment of accountability, culpability, and even the appropriateness of demanding to be cared for requires a rethinking of the politics of care and protection that encircles families and the state, and which frequently excludes questions of love, pain, and desire as important mitigating factors in Black women's lives. Bessie didn't often reminisce about the men in her life, either those who left her or those whom she left, but when she did it seemed the passage of time allowed her to be fairly generous in her assessment of each man. She talked about JoJo's father with a careful attention to the details of their early courtship and what it meant for both of them to be too young to know that it could be "dangerous to be so full of hope." Gwen and Ruby's father, however, was defined by Bessie's indifference. She understood why it was hard for him to find steady work, combat the overt acts of daily discrimination, and still find a way to "tuck that all away to come home and care for his family," but that understanding did not translate into approval of him, and his name rarely passed her lips. When Bessie mentioned the father of Donna, Phillip, and Bip—the man who received the surprise visit in Ohio—it was as if she was talking about a disobedient but well-loved child, one whose selfishness she shook her head at but whose audacity she begrudgingly envied.

In the late 1990s, the twins were rediscovered by an underground international blues network, which enabled them to record three albums. In "Pursue Your Dreams," the title song of the second album, Samuel sings:

If you gotta dream, please go out and pursue your dream.
Yes, if you got a dream, please go out and pursue your dream
Cause if you don't
You gon' be a messed up chile.
Why you sitting there staring at them four walls?
Tell me why, why standing there praying at them four walls?
Well, you know you can do better,
You can go out and pursue your dreams.
Life is too short to find you done messed around with your life
Time is too short, honey, for you to mess around with your life
For it's all over, It'll be all over for you.

Samuel's tone is beseeching and carries a possibility-tinged desperation of the blues even though the naivete of the explicitly motivational lyrics is uncharacteristic of the Delta blues in particular. The twins warned that—given all of the factors that collude to disrupt lives and thwart plans, especially when you are Black and poor—not pursuing your dreams despite these realities is ultimately what can mess you up. The first generation of the Browns left Alabama with this belief. Bessie reads the actions of the twins, the fathers of her children, and her children through this lens of agency in the face of constraint, and she has compassion for her family's shortcomings and failures to a large degree because of this perception. She is not blind to the limits of individual motivation and bets on the fact that promises made in the pursuit of a dream are likely to be broken. But the ability to construct a vision for your life and to act even in some small way to move toward that goal affirms humanity in the face of continual dehumanization. Obligations to family can be obstacles in this pursuit, as Bessie well knows. Yet—although all members of her family are Black, undereducated, and marginally employed—not all members of her family are authorized to pursue dreams, or even to dream, with the same sort of unfettered mobility.

Mothers and Aunties

As we made our way back down Wesson Street at the end of our walk, I could make out someone who looked like Gwen talking to Phillip in the driveway. She placed her hand on his shoulder in a way that indicated she needed support, and he reached out to take her free hand. They were conversing like that, as if about to waltz, when Bessie and I walked by them.

"You can't speak now?" Gwen took her hand off Phillip's shoulder to point at me in mock anger.

"Oh. Hey Gwen, I didn't want interrupt." I gave her a hug as Phillip walked back toward the house.

"I thought you needed to be somewhere." Bessie playfully swatted Phillip on the back of his head.

"Nah. Gwen's home early." Phillip ran up the steps and disappeared into the house with the glasses Bessie and I had left on the back landing. Gwen is about a half-inch taller than five feet. I could see the defined muscles in her legs through her dark blue work pants when she shifted her weight from side to side to accommodate the pain in her bad leg. When she was sixteen, Gwen was caught in the crossfire and hit in the thigh by a stray bullet during an altercation between her neighbors. Ever since, she has been in chronic pain, which made standing for any extended period of time excruciating. The office in the local Department of Labor that managed disability and workmen's compensation would not recognize Gwen's disability, so she had become dependent on Advil, which only reduced the pain enough for her to remain upright. Crystal calls her mother "a general labor," as a way of describing her work on the late night shift at an automobile plant in Livonia and the part-time custodial services she provides to a local elementary school. Both jobs require Gwen to spend the majority of her eight- to twelve-hour shifts on her feet. Janice explains her grandmother's invitation for her mother and Janice and her siblings to stay in Bessie's home this way: "When she [Gwen] got home, she couldn't even take her clothes off. It was crazy. So Momma [Janice's grandmother] was like, 'you got to stay with me 'cause you can't even take care of yourself, let alone the kids.'" Janice's aunt Ruby, Bessie's third daughter, was already living in her home when Gwen and her family moved in. Ruby had been diagnosed with schizophrenia in her early twenties, and her struggles with mental illness and inability to receive quality health care made it impossible for her to maintain steady employment.

By 1987, the same year that GGC opened and two years after Mary's death, Bessie was living in the house on Wesson Street in southwest Detroit with her two young sons, Phillip and Bip; Ruby and her three-year-old son and one-year-old daughter; Gwen and her baby daughter, Janice; and Donna and her one-year-old daughter, Karlyn. All twelve people lived in a three-bedroom apartment. Ruby and Gwen contributed to the family income by working overnight janitorial shifts in office buildings and restaurants. Donna, then seventeen, found her time protected by Gwen and Ruby while she worked on her General Equivalency Diploma (GED) and took care of Karlyn. JoJo was already living on her own, and Donna moved out of Bessie's house shortly after earning her GED. Of Bessie's six children, Donna is the only one who earned her GED. JoJo dropped out of high school in her freshman year, and both Ruby and Gwen dropped out in the eighth grade. Phillip left in his sophomore year and Bip in his junior year.

Gwen swung her arm around my shoulder, encouraging me to walk with her back toward the sidewalk. When we reached my car, she asked if we could sit inside.

"Gwen, are you nuts? It is hot as hell in there, and you know I don't have air." It was so hot I hesitated to touch the door handle, gleaming in the blazing sun.

"We can sit with the doors open. No hotter than that house right now." Gwen smiled and winked, and in that moment looked exactly like a smaller version of Janice.

I sat on the small patch of grass on the passenger side of the car, where Gwen reclined with her legs extended under the dashboard. I propped my feet on the base of the car just inside the open door and folded my arms over my knees. Even though Gwen's eyes were closed and I felt like taking a nap, I leaned in to look as if I was ready to listen, knowing she wanted to talk.

"Phillip look taller to you?" I could tell that even as she asked, Gwen knew this was a ridiculous question since Phillip was twenty-seven and not going to get any taller (at over six feet, he was by far the tallest in the family). "I mean maybe he's just getting skinnier. He don't eat," Gwen added. I fidgeted on the grass and waited for what Gwen really wanted to say. I knew she loved all of her siblings but had a special relationship with Phillip and Ruby, who went out of their way to foresee her needs and watch over her physical health. I imagined Phillip's staying home that night had something to do with looking after Gwen, who had come home unexpectedly early. Crystal often called her uncle Phillip "a hustler." When she speculated on where his income came from, she told me that he "gets his money any way he can but not drugs . . . I don't think. I really don't know, to be honest. He got a bunch of bubbleheads, though, that probably give him payouts and stuff." Bip, on the other hand, was an aspiring rapper, and Crystal assured me he could "rap his ass off"—although she said that he did so primarily "on the streets and in Momma's house when we trying to watch TV." Bip was four years younger than Phillip and moved with a flowing grace that was in stark contrast to Phillip's always anxious and frenetic movements. Bip's voice was as smooth as suede, and it wasn't difficult to imagine him rapping with skill. However, I never got the impression that he, unlike his cult-favorite uncles, was on his way to a recording contract. Janice offered a more feasible explanation for Bip's source of income: "He on that child-care scam. He take Lelah's child-care check and act like he watching her baby, when most of the time Jasmine with her young ass be the one watching Lil Bip. He sometimes will give Jasmine some change, but usually he keep the check." A child-care check for one baby would amount to $120 per week for Bip.

"How's Janice?" Gwen's eyes were still closed. She folded her hands in her lap and turned her head to me. This was what I knew was coming. Janice and her cousins had been participating in GGC programs for over four years now, but this was the first time one of the Brown girls sought admittance to Fresh Start. "She ain't homeless. That makes zero sense," Gwen said. Her eyes were open now, and she was looking to me for a logical response. Although Fresh Start had a relatively nuanced definition of homelessness, I felt uncomfortable explaining that the nature of their current living situation in the very home we were parked outside of made Janice eligible for residence in the shelter.

For the first few years that I knew Janice and Crystal, I met a new brother, cousin, or nephew each time I dropped by. I watched a segment of the third generation of Brown women in Detroit progress from preteens to mothers and watched the second generation of women get smaller and more tired every time I saw them, which was about once every two weeks what with their hectic work schedules. All of the Brown girls cite first Bessie and then their mothers as their strongest sources of inspiration. Jasmine said that her mother, JoJo, made her proud because "she took care of all of us and did it by herself. Six kids . . . and her sisters and brothers. She's the oldest and was always helping out Momma." Janice also identified the women in her family as productive examples for adulthood: "I say my mom and Momma are the only role models I ever had. And some of my aunties, because they surviving in Detroit right now. Especially right now. Props to anybody who can do anything right now." On the day Janice decided to complete her Fresh Start intake paperwork, she also said: "I think I just don't want to be the same way or I just don't want to fall in the same way. I don't want to live with Momma. Yeah, I just don't want to be like a burden. I just don't want to become one."

"Struggly" and the Nuances of Struggle

Although the first and second generation of Brown women were able to manage despite physical and mental illness, men who refused or were unable to contribute to the families they helped make, insufficient income as payment for backbreaking work, and homes that landlords refused to maintain, the third generation of young women wanted to craft lives for themselves that were based on more than what they saw as survival. In the various Brown homes, the example set by Bessie and their mothers provided a counternarrative that allowed the younger women to understand struggle and the physical and emotional strength it demands. They admired the older women's fortitude but did not envy the multiple reasons why they required so much of it. Bessie's grandchildren often used the term *struggly* in talking about Bessie's and their mothers' lives. *Struggly* is different from what they defined as *a struggle* or *the struggle* or as *struggling through* something. *A struggle* meant the cost of being alive and confronting the daily challenges and disappointments that come with being human. *The struggle* referred to the status of Black people in the United States and was usually used in conjunction with identifying an act or situation as racist. *Struggling through* was completing something difficult and sometimes distasteful, with the understanding that you would be better off afterward. But *struggly* was doing difficult and distasteful things with no promise of reward. *Struggly* requires strength to get through but does not offer strategies to get out.

Janice appeared to be on her way to the type of mainstream success grounded in educational upward mobility when she passed the entrance exam for Monroe High School, Kwame Kilpatrick's alma mater. With over 95 percent of its graduates enrolling in four-year colleges, Monroe was considered the best public school in Detroit. Janice's previous academic record was spotty and her grades below average, but she was admitted to Monroe nonetheless because of her off-the-charts scores on the placement test. Despite Monroe's reputation as an undisputed academic powerhouse, it was not the academic challenges that discouraged Janice. She said it was "more of the social than the educational" that made her want to drop out of Monroe, since she felt that the "classes were like fairly easy. And for me to be in honors classes it wasn't that hard, but it was still a challenge." The real challenge for Janice was facing the contradiction between the educational mantra of "be smart, work hard, and love learning" and the myth of meritocracy played out through the failure of the politics of respectability tied to conspicuous consumption:

> I hated Monroe. There is so much hype about it being the best school, but to me it was just a bunch of snobs. Every day you had girls looking at you all up and down to see what you got on and just spending their time talking about what boy was doing what. I just didn't want to be there anymore. Every girl had a weave or something, and you know how I roll—I don't even care what my hair looks like, you know I'll get it braided or whatever, but they were so caught up in all that crap. You had to, like, have a Coach bag or Vuitton to go down these certain hallways. I liked the classes, but the other stuff was a trip. The other girls were so bourgie. I was into school, but I couldn't take the other stuff. The teachers tried to get me to stay, but I told them I wanted to go and

my mom was like, finally, you know, "You can go. Just go. If you hate it so much, you don't have to stay."

I wondered if Janice saw a long-term advantage in graduating from Monroe she could have endured the social frustrations and exclusion she felt outside of the classroom. The "bourgie" girls she talked about were predominantly from middle- and upper-middle-class Black families who knew that outside of a private school diploma, Monroe was the best route to elite institutions of higher education. Monroe had the kind of cultural cachet that makes an impression on college admissions committees as well as on the local social elite. Janice's decision to leave Monroe, a decision that was ultimately supported by her mother, represents a complicated intersection of issues. Embedded in the narrative she employed to talk about why she dropped out of high school and enrolled in the Job Corps are examples of the layered and contradictory forces that affect the decision-making processes of many young Black women living in environments that are short on resources.

The Job Corps used all of the language and symbols to recruit low-income youth of color that Janice usually despised. The terms *at-risk* and *high-risk* to Janice were "other ways for people to say that Black people are messed up." Yet the frequent use of these terms throughout the Job Corps's glossy brochures and on its colorful website did not bother her. When I grimaced at the Job Corps materials in my hands, Janice yanked them from my grip and said: "At least they telling it like it is—like they see it. They may be saying, like, 'Yeah, you don't have this or that. You are poor and your schools may suck, but we are going to help you get a job and get that high school diploma. I mean, at least they realize that there is a problem and it isn't just about Black kids not wanting to do well. They are looking at the whole country as a problem." I raise my eyebrows, but I have heard similar comments from too many other Black girls to discount her statement. What seems initially most appealing about the Job Corps to many of the young women I have met who have either attended it for short periods of time, been kept indefinitely on the waiting list, or even graduated from the program is the plain talk and clear expectations. "Job Corps is about getting you a job"—that statement reflects young women's beliefs that despite what they have been told about staying in school, it is the social service programs outside of the school that operate under the most realistic curriculum guidelines. Janice continued: "They call it what it is and teach you exactly what you need to know to get hired. It ain't about all that extra, 'for show' stuff that I was learning at Monroe just to demonstrate to somebody I was educated. When will I speak Latin? Never. But I can learn how to repair a computer today and get hired by somebody tomorrow."

I don't know if Janice chose to forget or changed her mind about how she wanted to express her recollection of her experience at Monroe, but I distinctly remember the "for show" stuff and the liberal arts part of her experience being what most ignited her interest in the educational process at Monroe and helped her decide that it was a good thing to "be open and try things that you may think people like you shouldn't or couldn't do." In the end, Janice stopped going to her classes at the Job Corps after fighting with instructors and administrators over the fact that young women were overwhelmingly put in the clerical studies and certified nursing assistant tracks instead of the more lucrative and viable computer repair courses, where young men were directed.[7] The day after she was "dishonorably discharged," she seemed both relieved and confused as we sat in the park eating ice-cream sandwiches as a half-hearted attempt at celebration. The Job Corps presented Janice with the role and status expectations for a Black girl with her life story, which were more subtly implied through the middle-class exclusions she felt at Monroe. The unevenness in the outcomes of these institutional engagements added to Janice's difficulty in coming to conclusions about what success could mean in her life. At the time, her cousin Gina was enrolled in the Job Corps's medical billing track, and her cousin Anita was in the carpentry track. Both of them had confidence in the Job Corps's guarantee that they would be placed in jobs shortly after they received their vocational certificates. Gina had left Wayne State University for the Job Corps, a choice that appeared to pain her professors and baffle the caseworkers at GGC.

Gina and Anita left their children in Bessie's care while they worked toward their certificates. Along with Anita's three-year-old twin boys and Gina's two-year-old son, Bessie also cared for their older sister Sharon's two daughters and Karlyn's daughter, Alani. The child-care subsidies that her grandchildren received through the Family Independence Agency barely covered the expenses involved in providing daily care to six great-grandchildren. With children always under foot and ends that could rarely be made to meet, Janice's ever-present concern for her grandmother's physical and emotional well-being was understandable. Bessie, however, talks about her grandchildren's pursuit of vocational certificates in relationship to her own migration to Detroit and youthful ideas about security and family: "Education is how you get it done nowadays. I ain't studyin' that then. I had JoJo, but that didn't matter 'cause I was coming up here where there was money to be made. But jobs ain't stable always, and you can't count on no man to be the one providing. I think all my girls thought some man was going to bring home the money and they all could be stayed up in the house taking care of kids, cooking, cleaning." Bessie talked about the promise of economic gains to be made in the move to Detroit as the reason why she was not concerned with finishing high school, even though it may appear as if an early pregnancy was her obstacle. Her view was, "Who needs an education, when you can get along without it?" She thought this way primarily because she did not know anyone in her family or immediate community who had gotten ahead because of education. There was no model of how education might translate into success. Bessie framed her daughters' orientation to education and work as tied to their ideas about the traditional gendered roles for women in the home. From her perspective, JoJo, Ruby, and Gwen did not see education as a necessity when there was a man who could provide for them financially. Unfortunately, this heteronormative model of a financially stable nuclear home was not within the grasp of the Brown women.

In addition to relying on men for economic stability, Bessie also cautioned her granddaughters about the dangers of falling in love. Essentially, Bessie believed that relying on men for economic security or love was a mistake. *Getting caught up* was a term used interchangeably with *falling in love* to connote the lack of discernment that comes from loving the wrong person too deeply. As Crystal explained her older relatives' attitude, "They feel like they was tricked or something. Like these dudes was pretending to be in love and then left, like 'peace out.' And, I guess, they don't want that to happen to us." To Bessie and her daughters, "getting caught up" could lead to parenting on your own and working double shifts on an empty stomach so your children didn't have to miss a meal. And yet—similar to the mother's sentiment expressed in the epigraph to the Ntozake Shange novel *Sassafrass, Cypress, and Indigo*—Bessie wanted, more than anything, for her daughters to find happiness regardless of the route they traveled to get there.

I think about the ways Gwen may feel that she got caught up as she massages her thigh and leans further back in the passenger seat. "I guess I can't be mad," Gwen starts again. "She will make sure she gets what she needs." Gwen starts laughing about an earlier example of Janice's self-care tactics that had been no laughing matter at the time. A year ago, motivated by the difficulties she encountered at Monroe and the absence of the adult women in her life who spend most of their days working around the clock, Janice demanded that her father acknowledge her and become involved in her life, even though none of her siblings have a relationship with their fathers. She found his address on a piece of documentation that her mother was holding onto and went to his house. He reluctantly and briefly spoke with Janice that first time, mainly out of shock, but she persisted:

> I was like on the bus every week to his house. His girlfriend was all pissy and I was like, "Look, I am not here to see you, talk to you, or get to know his other kids. I am here to see my father. Yes, my father. And he will act like a father." So now we hang out, and I went to my aunt's funeral—my aunt on his side. I guess his aunt, my great aunt. And all these people was like, "Whose child is you?" I was like, "Bessie's my gram momma," 'cause I know they all knew who Bessie was even if they didn't know me.

When she got to the part of the story where Janice met her father at his door, Gwen imitated the face she imagined he had made and leaned forward in her seat, hands on hips, to paraphrase the monologue Janice had performed for me on more than several occasions. Gwen was animated now, and I laughed with her, hoping her leg hurt a little less. I walked with her to the back of the house and headed to my car, absent-mindedly kicking the pebbles in the driveway. On my way home I passed GGC and realized at the stoplight in front of the shelter that I had never told Gwen how Janice was.

Remapping and Retelling

Now, in 2013, as Bessie moves into her late sixties, her daughters continue to work and negotiate relationships of care and support, and Janice's generation makes the transitions from middle school and junior high to parenting and adulthood, the Brown family continues to illuminate alternative versions of the residue of Detroit's history. The city filed for bankruptcy, and the many people ready to assign blame have generally looked in the usual places—in the actions of politicians as distant as Coleman Young and as recent as Kwame Kilpatrick, the aftermath of white flight, deindustrialization, decades of crumbling local infrastructure, disinvestment in the city by the state and federal governments, and a populace thought to be motivated by uninformed anger. The bailout that rescued the automobile companies was narratively cast as a temporary support to a worthy, but challenged, industry—an agreement of financial backing and promised payback among corporations embodied by men. The bankruptcy, however, was told as the final and decisive chapter in the history of a fatally troubled city. Detroit was first taken over by the state (who appointed an emergency manager) and then declared bankrupt, and discussions of both moves had undertones of failure that was feminized in the same way that poverty has become over the past five decades. The unthinkable spectacle of a city filing for bankruptcy is, like the riots of 1943 and 1967, an event that has fossilized Detroit in the popular imagination as the symbol of economic decline in the United States.

But Detroit's history is more than a series of tragic events and unfortunate circumstances. Similarly, the Brown family is, despite what normative analyses would have us believe, "more than a tangle of pathologies and misfortunes" (R. Ferguson 2004, 1). As Bessie demonstrates in her reflections on the 1967 rebellion, the singular events that mark time in official history do not adequately convey the quotidian history that shapes the way Black women and girls live through their cities and are contained by the physical and symbolic territories whose creation they both contribute to and contest. I am interested in what matters to Black girls and women, like those in the Brown family, as they are talked around and about historical narratives that constitute how they are able to live and imagine in the present. The Browns represent, in many ways, the Black women who came to Detroit during the late Great Migration to find that even low-paid clerical work was not an option for an undereducated, poor woman of color. The promise of prosperity in the North in all of the ways that it was often defined—through economic resources, access to education, and the ability to establish a nuclear family headed by an employed man and sustained by a hardworking woman in the home—did not apply to Bessie Brown. This promise was made to white, heterosexual, able-bodied, economically viable males and, by default, their wives.

Enumerating the ways in which the Browns deviate from white middle-class norms and sensibilities or violate codes of respectability for the sake of detailing points of rupture and dissent is not only unhelpful, it is dangerous. Instead, I argue that their experiences and their processes of self- and social reflection can be the sources of a generative politics of transformation. As Bessie, Gwen, Ruby, and Janice renarrate Detroit as rhetorical space, they also plot the city's physical landscape. The Brown family charts new routes with the intention of providing for more, albeit still limited, freedom and marks potential sites of care and protection.

In these territories, the urban tale of Black men and boys as forever in danger or dangerous and Black women and girls as the facilitators or perpetuators of this dynamic loses legitimacy as it is replaced by more complicated and intractable structural realities. Yet Black women move "through and beyond practices of domination" in their structural realities to demonstrate that geography is, as Katherine McKittrick notes, an "alterable terrain" through which they can "assert their sense of place" (2006, xxxi). What this precipitates is a shift in the shape of the city from the perspective of the Black women and girls who appear to exist on the outer rim of civic life due to, among other things, their status as single mothers of multiple children and part-time workers providing surplus labor. In the process, Black women and girls, as evidenced by the Brown family, enact and claim family in ways that force a rethinking of home, home spaces, and homelessness.[8]

In many ways, the Brown family experiences citizenship as a series of closures and exclusions. Boundaries (geographic, material, and ideological) attempt to order and constrict their worlds within and beyond the space of Detroit. There is an important spatial and temporal shift, however, that occurs when the Browns are positioned at the center of the well-worn tale of Detroit's fall from industrial grace and the subsequent challenges created in Black lives. Detroit has been captured and suspended in time by spectacular events and inconceivable moments like the demise of the supposedly indestructible automobile industry and the audacious corruption of the Kilpatrick campaign. In what has come to be known as Detroit "ruin porn," professional and amateur photographers showcase images in online forums of eerily dilapidated houses and empty lots so overgrown with weeds and other vegetation that the streets look like Mississippi in the early twentieth century. The "fascination with images of first-world urban decline" (Leary 2011) and the powerful visual symbolism of deteriorating spaces in Detroit's landscape fix the city in time as a cautionary tale spun from the nation's industrial past. At the same time, because Detroit is characterized as presently irredeemable, it is the site of continual theoretical speculation about ways of living and producing capital in the future. In a future Detroit, empty lots may be the solar-powered urban gardens that both feed and create new communities while providing skills for local economic markets that may challenge the destructiveness of global capitalism. Detroit is, thus, constructed in the past and future tense but rarely in the present.[9] It is easier to discursively erase real live human beings in the past and future than it is in the present.

In "Detroitism," John Leary identifies three of the most common narrative tropes used to discuss contemporary Detroit: Detroit as a metonym for the auto industry; the Detroit lament, which dramatizes Detroit's history through "spectacles of degradation"; and Detroit Utopia, which envisions a future perfect Detroit that offers an experiment for the future emerging from a failed past (2011). The primary subject for the second trope, lamentations on Detroit, "is spatial—the empty lots, the derelict buildings, the overwhelming vastness of a city mutilated by freeways and marked by more vacant land than it can ever plausibly develop" (ibid.). The Detroit Lament and the preoccupation with Detroit told and visually represented through a series of material relics is an aesthetic of poverty that depends on both the absenting of people and the stagnation of time through encapsulated events. The Detroit Lament, I argue, works in tandem with what I term the Black Women's Lament to establish the parameters that all generations of the Brown family live and work through. The Black Women's Lament echoes throughout social science literature on poor Black communities and is carried over into popular media and urban policy reforms. Similar to the Detroit Lament, the Black Women's Lament also locks time and space. But here Black women and girls are the frozen embodiment of anxieties about the interdependency of the normative family structure and capitalist exploitation. The pathological Black family at the center of Daniel Patrick Moynihan's report (1965) became codified through the image of the Black matriarch who is domineering and emasculating, yet not competent enough in her powers of control to sustain a healthy family environment. The failures of Black motherhood that Moynihan promoted extend to an overall denigration of Black womanhood and evoke the additional tropes of the hardheaded and mean-spirited Sapphire and the sexually promiscuous Jezebel. These tropes easily morph in name, but not deed, into the welfare queens of the late 1980s, the ghetto hood rats of the 1990s, and the ratchedness of the new millennium. However, Janice and her family disrupt the narratives that bind Detroit and Black women in mutually constructed geographies of dysfunction by revealing the boundaries of exclusion that mark off and enforce this physical and psychic territory. The Browns also show us where we might be able to locate a space from which to theorize and practice a politics that provides young Black women with a "definitional power" (Cacho 2012, 48) that could be employed in not just naming their current experiences, but also in experimenting and modeling ways of being that are now unimaginable.

Motherhood, neighborhood, and work are the broad categories that constitute the boundaries of exclusion legitimizing the Browns' partial citizenship in a politics of care that spans the private realm of mother-daughter relationships as well as the relationship between young Black women and the state. In the following section, I trace how these boundaries have been erected and have merged over time. I then discuss entitlement as the important shapeshifting intervention the Browns suggest for enacting a different politics of care that is fluid and responsive to the needs of Black women living in stressed environments. Both the Browns and I operate from the understanding that the present state of exploitation and subjugation that creates these environments cannot continue into the future.

The Public and Private Policing of Race in Detroit

By 1943, two years before Bessie was born, the number of Blacks living in Detroit had risen to 200,000, which was double the number in 1933. Overcrowded and unsafe rental apartments were the only options for low-income Blacks, who lacked both the money for and the social access to better housing. A crucial turning point that precipitated the 1943 riot was based on the fight for housing in the city and the militant policing of geographic boundaries that marked off the limits of white and black spaces. With no other room to build on or move the black population to, the city constructed the Sojourner Truth projects on land in a location considered a white area. Verbal and physical confrontations between white protestors and black would-be residents accelerated into what has gone down in history as the race riot of 1943.

It is important to note that the rumors that ignited the actual acts of rebellion in the summer of 1943 were differently cast in the white and Black communities, but in both cases the rumors relied on motherhood, gendered femininity, and race. The story that ignited Blacks was that a mob of white men had murdered a Black woman and thrown her baby off the Belle Isle Bridge. Whites were mobilized by the rumor that a group of Black men had raped and murdered a white woman. Collective reimaginings of riots and the acts of physically performed emotion associated with them are generally cast as masculine or enacted primarily by men with women (both Black and white) as the victims. This may be why the action taken by a group of white women during the Sojourner Truth housing project standoff presents itself as an act that was ripe with a differently enacted form of gendered and raced symbolism.

A group of white women with baby carriages and American flags patrolled the outskirts of the project, demanding that their neighborhood be protected from the migration of Blacks with no other place to go in a city growing in leaps and bounds. These women strategically and simultaneously shielded their homes and themselves from the geographic, site-specific breakdown of their racial boundaries, which had been unchallenged until this time.[10] Blackness, however, was making its way into their world, and they found motherhood and nationalism to be their strongest symbolic weapons. Motherhood embodied in the physical form of white femininity has been constructed into a sacred institution in the United States. Black motherhood, which has historically been portrayed in the instinctual nurturing quality found in the nanny or nonmother caregiver happy to soothe and protect all children except her own, but the white mother is of the white family, one of the pillars of society upholding social norms and a cornerstone of American culture (Feldstein 2000).

It was not just bodies that stood in protest and physically performed the process of making and defending boundaries. Prior to the riots of 1967, in attempts to prevent housing integration, white residents erected a six-foot-high, one-foot-wide concrete wall along 8 Mile Road[11] as a material reminder and threat to Blacks considering purchasing homes or renting apartments out of their bounds. Policemen in groups famously called the Big Four patrolled the streets of all Black neighborhoods, looking for young Black men to pull aside and search for identification to reinforce the violence of social isolation and restricted mobility that the wall represented. If concrete edifices and flag-waving mothers could not keep the Black population confined and at bay, perhaps the humiliation of having to legally and continuously prove themselves as legitimate beings would. Certain documents or papers lend credibility, confer or deny citizenship, and allow or restrict access to resources and places. Police officers, representing the state, are authorized to control public spaces by, among other things, demanding that individuals prove their identities and right to occupy those spaces. The Big Four mentality has a long history, rooted in plantation slavery and fears that Black bodies perceived to be only property and labor would escape and claim their rights to full personhood. The contemporary policing of Black men and boys, like the 1960s and earlier criminalization of Blackness, is predicated on the valuelessness of Black life outside of labor and the potential to be turned into other sources for commodification.

Historically, the focus on the policing of Black women and girls has been in the home, intimate relationships, and the politics of respectability that govern that private context with significant implications for being in public. Given the realities of the raced, gendered, and classed reproductive labor market, low-income Black women have never been confined to the home and have always had to devise strategies to protect their bodies, minds, and spirits as they necessarily crossed and transgressed social and geographic boundaries. Like Black men and boys, Black women and girls have had to understand the creative negotiation of public space as a matter of life and death. Janice notes this fact in the van when she sees her cousin's friend Troy in the street. "Nobody really wants to see us out here," she says, addressing the ever-present risks Black boys and girls encounter when their bodies meet the street. Although Janice uses the pronoun "us," it is clear that she feel less certain about the prospects for Black boys. She takes up the concern for the viability of Black males that is reproduced in urban studies literature and public debates. Janice's grandmother, mother, and aunts exhibit a similar concern in how they discuss the men in their lives, particularly Bessie's sons, Bip and Phillip. What does this mean for how the future is conceptualized in the Brown family for and by Black girls? Janice and her cousins are the first members of the family most likely to be charged with devising alternate plans when the occupancy rate of one of the homes becomes too high. Their repeated acts of place making beyond any one location identified as home refers to their mothers' and grandmother's fluid movements within notions of home and family.

The Artistry (and Privilege) of a Self-Made Life

Bessie talks about her twin brothers with affection and envy. Even when they all lived together in Florence, Alabama, Samuel and Simon were encouraged to bring music into the home and follow their own rhythms in life outside of the domestic space. The twins were blues men and, because they were artists and men, were expected to be mobile, following self-directed paths. Their love of music did not mean that they were unaware or uninterested in the real possibility of economic security promised through work in Detroit's automobile industry. Dividing their days between the predictable routine of the plant and the sweet release and leisurely excitement in the clubs in the Black Bottom, a predominantly Black neighborhood in the city that was demolished in the 1960s, they experienced Black Detroit at work and play and blurred the distinction between the two.[12] Bessie was never under the impression that her life would flow as seamlessly from Alabama to Detroit as was the case for her brothers. But she always held out hope that she might be able to live on her own terms. When Bessie excused the twins' absence from the family and their failure to share the responsibilities of caring for their mother, she does so with the understanding that the life of an artist means that creativity is attracted and led to the spaces through which it is fed. I am interested in how Black women like Bessie sustain an investment in creativity and artistic self-making despite the realities of their socioeconomic status and the multiple exclusionary practices that challenge their mobility and personal efficacy.

Aspects of the lives of Janice and her peers point to the ways that creative self-making, or shapeshifting, can be reclaimed by Black girls and women through the exercise of critical entitlement. A sense of entitlement exhibited by Black girls is one that explicitly acknowledges the intrinsic value of all human life and the right to be protected and cared for. Bessie yearns not for a life that is unfettered by responsibilities to loved ones but for one that allows her to explore, travel, love, and establish relationships to people and places without confronting sanctions or surveillance—a life in which her intrinsic value as well as her desires and dreams are honored and protected. This is something that Janice attempts to claim for herself, and whose lack in her grandmother's and mother's lives she describes as "struggly." Both entitlement and struggliness is evident in the women's blues tradition, in which Black women like Ma Rainey and Bessie Smith "bore witness to the contradictory historical demands made of black American women" (A. Davis 1999, 22). As Angela Davis states, "women's blues cannot be understood apart from their role in the molding of an emotional community based on the affirmation of black people's—and in particular black women's—absolute and irreducible humanity. The blues woman challenges in her own way the imposition of gender-based inferiority" (ibid., 36). Samuel and Simon were not the only ones in the Brown family to carry forward a tradition of creatively and critically bearing witness, even if they were the only ones to do so on albums and international tours. Bessie and her daughters challenge gender politics through the shape and form of their families and the roles they take on inside and outside of the home as democratic heads of households and members of a team of breadwinners.

Bessie was never opposed to marriage or the idea of a nuclear family. Her ability to achieve heteronormative familial and romantic relationships was thwarted by mainstream cultural representations of Black womanhood that construct Bessie, Gwen, Ruby, Janice, and her cousins in opposition to these ideals. The conditional nature of citizenship for the women and girls in the Brown family means that they are challenged with attempting to live according to tropes of white femininity and motherhood even while their failure is predetermined. This contradiction is supported by the "nation-state's attempts to naturalize the splitting of self into that which is—always incompletely—integrated into the state as citizen and that which haunts that project by imagining ways of being and communal identifications that transcend, ignore, displace, upend, or undermine the singular predominance of these administrative investments and arrangements" (Iton 2008, 32). Women's blues traditions express these contradictions and impossibilities as well as, more importantly, the possibility of embracing so-called alternative ways of living as essential work for asserting the entitled ownership of one's self.[13] Black women, particularly poor Black women, have been held physically and psychologically captive through colonial practices that are still evident in the exclusionary boundaries of traditional definitions of womanhood that exile them from geographic spaces and sites of potential capital gain—such as neighborhoods and jobs that provide a living wage. This makes claiming ownership of the self a radical act within a history of Black struggle. The Brown girls read the struggly experiences of the women in their family in attempting to claim ownership of their lives as examples of the responsibilities of citizenship without the corresponding rights, and through this critique they offer insights into how a politics of care as actualized by Black girls might work differently.

Take Care

The concept of care shows up in the Brown women's lives in several ways that are openly referred to and inadvertently challenged by the third generation. Even before she came to Detroit, Bessie was part of the reproductive care industry, taking care of other families' homes and children. In Detroit, she continued to work caring for other households while building and maintaining her own.[14] Shifts in the economic terrain meant that Bessie and her daughters labored in the service industry, providing a different sort of widely accessible care to the general public. Gwen and Ruby worked in food service, retail, and other service industry jobs while often working shifts in automotive plants in the nearby suburbs or working overnight as security guards. The physical requirements of this work taxed their bodies, which were already weakened by self-care home remedies that replaced the professional health care made available only inconsistently through their jobs. The expenditure of emotional labor in their service industry jobs compelled them to provide care for their own children in a state of exhaustion. Yet, in the brutal irony of working in the care industry without reciprocity, the Brown women fought to create homes where joy and collective caregiving existed.

The homes of Ruby, Gwen, Donna, and Bessie are a network of spaces of care that map Detroit for the Janice and her cousins. Their routes through the city start from home spaces that are more than just the physical location of any one house. The younger women additionally find and make home in the places like the street where a cousin's friend thought to be out too late at night is briefly seen and looked after as a young person in need of care instead of as a threat to public order. When the house of Bessie or one of their mothers becomes uncomfortable with too many bodies and not enough people honoring the familial contract of care, the younger women move through the city to locate a different home where the contract is presently intact. In considering the connection between Black bodies and risk, Katharyne Mitchell argues that "certain bodies have become vessels for concepts of risk formed in anticipation of an inevitable future" (2009, 239). Race as historically and spatially formed determines who is both deemed valueless and identified as a future failure. "The link to pre-known spaces of failure is crucial as it both constitutes Pre-Blackness (being in the wrong alley or park with the wrong kind of body), and it also provides the punishment—exile from those spaces" (ibid., 254). According to neoliberal logic, Detroit could be considered a space of postfailure and the Brown girls considered post-Black bodies that have failed because of the unwieldy combination of their race, gender, and class. In this scenario, Black girls belong in a certain sense in and to Detroit but are out of place outside of the home, the historical site that constructs their presumed dysfunctionality. Deviant, but predictably so, in their homes and in danger or dangerously misplaced in public spaces and institutions, Black girls are compelled to occupy the realms of the private and public with a skill that supports their interest in care, protection, and independence.

Despite the incredible labor involved in providing care across settings to people and institutions both intimately familiar and far removed,

Ruby's and Gwen's multiple jobs outside of the home and low wages su-perficially and simplistically support the trope of bad Black motherhood. They are often away from home for more than a day at a time, working back-to-back eight-hour shifts in locations too far from home to allow them to return late at night, given the unreliability of public transporta-tion. They may stay instead at the home of a co-worker or friend who lives closer to work. The inadequate wages they make despite all of this home shifting, bodily wear and tear, and emotional stress generally only give them enough money to buy food, to make small partial payments on utility bills, and to pay for transportation—and thus to continue the cycle of stressful work that provides the bare minimum of food, shel-ter, and transport. These sacrifices and strategic communal practices of survival are presented through conservative neoliberalism as disorgani-zation and calculated laziness designed to swindle resources out of the state. This is a different sort of entitlement, a state-generated falsehood that works to define poor Black women like the Browns as undeserving through stereotypical narratives of entitled greed. In the times when the Browns needed the support of public assistance, Mary's suggestion that welfare "is shameful" competed with Bessie's question: "Is it shameful to eat?" The decision to live and care for oneself and one's family was, thus, always already wrapped up in a politics of surveillance and respectability and the threat of shame. In addition, "the rights of citizenship—uniform on paper, but varied in practice—become interrogated and contested" as women like Bessie and Mary attempt to "lay claim to 'help,' broadly defined" (Watkins-Hayes 2009, 3). In these instances the Brown women were responding to the powerful and fantastical representation of the Reagan-era welfare queen sitting on top of a stack of money, continually bearing children and manipulating men and the state to feed her greed. The state's care for low-income Black women is, thus, shamefully nonex-istent in the face of the care that they provide to the state in spite of the threats to their own physical, mental, and emotional health.

Entitlement

The language of entitlement in welfare discourse paints recipients (who are also inaccurately portrayed as all female and Black) as demanding finan-cial resources and services that go beyond the bounds of their rights. Their demands are considered suspicious because the true right-bearing citizen is seen as making enough to support him- or herself and a family and as upholding the state through the production of highly valued specialized labor and the consumption of goods that feed the global economy. Poor Black women, although historically and currently supporting the workings of capitalism through their often forced reproductive labor, do not match this prototypical citizen. Entitlement in the language of welfare reform is the language of historical erasure articulated through the grammar of racist tropes. A libertarian notion of entitlement, on the other hand, proclaims that citizens (here, we can assume the term means only the white and wealthy) have the right to the fruits of their labor and the right to acquire property without interference. According to this view, "racial discrimination in education, employment, and housing is, thus, historically understood as private property" (L. Davis 1976, 74). Janice's version of entitlement, however, is something entirely different.

According to Janice, entitlement for a Black girl recognizes the value of all people and takes it for granted that individual actions always have larger consequences for the community. These fundamental beliefs are the foundation for Janice's demands to be, first of all, accurately seen and, subsequently, properly cared for and protected.[15] Within the habitus, if you will, of the Brown family we see this in the contract of care among Gwen, Ruby, Donna, Bessie, and—to lesser degrees—Bip and Phillip. To the best of their ability, at any given time a member will take the lead in maintaining the home, providing a combination of material resources and physical support for the other members. Although the adults are the primary caregivers in this network of homes, houses, and variously employed and variously healthy individuals, the roles that the girls in the third generation play in keeping the balance in the home are significant.

In the years that I have known the Brown girls, they have talked openly about overcrowding and the lack of material resources and have insisted that their decision to leave when overcrowding occurs is never a response to violence or the threat of bodily harm or violation. Because the Brown girls had been open about these threats in other areas of their lives, I have no reason not to believe them when they discuss leaving home as a decision tied primarily to the allocation of resources and an assessment of who can be the most mobile, who has at that time the ability to shift spaces and make a home out of the available options. These people tend, from the perspective of Janice and her cousins, to be the young women in the family. Yet given the statistics on the occurrence of sexual assault among Black girls in the United States, which tell us that 60 percent of Black girls experience sexual abuse from Black men before the age of eighteen,[16] I felt it naive to assume that overcrowding in their homes was the primary reason the girls felt compelled to leave. The realities of sexual abuse that Janice shared with me years later, after I was no longer working at Fresh Start and no longer living in Detroit, speak to the several interconnected and deeply troubling forces that contribute to the normalization of violence and abuse in the lives of young Black women and the silence about abuse that occurs in the home.

The adult men who live in the Brown homes rarely contribute resources in the form of money, food, or assistance with household maintenance that would mean professionals would not have to be paid to fix things like plumbing or electricity. And, in certain cases, what they do provide contributes to the physical and emotional pain experienced by the girls and women in the home. The men and women in the Brown family compel us, however, to hold several things in tension. Bessie's sons are not expected to provide income and sustain the functioning of the home, unlike Gwen and Ruby—who work multiple jobs while attempting to manage daily domestic routines. Although the Brown women express frustration with their brothers and the men who are their inconsistent lovers and live on and off under their roofs, they rarely demand that these men leave, find employment, or contribute financially. Even when work becomes untenable for the women—as was often the case for Gwen, given the pain of her disability—not working or not at least finding some way to bring money into the home was not an option that they considered. The distinctions between the value placed on the lives of Black men and Black women were always evident to Bessie. The twins had talent, no doubt, but they were also able to experiment with and develop that talent because they were men. They could both work and play in Detroit. And even though both prospects required resilience in the face of racism and economic exclusion, the twins still had room to direct a great portion of their lives. Bessie's limited education and minimal experience working outside of domestic spaces unfortunately meant that she fit perfectly into the shifting postindustrial economic landscape as a low-wage service worker. In Alabama, she and her mother developed intimate (yet still obviously based on power inequities) relationships with the families for whom they worked. This meant that their employers often made certain concessions, such as providing transportation to and from work and offering advances in pay, that would not happen at Bessie's service industry and retail jobs in Detroit where she was just another worker expected to perform and serve.

Bessie said more than once that "it was much harder for the girls—Gwen and Ruby and them. They worked for bosses who couldn't bother to learn their names. So, something go down at home where they couldn't work, they was still supposed to or it was a wrap for them. No questions asked. Or they just looked to the next girl in line." But, despite the anonymity of Black women in the service industry in Detroit, Bessie believes it is even worse for Black men, who she says "can't even get looked at to get hired." It is curious, then, that Bessie also believes that "having men in the home is good luck. Means there is a chance things will start coming your way." Gwen and Ruby have expressed similar sentiments in that they see men as "lucky" even when men's actions contradict that view. The value of men, simply as men, in larger society appears to translate to potential sources of capital to the Brown women. In the context of an unpredictable economy where, no matter how it rises and falls, Black women are inevitably at the bottom, betting on the individuals who have the most intrinsic value within the systems of patriarchy that support their marginalization is logical. Add to this the fact that Black men have been discursively constructed as both dangerous to and in danger of failing within traditional American culture, and Black men become vulnerable in addition to being favored in the eyes of the Brown women.

The perceived status of being most vulnerable to the state yet more likely to achieve the benefits of inclusion and acceptance within the state validates the men's presence in the home even when their vulnerability or capital gain are negligible there. It also means that when Black girls are sexually assaulted in the home by Black men, the failure to act on the part of the mothers and aunts likely stems in part from this devastating confluence of human devaluation. There is also the popular assumption that Black women have a fear of contributing to the vilification of the Black man and making him further susceptible to the criminal justice system. But where does this intense focus on Black men leave the young Black women who are perpetually under siege by state attempts to regulate and contain them and by perpetrators, often within their own homes and communities, who feel invested with the power to claim ownership over their bodies? And, how do we imagine that love, desire, and attachment figure into all of this?[17]

Entitlement means that the young women in the Brown family do not think the struggles that take place within their homes—mostly shouldered by their mothers, aunts, and themselves—are just the way things should be. For Janice, the generation of older women's lives are "struggly" because these women have no possibility of moving forward to live in ways that reflect their capacities, hopes, and desires. Janice comes to Fresh Start not because she does not have an actual house where she can lay her head down and find a meal, but because she believes she is entitled to more than the means of survival and has the right to be protected and free from bodily, emotional, and mental harm. Within a political economy established on an ideological framework that refutes the humanity of Blacks, Black men and women living in poverty can attempt to prove their value only as contributors to the economic systems that exclude them from any real substantive engagement as social actors, citizens, or human beings worthy of being seen and protected. The stakes are highest, however, for Black girls, who live at the dangerous intersection of Blackness, girlhood, and poverty.

Although Janice's analysis of why she did not stay at Monroe and make the most of her apparent scholarly potential is contradictory, her demand to be educated without the distraction of having to accept middle-class economic status reflects a sense of entitlement to receive the benefits from public institutions that they were established to provide. The ostensibly wealthier students at Monroe constituted for Janice a judgmental gaze that highlighted the importance of middle-class norms within a predominantly Black space. The Job Corps, in contrast, exemplified the gendered limitations for economic mobility, even though it was through the Job Corps that Janice managed to attain her GED and apply for admission to Wayne State University, despite the fact that she failed to complete the program. Janice criticizes both institutional spaces for their failure to educate and afford opportunities free of class- and gender-based exclusions. She knows that she and other young Black women are entitled to more. This does not mean, however, that she ultimately took actions that could have helped her in successfully navigating either institution or disrupting the status quo according to which they operated. Nonetheless, I think it is important to consider how Janice asks new questions based on conversations that link cultural capital and social mobility. In this regard, I am influenced by Alford Young's ethnographic research with marginalized Black men and Prudence Carter's work on minority students' deployment of cultural capital, both dominant and oppositional, to gain status in schools. Young argues that in the long tradition of research on urban poverty, poor Black men have been assessed through frameworks that focus primarily on values and norms. What gets lost in these analyses are the complex ways in which social actors are continually assigning meaning to the world around them and operating from beliefs based on "weighing various possibilities for their futures and making conscious choices" (2004, 6). Carter's research reveals that minority students do not respond in just one way to the dominance of mainstream cultural practices in schools that marginalize their ethnic and racial cultures. Code switching is not linear nor uniformly accessed by students navigating the styles of behavior, values, and linguistic mandates related to dominant cultural capital. In critiquing the oppositional framework traditionally employed to explain academic achievement gaps, Carter writes that it "ignores the full spectrum of why and how culture becomes a social and political response to schooling by discounting the positive values and functions of these students' culture, instead focusing on their culture as a maladaptive response to social marginalization, and consequently paying no attention to the roles and values of non-dominant cultural practices in the lives of many minority youth" (2005, 8). The experiences of Janice and her peers offer the possibility of theorizing marginal status and assessing prospects for social mobility differently. It is important to pay attention to Janice's beliefs or, in Young's terms, to what she believes are the likely and possible outcomes in the various realms of her life. It is also important to consider how she manages code switching and strategies for maneuvering through educational and training spaces. However, Janice's apparent failure at a traditional, academically rigorous high school despite her ability to succeed intellectually in this space may point to another possibility that needs to be more thoroughly explored. Rather than devising plans and implementing new methods for climbing various social ladders or for struggling and failing through oppositional practices, Janice proposes the option of kicking the ladder out from under mobility and achievement. She does not avoid social institutions charged with educating, training, and employing, but—through a profound sense of basic human entitlement—she does demand that the terms of these institutions shift. Instead of changing and managing her body, behavior, and desires, she demands that schools and programs live up to their stated and official missions to provide services for her. Janice asks for the reciprocity in the politics of care that she sees as denied to her mother, aunts, and grandmother.

In her family, where she undoubtedly loves and admires the resilience of the women, Janice still expresses her entitlement to a home that provides the material comforts and stability that nurture the physical and mental health that proved elusive to Gwen and Ruby. She also expresses the fact that she and all generations of women and girls in the Brown family are entitled to experience loving relationships and romantic partnerships in ways they define as fulfilling. Janice's investment in performing academically and socially at Monroe is tied to her assessment of Monroe as an institutional space that is unlikely to reward her for her efforts once she leaves the school—whether returning to her life on Wesson Street at the end of the day or transitioning into the world of work and career opportunities after graduation. She acts, or not, based on what has proved to work for her in the contexts in which she most frequently finds herself and, therefore, she has the most experience with in terms of devising strategies that serve her shifting interests and needs. Her assessment of the sorts of behaviors and attitudes that are valuable and beneficial does not necessarily translate to other, less familiar or culturally well-aligned spaces and interactions. But the assessment is useful in those spaces where she is able to successfully predict outcomes. Janice's actions and her rationale for them are not simply emblematic of how young people of color living in poverty exhibit the impact of ghetto culture.

All social actors across status positions, races, genders, and ages determine the most beneficial course of action to take, as well as how and where to invest their labor and time, depending on their relationship to their environment. Actions that may be helpful in terms of surviving, protecting one's body or reputation, or permitting greater access and mobility in one space may very well be detrimental in another. It is generally the case that the spaces with which individuals are most familiar or comfortable are those where their bets on the most beneficial ways of being will pay off. Individuals privileged by virtue of their wealth, whiteness, and maleness, for example, most often find themselves betting and winning in the spaces that hold the most power. If individual motivations are understood in this way—as perspectives that inform acts that are inflected with agency and subjugation—we can dismantle "essentialized notions of culture that view culture as an immutable set of negative traits passed down from generation to generation as explanations for inequality" (Mullings 2000, 19).

In a conversation I had with Janice and Karlyn that flowed from the training opportunities at the Job Corps to how work influenced family dynamics, Janice said: "It seems like everybody in my family is a caregiver, and then they come home and still taking care of people. Like grown folks who should be able to take care of themselves."

Assuming that Janice was talking about the new boyfriend of Donna (Karlyn's mother), Karlyn chimed in, "Yeah, Marcus is the worst. He act like he running stuff. He act like a big ol' kid. I don't like him. He don't own nothing. He don't own nothing. Not himself. Nothing."

Encouraged by Karlyn's agreement, Janice continued: "Your mama is too nice to him, and I don't like that. She treat him like one of them old people at the nursing home."

Karlyn looks at me before responding this time: "Right. She comes home still in work mode so strong she don't even notice she taking care of a kid."

Janice moved from beside Karlyn and positioned herself in front of both of us to get to what appeared to be the point of bringing up Marcus in the first place:

I asked your Mama one day, "Donna, what's love?" And she was like, "Something. I don't know. Ask me later." I mean, how can you be with somebody for so long and not know what love is? So I just started breaking it down, you know, like . . . they gotta be like a friend. You know, someone that we can talk about everything on every level. Someone you can express yourself with. Someone who is going to be a support system instead of just a burden. Somebody that is going to challenge you to be better. I don't need somebody to bring me down. I don't need nobody who is still childish. You best believe you won't see me working all up in the struggle while he lives off of me.

Karlyn and Janice make the connection between Donna's low-wage gendered work providing care in the service sector and the role she has taken on in the home as everyone's unconditional caregiver. In this regard, Karlyn and Janice experience gender as an additional trap that, along with race and class, threatens to contain them in unfulfilling, disrespected positions unless they find ways to escape. One significant strategy may lie in the ability, as Janice articulates, to envision and demand a healthy, mutually supportive relationship when choosing a partner. The intersection of gender, race, and class in the Brown girls' experiences influences their ability to make sense out of "acting like a dude" at the Job Corps and to identify the types of career paths and relational roles they want to avoid in the future. Although Karlyn and Janice disagree with Donna's acceptance of Marcus's behavior, they use her model of "working in the struggle" as a lesson and warning as they move through possibilities in the workplace, in educational institutions, and at home.

While in the Job Corps, Janice's cousin Anita began an intimate relationship that developed into a fairly long-term partnership with another young woman in the program. When Anita and Stephanie first started dating, Karlyn told me that she felt Anita was working too hard to perform the requisite masculinity for being in the more lucrative tracks for manual labor and technical fields. After the couple had been together for some time, moved in together, and established their own home, Karlyn rearticulated her assessment of the relationship. "They have the love," she said, "that I feel a lot of women in this family have been trying to force from men and trying to make happen in ways that are not working. I think love is supposed to make you feel protected, is about knowing that at least one person knows you. It shouldn't matter who that is." Bessie often cautioned her daughters, in a warning that trickled down to the granddaughters, to avoid loving someone so hard you "get caught up."

Regardless of the outcome, Bessie told me she never regretted being in love because it was one of the ways she was able to express herself. I imagine that even though Bessie wanted to protect her daughters from the pain of love, the act of being able to care freely and to decide who to love felt like an important part of creating a self that could not be managed or owned by anyone else. Loving, whether recklessly or with caution, is an art, a self-defining moment. Yet loving is not free of obligation. Bessie demanded that Donna's father care for Donna when she was too exhausted to do so, in an act that was referred to in the demands that Janice made decades later of her own father. The who and the what of love are questions that, based on the experiences of Bessie and their mothers, the girls in the third generation of Browns realize are less important than the how. The process of showing care in relationships should extend, according to Janice, from spaces we categorize as either private or public and from social actors we are bound to through an interconnected web of entitled care. It must also include the right to participate in the processes of citizenship—even as young Black women like Janice question its inequitable terms.

Specifications

"We don't see the American dream. We've only experienced the American nightmare." Denzel Washington's voice trailed through the activity room like a charged whisper instead of a booming proclamation. Since it was already approaching midnight, the volume had been turned way down, and the VHS player hummed and warbled over the muted dialogue in a way that made it seem about to smolder and catch on fire. The film was over three hours long, and it was started every night after dinner and continued through chores, down time, and the interminable stretch to lights out. For the past three weeks, Spike Lee's *Malcolm X* had been the film of choice for the residents of the Fresh Start shelter, and they alternated between watching each frame intently and letting it play in the background as a quasimilitant backdrop to the evening routine. Lights out meant different things to different residents, since some of the young women were just getting in from work that ended late in the evening and others were preparing to leave for 11:00 PM shifts. The staggered comings and goings of the residents made the enforced times for eating, cleaning up, and sleeping seem irrelevant and suspiciously counterproductive to the rhythms of most of their lives. Charlene, one of the resident advisors (RAs) on duty, fumbled though the wicker basket of VHS tapes next to the television, tossing to the side the ones that she would view after most of the residents had fallen asleep. I was sitting on the couch with the chore list in my lap, waiting for each girl to approach me so that I could check off her assigned task. Charlene glanced at me out of the corner of her eye as she gathered the tapes in her arms (there were too many to watch in one night) and walked past me with a sigh that I heard as annoyance.

Two RAs worked the shift from 3:00 PM to 11:00 PM, and one worked the shift from 11:00 PM to 7:00 AM, called the midnight shift. The RA who usually worked the afternoon shift with Miriam called at 2:00 PM to say she couldn't come in. Normally the shelter manager would stay to cover the shift, but since she had been laid off, I was pulled out of a budget meeting to handle the situation. We were severely understaffed, and our list of on-call RAs was thin and becoming increasingly irrelevant, since the most common response we received when we called people on the list to cover a shift was, "Why y'all always wait to the last minute?" The general attitude seemed to be that *on call* meant something other than being, in fact, on call. So in what was becoming quite a frequent turn of events, I worked the afternoon shift with Miriam. Miriam was in the RA office trying to finish writing up the shift report, but she kept getting interrupted by residents who wanted to talk to her about the recipe she used for the homemade chicken soup for dinner that night. Technically, the residents were supposed to prepare and cook dinner as part of their rotating chores, but Miriam said that making dinner for the residents was her favorite part of the shift. Her family had moved to rural Georgia from Puerto Rico when she was fifteen years old, before finally settling in Detroit a few years later. You could taste influences from these migrations in Miriam's food, and we liked guessing what spices she used, often surprised to learn that what we thought we tasted wasn't actually there. Charlene, who had effectively ignored me for the hour that our shifts overlapped, came back from dropping the tapes in the office and sat down next to me on the couch.

"You know, it trips me out how some rules get overenforced and other rules get to slide. Or does it just depend on who's breaking the rules?" Charlene raised one eyebrow and looked out at me from over the tops of her low-hanging glasses.

"What are you talking about?" I asked, even though I knew that she was trying to make a case for Miriam's cooking as a continual violation of shelter rules.

"Never mind." Charlene shifted forward to the edge of the couch as if getting ready to stand. "You make the rules, I guess you get to decide who breaks them. But don't be surprised when the rules you care about getting broken get broke."

Before I could respond, Terri, one of the residents, sat on the couch between us and handed me a piece of paper that looked like a letter to her manager at Claire's Boutique. She said to Charlene, "You stay complaining about Miriam. But you be the first one in the kitchen trying to eat the leftovers."

Charlene looked at me and rolled her eyes at Terri, barely concealing a smile.

"Am I lying? Tell me I'm lying, Char." Terri's laugh was infectious. "I see you all up in that fridge when you think no one is looking."

"Most of the residents work during dinner time," I observed. "We actually need the RAs to help out with meals, among other things. We talked about that at the last house meeting you missed."

"Mmhmm." Charlene was obviously unconvinced, even though her rule violations were too numerous to name—starting with her use of the shelter's washer and dryer to do her own laundry while ignoring the long line of residents who needed to wash clothes for work or school.

Terri put her arms around both of our shoulders. "Can't we just all get along?" Her expression of mock sincerity made all three of us laugh.

"I still love you, anyway." Charlene stood up, blew a kiss my way, and added, "But can you go now? The midnight shift started over an hour ago."

I got up to see if Terri had finished mopping the kitchen floor, and the letter she had handed me fell on my lap.

Dear Meghan,

I am writing to you because when we talk there is always a problem. I don't want you to get me wrong. I like working at Claire's but some things need to change. We should have staff meetings so we can let you know our side and how we feel. I also been meaning to talk to you again about wanting more hours so I can make more money. As you know I am living at Fresh Start but am looking to move out sooner than later. I look forward to what you have to say.

Top employee,
Terri

To Charlene's obvious disapproval, I stayed in the shelter for most of the midnight shift. There were seventeen residents in the shelter at that time.

The young women who worked during the day or were unemployed and job searching were in their rooms, either already asleep, reading, or discussing the day with their roommates. Terri should have been one of these young women, but she stayed in the activity room to discuss her letter.

"Do you think I should give it to her?" Terri was laying belly down on the carpet, flipping through a magazine. "I mean, do you think she'll get what I'm trying to say to her?"

"You've said before that the communication is really strained between you two," I said. "So yes, I think a letter makes sense."

Angel entered the room with her one-year-old son, Rico, just as I was beginning my sentence. He wasn't crying but seemed fussy, and Angel looked like she had been abruptly awakened from a sound sleep.

"You still talking about that letter, Terri?" Angel walked toward Charlene's outstretched arms and handed Rico to her. "How many times you gonna have the same conversation about this chick? She does not like you, so let it go."

"Not asking her to like me." Terri sat up. "She should listen, though. It ain't just about me, A."

Terri was the youngest employee at Claire's boutique and had been working there for two months before she arrived at Fresh Start. For the most part, she seemed to like her job. The other residents liked it, too. At the end of the week, Terri would return to the shelter with a bag full of unsellable damaged jewelry—earrings that were missing posts and necklaces with broken clasps that the residents half-fixed with glue and string. They wore the plastic and alloyed metal adornments until they fell off and were lost until a girl with the chore of vacuuming heard them clanking against the machine. Terri was making minimum wage and working four shifts a week at Claire's, either 10:00 AM to 4:00 PM or 5:00 PM to closing (10:00 PM). Although she had asked for more shifts, Meghan said that was out of her control. Every employee was kept to under three shifts a week. She was doing Terri a favor, Meghan said, by giving her a fourth shift. Inspired by the weekly house meetings in the shelter, Terri had also requested that the staff have the opportunity to meet once a week with Meghan and the other managers to discuss problems and "smarter ways to do shit."

"I don't even really have problems besides wanting more hours. I said that meeting stuff for the other girls who complain all damn day long but don't want to open they mouths." Terri sat down next to Angel. Angel yawned and lay down on her back, putting her head in Terri's lap.

"I said get off the phone, heifer!" The voice, unmistakably Javon's, came to us from the hallway.

"You going to hold him or go check it out?" I asked Charlene, who appeared to have already settled Rico down.

"Probably shouldn't move him." Charlene smoothed the little bit of hair on Rico's head. Angel's eyes were already closed.

When I went into the hallway, I saw Javon's foot in its Tweety Bird slipper wedged in the doorway to the pay phone room, a small cubby with a chair in front of the phone that residents regularly fought over and access to which the RAs unsuccessfully used as a form of reward and punishment. Inside one of the residents, with her back to Javon, kept talking to whomever was on the other end.

"What's up, Javon?" I opened the door wider, encouraging her to move her foot and then closed the door again.

"Hey, Miss A."[1] Javon seemed only slightly surprised to see me at this hour. "Look, we can have a whole conversation about this later, but right now, I just need you to kick her ass off the phone, please."

The young woman on the phone was now standing up and looking at us through the cubby window, still in conversation. "Just some bullshit" was audible through the door.

I knocked on the glass and gestured for her to hang up the phone and step outside.

"First of all, nobody should be on the phone. It's after midnight." Thinking it was a good idea to start by stating the obvious, I continued, "And what's so urgent, Javon?" Javon was tapping her foot and nodding her head more in impatience than agreement.

"Doesn't even have to be that deep. Stay on the phone, heifer. Can I use the office phone, Miss A?" Javon said all of this through one big sigh.

The young woman who had been on the phone shook her head, mumbled something under her breath, and walked back down the hallway to her bedroom.

"I'm trying to call T to see can she pick Dani up when she gets off work," Javon seemed less anxious now.

Danita (Dani) and Javon were close friends, entering the emergency shelter on the same day and both participating in the transitional living program for close to four months. They were roommates and shared clothes, CDs, books, and almost every other material thing they owned. Javon was working as a home health care aide during the day for an elderly woman who lived on the east side of Detroit. After Danita became a certified nursing assistant, Javon found her a job through the same agency that had placed her. Danita's hours were less regular than Javon's because the children of the woman she watched needed her assistance at unpredictable hours of the day and night. On this day she was working overtime in a part of town where, like most parts of the city, bus service was spotty at best. And of course standing at a bus stop alone in the middle of the night was one of the most dangerous things young women in Detroit could do.

Stories about one or more men yelling threats or opening the doors of slow-moving vehicles as they passed were so frequent among the residents that they had stopped being noteworthy. Some of the boldest predators actually left their cars and attempted to physically coerce the young women to get in their vehicles. Whether or not the men assumed the residents to be sex workers was rightfully irrelevant to the young women. "I don't give a fuck what I do or who I am," Danita stated the last time she was approached at a bus stop. "You do not have the right to demand shit from me or put your hands on me." The Fresh Start staff understood and was sympathetic to these risks, and the agency maintained an account with a taxi service for this and other reasons related to both safety and efficiency.

"Javon, I planned on calling a cab for Danita anyway," I said, "and Charlene knows her schedule, too. Why are you tripping?"

"Look, can I just call my cousin, T, so she can go get her? Please?" Javon was pleading, something she never did. I let her use the office phone.

When Danita walked into the activity room nearly an hour later, she handed Javon a paper shopping bag full of clothes. T was Javon's cousin and lived with her girlfriend near the home where Danita worked. She had picked Danita up so Danita could collect the clothes that Javon had left at her mother's house months ago, when she came to Fresh Start. Javon refused to set foot in the house where her mother still lived with her younger brother and the boyfriend who had attempted to sexually assault her on more than one occasion. T couldn't pick up the clothes because she had been banned from her aunt's house after an altercation with the aunt's boyfriend. T had rang the doorbell and punched the boyfriend on the jaw after finding out that he had tried to assault Javon. As the story goes, the boyfriend had tried to fight back but had been no match for T's strength and quickness. It couldn't have helped that he was also high and still holding a joint in his hand.

"This is old, but I might still be able to fit it." Javon stood and held up an emerald-colored polyester dress that was clearly too small for her. It ended at her upper thigh, and the silhouette was just inside the lines of her body.

Charlene chuckled under her breath. She was still holding Rico, who had fallen asleep almost as deeply as his mother, whose head was still in Terri's lap.

"You clearly lost your mind." Terri rolled her eyes and reached for the bag before realizing that Angel was about to fall off the couch. In one deft movement, Terri pulled her up with one arm, slid out from under her, laid her back down on the couch, and sat down on the floor near Javon's feet.

"Here. Take this." Javon reached into the bag and flung a formerly white blouse over Terri's head. "Flaunt this professional shit next time you go to Claire's."

"This gray mess?" Terri took the shirt from her head, made a pillow out of it, and reclined on the floor with one leg crossed over the other.

Danita and Javon started folding leggings, jeans, polo shirts, and awkwardly sized hand towels and put them back in the now-ripped paper bag. Angel was snoring softly, her breaths keeping time with the visible rise and fall of her chest, while Charlene and Terri turned their attention back to the muted television and Angela Bassett's stoic face.

The Takeover

This was the beginning of my second year as the shelter director, and the executive director of the entire Give Girls a Chance (GGC) agency was on a year-long sabbatical. Her temporary replacement, Camille, was a retired corporate executive from General Motors. Camille had no previous experience working in the nonprofit social service sector, nor had she ever worked with young people in any type of training, mentoring, or educational setting. It may have been because of these unqualified qualifications[2] that the conservative and very vocal segment of the board lobbied for Camille to be the interim executive director, and increased her tenure in this leadership role in the agency to three years. The program directors had been confused by this hiring decision and wondered what statement was being made through the appointment of a woman who had been entrenched in the upper-level administration of the automobile industry.

Camille was like an arrow. Everything about her was streamlined and direct. She was in her late fifties, stood about five feet seven inches tall, was exceptionally thin, and wore her ice-white hair in a razor-sharp bob that hit precisely at her jaw line. She spoke in clear, efficient sentences devoid of extraneous superlatives or hesitation. And when she finished what she had to say, she simply stopped speaking. Camille was unbothered by awkward pauses or the uncomfortable reception her words often had. She was shrewd and intimidating, but her unapologetic boldness was appealing, and I was initially encouraged by the prospect of having a boss who supported all of the program directors in taking ownership of their departments. The agencywide vetting and drawn-out collective processing that had been the norm before Camille's arrival often prevented the timely approval of critical programmatic changes in the shelter. Several of the program directors and administrators in other parts of the agency were also frustrated by being held accountable for meeting goals in their program that had been established through a group-processing model that often felt sloppy.[3] Camille viewed these collective processes as signs of inefficiency and, above all, weakness in the directors.

Camille met with each program director individually to determine the intended focus of the program and convened the leadership team[4] to discuss the immediate and long-term goals and foci of the entire GGC agency. After these meetings, everyone seemed to be in agreement that the shelter should be the fiscal and programmatic priority for GGC, considering the impending expansion into the new building and the expected drastic increase in the number of shelter residents. Camille informed us that the agency's relocation to the $4.5 million building represented a transformation not only in the visible, external appearance of GGC but also, and more importantly, in the agency's culture. It was implicit in these early conversations that board members who had donated significant sums of money to the capital campaign were dissatisfied with the current state of the agency and wished to see systems established within each program that insured the efficient, cost-effective facilitation of program activities, along with increased professionalism among the staff. The majority of the board members who felt this way were the ones who also had experience in the automotive industry as high-level executives and believed the agency could benefit from leadership that exhibited the type of "business sense" cultivated in that environment.[5]

Professionalism was vaguely referred to and carried different meanings for the GGC staff. When we needed to hire an RA to help cover the midnight shift in the shelter, Debra, the program director in charge of supervising counseling services within the Fresh Start Shelter and Transition to Independent Living Program, and I found out what was essential in Camille's definition. Debra's close friend, Martha, had over ten years of experience working in residential care and had also taught in the public school system. Her experience working with young people was evident in the creativity and skill she exhibited in the interview with me, and I raved to Camille about finally having found someone to fill the unappealing shift. However, when Camille conducted a follow-up interview, it was a very different story. Debra and I sat waiting for Camille on the two chairs she placed outside of her office, in good spirits because we would no longer have to alternate coverage of the midnight shift ourselves. Camille opened the door for us to enter and started speaking before we could sit down.

"How could you even think of suggesting a candidate with Martha's weight issues?" she asked. I looked at Debra, stunned by this unexpected turn and also offended on her behalf by Camille's insensitivity. It was no secret that Debra was struggling with her own weight issues, as her desire to drop the sixty pounds she had gained when she was pregnant and following the birth of her child a few years earlier was frequently a topic of conversation. Martha was also Debra's close, long-time friend. Debra was silent, her eyes just beginning to well with tears. I stammered an explanation citing Martha's superior qualifications.

Camille, who until this time had been focused squarely on Debra, turned to me with a look that could cut steel. "That is nice. Unfortunately, I did not get that far in the interview since I could not get past how huge she was."

"I really have to question your judgment," Camille continued. She seemed to be conversing only with me now, as Debra appeared to have checked out, sitting back in her chair, one hand shading her forehead. "I would think you of all people would be concerned with the poor example of health that woman would set for the girls. It exhibits an unproductive attitude. And we certainly don't need any more lowered aspirations in the shelter."

"Because you think she is overweight?" I asked. "Well, thank God most of the staff was hired before you became the executive director, because half of us would not have even been interviewed if it were up to you."

"You're right." Camille's response contained no compassion. She said a few more words that demonstrated her "deep concern" for our ability to direct our programs if we ourselves "did not know how to discern productivity and a good work ethic," and then she dismissed us with a brisk, "You can both go."

During this meeting, Debra and I learned the prerequisites for being a good employee and a positive role model from Camille's perspective. Both roles required a productive work ethic and professionalism mirrored by the size and shape of the body. "Unmotivated," "slow," "weak," "dull," and "unimpressive" were some of the other words Camille used to define Martha even though she had barely had a four-minute conversation with her. Camille also discussed the size and shape of the bodies in the shelter as a problem that either needed to be solved or politely tucked away from public view. Large, presumably unfit bodies created an unappealing visual picture that conveyed a lack of self-control. Camille felt very strongly that thin bodies were a physical ideal that symbolized internal attributes. In fact, her beliefs verged on illegality when she used them to weed out job candidates.

For Camille, acceptable bodies, like acceptable workers (especially line workers), were neat, contained, efficient, stripped of any excess (stream-lined), and desexualized.[6] This physical aesthetic was not only associated with the shelter staff but also applied to the residents. Visible pregnancies, large breasts, exposed midriffs, and wide hips in tight jeans were not only a "personal affront" to Camille but, she implied, symbolic of what was wrong with the girls in the first place and partly to blame for their current situation of single parenting and, in some cases, even their homelessness. The corporeal readings and assessments that Camille and certain members of the board made about the staff and residents of the shelter were rooted in race and given credence through long-standing assumptions about the dangerous visibility of Black female bodies as always already representing material excess in addition to excess flesh (Fleet-wood 2011, 9), although race was rarely explicitly mentioned by the board or administrative staff members. Instead, they expressed a color-blind philosophy that was attuned to the gendered and class-based factors that collided in girls' economic and political lives in Detroit without naming the racial implications. Debra and Martha were white women. The notion of acceptable bodies and economic viability that Camille promoted in the shelter was concerned with an image and performance of the female body that required a racialized understanding of respectability and normative bodies that appeared to transcend race and be about the disciplining and containment of any body deemed excessive.

Renovation in the private, yet also exceedingly public, context of the shelter is an important theme that grounds the stories in this section as the bodies and behaviors of the young women residents and the shelter staff become the sites for remaking and making fit. The visible Black, young, female body carries the weight of economic anxieties and political uncertainties and thus tends to be read as either surplus or productive in the context of social service organizations like Fresh Start, where self-sufficiency in all areas of life is the explicit goal of the Transition to Independent Living Program. Here "the missing subject body in social science research" (Roberts 2013, 6) emerges as the space of disjuncture between the disconcerting options for social mobility for Black girls and their ability to present themselves as ready for mainstream mobility and productivity in capitalism. As the twin conveyers of education and employment become decreasingly less likely mobilizers in the lives of the residents at Fresh Start, the physical self is established as the most promising renovation site.

"We just moved in a few months ago," Sharita said. "It still smells freshly dipped in here. Why do we need renovations? Whose idea is this? Camille's?"

We were in our second house meeting that week. Generally, house meetings were held every Sunday night, but since the move to the new building daily meetings were becoming the norm. This Sunday meeting was devoted to the plans to renovate the shelter. Particularly in the shelter, where the prospect of falling short of stringent state licensing regulations and losing our residential status hung over Fresh Start's head like an ominous cloud, the anxiety about getting everything right in this brand-new space was almost palpable. There was much at stake for everyone. Because the shelter was a residential facility that housed minors and young women with children, it was automatically a space under strict surveillance by state child protective authorities, funders, law enforcement entities, other social service agencies in the area, and community residents. The move into the new building and the capital required to make this shift meant that the successes and failures of Fresh Start, as a physical space of shelter and as a program of supportive services, took on even more weight: it faced the prospect of becoming more visible to all of the stakeholders through the high-profile move. Therefore, the concerns of Camille and the board were not unwarranted. In fact, they reflected staff concerns about how to provide more comprehensive care so as to increase the number of young women who moved out of the shelter and into sustainable homes. Success, failure, health, and sustainability were differently configured and variously legible to Camille, the RAs, and the residents because they were concepts shaped by their own experiences, which in turn informed their perceptions of Fresh Start's ability to create positive outcomes for young Black women.

Rising through the ranks of General Motors had required Camille to "master a masculine leadership style" that she felt could bring a "much needed no-nonsense professionalism" to Fresh Start. Over the three years that our time at GGC overlapped, I would watch Camille struggle with her belief in the efficacy of a corporate leadership model within the shelter and attempt different ways of communicating with the staff and young women that tested the relevancy of her professional training in a social service agency setting. However, for the most part the staff and residents were not affected by Camille's internalized tensions and genuine desire to identify the most beneficial way to help the girls. Her hard-edged, blunt style was perceived by the shelter staff as evidence of her investment in strategies that were cost-effective and automated rather than focused on individual needs. "Agency excellence" became a term that both staff and residents believed to apply to them specifically, and to their individual bodies more pointedly. The news of Martha's interview spread like wild-fire through the shelter, evidence that supported the suspicions of the staff and residents.

Camille made a point of walking through the shelter at least once a day and tried to spend some part of the week observing the RAs or sitting in on casual conversations in the activity room. Her desire to be a part of the community and a familiar friendly face was challenged by the RAs' fear or loathing of her and the residents' confusion about "why this skinny white woman is always lurking," as Terri frequently asked. Unfortunately, the fear, disdain, and confusion that Camille inspired negatively affected the staff's ability to perform their regular work when she was around and hindered the natural interactions that residents engaged in with one an-other and the staff. Thus, to Camille the RAs often seemed stagnant or hostile, while the residents' self-protective behavior prevented any genu-ine connection. The texture, codes, and norms of life in the shelter were thus unavailable to Camille. In this way, the shape and perceived func-tionality of physical space and physical bodies took precedence and con-cealed the ways in which the young women constructed social space in and outside of Fresh Start.

Renovations

The top floor of the church where the shelter had formerly been housed was small and cozy and gave the appearance of a girls' dormitory. The new build-ing, however, was expansive and featured winding, disorienting corridors and a seemingly endless array of doors that created too many isolated, un-surveillable spaces in the opinion of staff members. The RAs agreed with the board that the main activity room, in particular, was sterile and unwelcom-ing. However, the staff was mainly concerned with the fact that the residents much preferred hanging out in each other's rooms, where it was difficult to monitor their activities, to gathering in the common room—even though it was equipped with a cable-ready television and a small stereo system.

Camille wanted as many residents as possible to assist with the shelter makeover by picking out paint colors and moving furniture, but mostly by presenting an amicable and grateful demeanor while the adults buzzed around them. The majority of the young women refused to take part in the renovation activities, and the RAs were just as uninspired by the blatant superficiality of the project when so many other life-threatening factors were at play in these young women's lives—factors that the board seemed much less interested in addressing.

The tape recorder ran on the coffee table in front of us during our sec-ond house meeting. Everyone in the shelter had become accustomed to it and my ever-present notebook, but now they were acting as if they were seeing it for the first time, taking care to direct their words toward the microphone.

"Why are we here? Who got time to renovate a shelter that we just moved into?" Sharita was continuing with her questioning.

Charlene and Miss Lucy were the RAs on duty. Miss Lucy spoke up first. "Well, I think it is nice that the board wants to freshen it up in here. I always thought that wall color was ugly."

Charlene rolled her eyes. "Ain't none of this got nothing to do with the shelter. We just moved in here. Don't trip. If they could, they would take that paint and paint all us over."

Terri was laughing with Charlene, and even Miriam was smiling and shaking her head. Sitting next to the coffee table, Terri leaned over to speak into the tape recorder: "Dog. Word. That white paint?! Instead of helping them we should just sit here like frozen, not saying anything and let them paint us into the wall."

"The way Camille and them be looking at us when they come through—" Florine, one of the residents, stopped herself in midsentence. The rest of the eight residents who had been able to make it to this house meeting were talking over each other now.

"I be feeling like them white ladies be having like special X-ray vi-sion. Looking all bugged out and crazy. Like what the fuck is you looking at . . . for real." One of the residents took over for Florine. "I be like [she hunched her shoulders and drew her chin down onto her chest, pulling her knees up so her feet were on the couch] let me just shrink up on your ass and disappear."

"You feel like that?" Sharita seemed surprised to hear someone else say how she felt.

"Who don't?" Charlene, whose sentiments were clearly aligned with those of the residents, said this almost like a threat, looking around the room as if she were daring someone to not feel the same way.

"Yeah. I feel like I want to disappear. Get smaller." Florine was back in the conversation now.

Some of the girls were getting up to leave. "So," I said, "I guess that is a 'no' on helping paint the shelter?" The meeting had already gone on too long, and the few girls who had not said anything were ready to end the conversation.

"I'll help," Sharita said.

"Pshh, no surprise, girl, no surprise." Terri stood and patted Sharita on the head. "You keep trying to make your damn self over. Let me know how that works out for ya."

Miss Lucy and I gathered the attendance sheets, pens, and staff log while the residents put the furniture back in its usual place. "You know, you really should think about reaching out to Lynnette," Miss Lucy gently pulled my elbow. "We could really use her here now. Y'all kind of think alike, and we need more support up in here."

Although the shelter was the focus of the capital campaign and the most profitable and visible of the GGC programs, as a living space it posed a threat to the concept of corporate order. The residents' living space as viewed through the eyes of the board members was in direct contrast to Fordist ideals of efficiency and interchangeable, almost automated, work-ers.[7] The shelter was deemed a stagnant space, and the bodies that filled that space were seen as unproductive and unacceptable in their current state.[8]

"Why are they always just sitting around in the middle of the day? It does not paint a good picture. They shouldn't even be seen during the day." What Camille meant when she said this was that it would be best if the residents were not seen at all. That way, they could be discursively created through fund-raising speeches and official agency literature that fit the rationale of those willing to donate to a worthy cause. In real life, as they were without the public-relations accoutrements of a target population in need, the girls seemed unworthy. Part of the agreement that young women make when they enter the shelter includes the understanding that they will be productive during the day—looking for a job, going to school, and so on. However, it was not always the case that all of the girls were out of the shelter during normal business hours. When I explained to Camille that the young women she encountered during the day may work midnight shifts, be in the later stages of pregnancy, have just been admitted and are waiting to meet with their caseworkers and have their paperwork processed, or have an appointment later in the day, she dismissed these explanations as insufficient excuses. It didn't matter to her why the girls were visible, just that they were.

The church shelter had been too much like a home, but the newly formalized structure of the shelter challenged the desire of the staff and board to have what they believed to be the benefits of monitoring the residents without the appearance of policing. The renovation was an example of all of our frustrated attempts to identify how home should take material shape in the shelter. The board members most invested in the renovation seemed especially torn by their competing beliefs that homeless girls should be provided with a space that mimicked the care and nurturing of home while enforcing the expectation of productivity and professionalism of a business. This tension was exhibited in the prevailing concern that a young woman be both comfortable and safe in the shelter—but not so much so that she stopped "working the program."

Lynnette and the Resident Advisors

Lynnette started working as an RA at Fresh Start in 1996, the same year that President Bill Clinton signed the infamous Personal Responsibility and Work Opportunity Reconciliation Act into law. For seventeen years Lynnette would work on and off in this capacity, occasionally leaving the agency for as brief a time as two months and sometimes staying away for several years. Lynnette was legendary. The staff of all three programs talked about how different the shelter felt when she was working a shift. There were never fights in the shelter while Lynnette was there. Former residents who left Fresh Start before giving birth would return so that Lynnette could meet and bless their babies, and current residents hung out in the shelter on the weekends rather than with their friends if Lynnette was on duty. Lynnette brought in fresh fruit on Saturday and Sunday mornings to cook fancy pancake breakfasts, over which she offered loving advice. But not everyone adored Lynnette. A few of the RAs called her "too soft" and felt as if her nurturing style did not prepare the residents for the harshness of the "real world." The RAs who did like Lynnette said that the others were just jealous because she made them look bad; she was not only persuasive with the residents but kept meticulously documented case files and log entries. Lynnette quit unexpectedly a few months before my hiring.

Since Lynnette refused to meet me at "that toxic shelter," I agreed to meet her at her home on the fifteenth floor of the imposing Lafayette Tower apartments. Twenty-two floors high, the east tower where Lynnette lived looked like the high rise that my ten-year-old Midwestern self imagined the "moved on up" Jeffersons to occupy in Manhattan. When Lynnette opened the door to me, the small pink gem on her forehead gleamed in the hallway light, and the smell of Egyptian musk wafted around her. Over her shoulder I could see intricately woven red and orange fabric on the walls. Given her hesitancy to meet me, I was taken off guard when she reached out with a hug that pulled me into her living room. Propped against chairs and leaning against the walls were photographs—each twenty-four by thirty inches—of adult and young Black women, white scarves draped over their heads and falling along their shoulders, their eyes cast down, their hands raised in prayer at their chests, and wearing on their foreheads *bindis* just like Lynnette's.

"Those are peace pictures," Lynnette said, watching me as I inventoried the dozen or so photographs. "I take those so that women can see their beauty from the inside out and discover a place of peace. Some of those are girls from Fresh Start."

"Oh, is that Danielle?" I asked, noticing a woman who was no longer a resident but who still came to the shelter for after-care services.

"Yeah. You almost didn't recognize her 'cause she looks so different out of that shelter," Lynnette surmised.

I stayed at Lynnette's for two hours, talking some about her photography, clothes design, and healing workshops for women but mainly about why she had left the shelter and what might bring her back. She said:

There was too much focus on keeping the numbers up at any cost. Making sure we met these grant goals for how many girls come through and graduate. But you got these girls up in here dealing with all kinds of mental illness and on prescription drugs and still getting high in the park. Girls are in emotional crisis, and they don't get the help they need. If we are dealing with a culture of people and they are dealing with deep-seated issues, it is mandatory that they be in some type of drug counseling. It should be a given. It should be mandatory that they should be in mental health counseling and drug counseling. If we don't address these issues, are we really committed to their health and healing? These girls are coming in with serious mental issues. Girls threatening to harm people. Our job as resident advisors is to keep them safe. This is our community. Our job is to keep our community safe.

Lynnette told me the RAs were the most important people at Fresh Start but were the least respected. Although the RAs played the most important role at Fresh Start in dealing with the issues that the residents worked hard to conceal and the emotional and psychological traumas that they faced, the RAs felt undermined in their ability to convince the caseworkers to address their concerns. Lynnette believed this was because the RAs were overwhelmingly Black and without college degrees.

"The RAs give the girls a truth they can build on. It may sound harsh, but we can say, 'You know, you really talk too much' or 'You kind of lazy' and they will hear us and understand that we know them and are speaking from a place of love, not telling them to fit some mold," Lynnette said. She continued, "We can show them the possibilities and how they can see theyselves and work on theyselves 'cause we see them and want the best for them."

However, in the past few years, with the hiring of relatively younger RAs as well as women who were former Fresh Start residents, Lynnette felt as if the tough love and constructive criticism that the RAs delivered with their particular brand of finesse was becoming mean-spirited and discouraging:

They get mad at me because they think I let the girls get over on me. But the reality is I let the girls get away with stuff so I can teach them something. I know when they lying or doing something sneaky. I let them do it, then say, "Let's talk about why you lied and then let's also talk about why you always mad because you say your boyfriend is a liar and your Mama lies to you. You need to see yourself so you can change yourself and stop attracting what you don't want in your life." The other RAs sit around in the office and talk about the girls behind they back and say stuff all the time like, "They slick. They can't be trusted. We have to stay on top of them." But I'm trying to teach them something.

When I left Lynnette's, she said she appreciated the visit but could not come back to Fresh Start. A few weeks later, I ran into her at a café downtown. "Just come by and see the new building," I said. Lynnette followed me in her car to GGC that day and came back to work at Fresh Start later that week.

Teshia, who had been a resident of the shelter for nine months, used the image of family to explain the relationship between the RAs and the residents, implying that the connection between them was natural and inevitable, although sometimes conflicted. The RAs "knew the real Teshia" and because of this earned a love and respect that existed in a realm beyond the confines of the Fresh Start shelter. This bond was one that allowed the young women and the RAs to find solidarity in challenging agency protocols based on cultural and class reference points that dismissed or devalued their experiences as Black girls and women. It was also a somewhat blurred relationship that fluidly encompassed the roles of sister, friend, "other mother," and staff member and caused concern among other agency employees because of what they assumed to be unprofessional boundary crossing.[9] But to the residents, the RAs were at least authentic, even if sometimes overly punitive.

In addition to the fact that residents and RAs had similar experiential and class backgrounds, there is also the issue of intimacy and the presumption of authenticity that develops from close encounters and the unstaged revealing of the self that can occur in off-hours in a residential setting. In this way, "being real" or "seeming real"[10] to the residents was related to how willing and/or able a particular staff member was to let down her professional guard and relate to the young women in a way that did not strictly involve her role and duties as defined by the agency. Working in a residential setting with young people as a direct service worker requires a certain type of emotional and intellectual capacity generally written off as personality traits or an ability to easily develop a rapport with youth. These qualities are devalued in ways that are similar to the downplaying of the work of women of color that is described as emotional labor (Durr and Wingfield 2011; Hwa 2012; and Brook 2013). Because of these devalued attributes, it was easy to discount the deeper merits of the work done by the RAs and ignore the high skill level needed to effectively run the shelter and keep everyone in it safe.[11] The devaluing of the close ties between the RAs and the residents was also connected to the idea that the physical distinctions between the two groups were blurred and murky. The conversations about the similarity of the RAs and the residents revolved around styles of dress and behavior that were discussed as products of cultural and class orientations.

Elaborate hairstyles that change on a daily basis and include cornrows, impossibly long extensions, detachable ponytails, bun attachments, and wigs are understood to be part of a ghetto culture associated with young urban Black women. Hence, the fact that RAs often exhibited the same hairstyles, in addition to wearing clothes whose labels were tied to hip-hop culture, identified them as being on the same social level as the young women in the shelter. This became problematic when considering the examples of success and upward mobility that some of the other staff members and board members felt should be presented by the direct service staff. The idea was that aesthetic and bodily markers of self-improvement were not supposed to reflect a young Black girl's current style of presentation; they should take her out of the ghetto, not locate her in it.

More Than a Day's Work

When I pulled up in front of Bessie's house, Bip was in the driveway talking to a man I hadn't seen before.

"Hey!" Bip paused his conversation and walked toward my car. "If you looking for Janice, she went to Donna's house."

Janice and I had made lunch plans late in the previous week, and I was supposed to pick her up at Bessie's. "Did she leave a message?" I asked, trying not to direct my irritation at Bip.

"Naw . . . she just said that she had to get something from Donna's. One of Karlyn's friends picked her up a half-hour ago."

I decided to take the long way to Donna's house even though I knew this might mean Janice would be gone by the time I arrived. But she was still there, and she got into the passenger seat with her Wendy's uniform on her lap. I asked, "If you knew you had to work today, why did you make plans to meet up?"

"Forgot," Janice said. "They be changing the schedule up. I ain't have to work Wednesdays in a long time."

"What time does your shift start?" I asked. "Do you want me to drop you off?"

"What time is it?" Janice glanced at the clock on my dashboard. "I'm already late. Can you drop me back by Wesson? I'll do Reesie's hair today instead of the weekend."

Reesie was a young woman in her twenties who lived a few doors down from Bessie. Janice made money doing her hair or babysitting when Reesie's sisters were unavailable. Janice was not as skilled a braider as her sister Crystal or her cousins, but she knew how to wash, blow dry, color, and use relaxers.

"Girl, you haven't even been there a full month," I said, referring to Wendy's. "You need to go even if you are a little late."

"A little?" Janice laughed. "I shoulda been there two hours ago."

"Why . . ." I sighed, not knowing where to begin. "Why were you at Donna's if you knew you had to be back over here for work?"

Janice seemed annoyed by my question. "Because I left my uniform at Donna's and I didn't feel like hearing it from that manager. Can't stand her ass. Didn't plan on being over there that long, but Donna was going through some stuff and was talking my damn ear off."

"You could have just told her you had to go to work." I felt like I was stating the obvious.

I suspected that Janice was rolling her eyes. "Whatever. Plus I make more doing Reesie's hair than I will on shift. I'll call in later and say I had an emergency."

This was Janice's second job in three months. She had left McDonald's after "getting into it" with a co-worker about whose responsibility it was to clean the oil in the fryer and walked out.

"What if you get fired?" I asked.

"Then I'll look for another job and babysit in the meantime." Janice was mad at me now. "Plus I probably need to quit that job anyway if I start at Wayne State."

So, I thought, this is why she wanted to meet. After Janice earned her General Equivalency Diploma (GED) through the Job Corps, one of her favorite counselors there, Ms. Ruggs, encouraged her to apply to Wayne State through an initiative that the Job Corps staff negotiated with the continuing education program at Wayne State. Nontraditional students like Janice who did not graduate from high school but had received their GEDs were guided through a special admissions process and required to take a remedial curriculum with a heavy emphasis on writing skills and mathematics. Ms. Ruggs liked Janice and believed that she "exhibited superior intelligence" even though she was "exceptionally fearful at times." Ms. Ruggs told me that "most people at Job Corps thought she was lazy and kind of a troublemaker—you know, the typical unmotivated girl that they think comes through here."

"So, you decided to move forward with your application?" I was excited that Janice was making this decision, especially since she had tremendous trepidation about what it would be like to commit to the academic and scheduling rigors of a four-year university. But I was also frustrated with her casual disregard for her current job.

After getting her GED results, Janice told me she had fallen asleep during the exam. When she woke up, she only had ten minutes to complete the entire English portion of the test. "And I still passed, of course," she boasted. There was something that both troubled and inspired me about Janice's approach to life. It was the same amorphous something that confounded the staff at GGC and the Job Corps, her mother and grandmother, and even some of her cousins. Janice seemed to assume that if she listened to her internal barometer of what seemed right, all of the external details orchestrated by other people, programs, and institutions would fall into place as they should. Why worry about missing a shift at a job whose low pay prevents you from meeting basic living expenses and whose intentionally inconsistent, arbitrary scheduling keeps you from finding supplementary legal employment? This perspective made sense to Janice especially since she would likely be starting college soon and could make more than she would on her shift working at under-the-table entrepreneurial activities like offering child-care and hair services to people in her community she actually knew and liked.

"Yeah. I don't understand the whole registration thingy, and I won't be able to stay in the dorms," Janice said in a less irritated tone, "But I think I'll give it a try. Shoot. Why not?" I dropped Janice off at Reesie's, and we made plans to meet up the following day to talk through the details of her application.

During the period that Fresh Start was moving into the new building and conducting renovations, the staff and administration were also contending with the realities of the economy in Detroit. The development staff and shelter team worked to find solutions to the dismal employment opportunities for the residents through grants that would enable us to hire a full-time employment specialist for Fresh Start. As I put it in a grant proposal I wrote requesting funding from a private foundation to support the establishment of an employment-services support program and the new position of employment specialist:

> With support from [the foundation], Fresh Start will launch a comprehensive employment support services program which will help formerly

homeless young women create clear career goals that are based in both the reality of their skills and interests, and in that of the market; and to help shape their vision for a productive, prosperous, and fulfilling career pathway. We intend to do what it takes to help our clients shift their employment and career aspirations from a survival level to a thriving level. Our program will guide young women through three distinct developmental phases: job readiness, job search, and job sustainability.

The shelter received the requested funding and proceeded in a matter of months to hire a new specialist, Alysha, and develop what was hoped would be employment services that would give the residents better outcomes. Job readiness involved fortifying the one-on-one employment counseling services with twice-a-day group seminars. We developed pre- and post-tests to assess areas such as knowledge of employment laws, communication and social skills in the workplace, expectations for a job, benefits, sources of pressure and stress, knowledge on the availability of jobs in various career fields, qualifications for various jobs and careers, and personal appearance. As for the job search component of the program, we had determined that, again in the words of my grant proposal, "McDonalds and Burger King are always hiring. The challenge is helping our clients secure long-term jobs with a living wage, health insurance and opportunity for a sustainable future." Fresh Start volunteers offered extra support with résumé writing and interviewing techniques and also formed a job bank committee to generate jobs with employers who understood the needs and concerns of Fresh Start residents. Job sustainability included more sophisticated tools to track employment outcomes, along with volunteer job coaches who contacted the young women twice a month via telephone to assist with solving workplace conflicts.

At first, the program produced a great deal of excitement among the overextended caseworkers and RAs, as well as the residents. Everyone seemed to be looking for some sign that the grim employment prospects could be overcome with a well-intentioned and well-funded collective effort. Alysha was a Black woman who appeared to deftly combine Camille's no-nonsense style with the RAs' easy kinship and cultural familiarity with the residents. She took the initiative to extend the terms of the grant by establishing an internship program in which young women were matched with employers (usually former or current GGC volunteers with an affinity for the organization) who provided crucial hands-on job experience without the threat of termination they would encounter in a real, paying job. It did not take very long, however, for the initial optimism that surrounded the program to subside.

Despite the concerted attention paid to the young women and their employment readiness and the marked improvement in their résumé writing and interviewing skills, the employment program could not alter the economic terrain of the city or expand the pool of jobs available for young Black women. The young women were still primarily qualified—based on their age, education, and previous experience—only for the low-paying and low-prestige service industry jobs in fast food and retail. And even these opportunities were decreasing significantly. Welfare reforms and work requirements made the options even less tenable they had been. Temporary Assistance to Needy Families (TANF) benefits and food stamps combined still left young women with children who were young enough to excuse them from fulfilling the mandatory work and training program requirements living below the poverty level.[12] The young women without children were eligible only for food stamps. Since they received three meals a day in the shelter, they sold the food stamps outside of the shelter and used the money to get their hair done, pay cell phone bills, or provide loans to relatives and friends. One of the job coaches, a long-time GGC volunteer who owned a boutique in the city near Greektown, met me at my Fresh Start office one day to talk about the young woman who had been interning with her over the past few weeks.

"Really," I began, "Alysha should be included in this meeting since she is the primary employment program coordinator."

"I understand," the volunteer said, "but I hate to discourage her with this news. I think the issues you all are facing are much larger than what she or the program can provide."

"What is happening?" I asked, anticipating a response that was not likely to be resolved through any discussion we would have that afternoon.

"You do know that Kim can barely write?" She responded with the question I had already asked Alysha after Kim's initial program assessment screening, and one that almost every staff person in the shelter had found ourselves asking one another lately.

The number of functionally illiterate young women increased steadily in the first year of my tenure as director of the shelter. The education coordinator and Alysha were not equipped with the institutional resources or skills it would take to adequately address the gaps in young women's educational histories. The other educational institutions in their lives, which included public schools, GED preparation programs, and Wayne County

Community College, either had already failed to provide an educational foundation for the young women or were unable to do the remedial work of meeting them where they were in their development. I acknowledged all of these complicating factors to the volunteer and watched her nod in reluctant agreement.

"And it's not just that," she continued. "She has serious issues making eye contact and greeting my customers. I am really just afraid she's bad for my business. I wanted to help, but this isn't working out." And with that, our first employment supportive services intern was fired.

In lieu of actual financial capital and job options, the shelter staff and I worked as creatively as possible to establish opportunities for the young women within the structure of the shelter program. Although the other program directors and I participated in several social service networks and policy action entities at both the local and state levels to collectively address systemic issues facing the vulnerable populations with whom we worked, everyone involved in these collectives was battling the same entrenched issues that resulted from intractable poverty and were sustained through neoliberal practices that increasingly valorized personal responsibility over collective accountability.

I organized a week-long on-site planning retreat for the entire shelter and casework staff to brainstorm about how to improve the employment and educational components of the shelter program. Following three days of fiery debates and dramatic exits from the conference room where we were meeting, the RAs and the caseworkers were able to agree on the details of a token economy system based on the model I provided. The token economy was based on color-coded Fresh Start bills that came in denominations of $1, $5, $10, $20, $50, and $100. The residents earned "Fresh Start money" for actions such as completing chores and making dinner; assisting other residents with child care or homework; attending life skills workshops; keeping appointments with shelter staff and showing up on time; and facilitating house meetings. Residents used their "money" to pay for fines incurred from cursing in the public spaces of the shelter, threatening another resident or a staff member, or missing appointments and meetings. They also used the money to pay $100 a month "rent" at the shelter and to purchase clothing and luxury toiletries from the linen closet that the staff transformed into the "Target Store."[13] On the last day of the retreat, the token economy system was introduced to the residents as a way for them to practice budgeting and establish priorities in terms of both material needs and individual actions within the Fresh Start community. We also used this special house meeting to solicit the young women's thoughts on how we might provide better support.

"Now, this shit might actually work." Terri was enthusiastic, mirroring what appeared to be the general consensus among the residents, and she dramatically pulled out a brand-new yellow Fresh Start $5 and handed it to me. Everyone laughed as she gladly paid the fine she had intentionally incurred.

"I have a suggestion," Florine said. "I like the internships. I mean I ain't on one right now, but I like that idea. I think it's a good one."

"But . . ." Terri prompted.

"I think we should have internships here at GGC." Florine seemed to be trying to convince herself that it was a good idea. "We could work with that white man in the finance department or help out with the kids in the Early Start program or . . ."

"I like that idea a lot," Lynnette agreed.

The rest of the residents were nodding and saying "mmhmm," and Florine rode the wave of encouragement. "I have another idea but don't know if y'all [looking around the room to indicate that she meant both the residents and staff members] be feeling this one. I think we should stay in the shelter longer."

"No one gets kicked out if they are doing what they are supposed to do," was the response from one of the caseworkers.

"Yeah, we know," Davita entered the conversation in support of Florine. "But it feels like we need to be working the program like in a rushed way. Like get you a job, even though there ain't none, get your master's [chuckles rippled through the room], and get out before the end of the month."

"We need more time." Florine made her voice heard over the laughter.

"And maybe you mean more understanding, too?" Miriam said, looking at Lynnette as if knowing that she would approve of this empathetic observation.

"Yeah, just some more like . . . some more support to know we aren't bad or wrong . . . that it takes more time and stuff than we have just in ourselves." Florine had everyone's attention and was speaking to a virtually silent room now.

I wasn't surprised that Camille was impressed with the token economy, although it did make me wonder if I was drinking personal responsibility Kool-Aid. We were all shocked that she was especially enthusiastic about the in-house internships and the proposal to intentionally support young women's staying in the residential facility as long as they needed. As is probably evident, these changes in the shelter program were by no means a cure-all for the intersecting economic and political forces that informed the residents' experiences.[14] Even though the token economy system is still being used over a decade later, and residents still fight over Fresh Start "dollars" they find between couch cushions, the most decisive shift came from Florine, Terri, and the other residents. Their ability to separate themselves from the problem, the variable in need of making over and fixing, compelled the entire shelter staff to acknowledge the implicit, undercutting tension in the program—that young women were both the problem and the solution, the disease and the cure. The young women were saying that Fresh Start, like many stressed and underresourced social service agencies, was placing "an overemphasis on rapid-employment services at the expense of tailored and in-depth case management" and implicitly calling us out as "a workforce ill-equipped to effectively identify and respond to client skill deficits, health issues, and other barriers to employment" (Watkins-Hayes 2009, 4). As difficult as it was and continues to be, the residents were asking for a solution that required our collective engagement with the structures beyond the shelter that created the need for shelter services for girls and young women in the first place. The residents were asking that the terms of their citizenship in the shelter and the city of Detroit be determined by more than their responsibilities to the social order. They were demanding the right to live the lives they imagined and the right to have this basic need met by something other than their own resiliency and will.

Painted Figurines

"Now for the eyelashes, ladies. This is the really important part. These details really really matter. Are you listening?" Miss Hannah, as she asked us to call her, was standing by the sink in front of the GGC art room, holding a four-inch ceramic Santa in her left hand. With her right hand she dipped a thin paintbrush into a small pot of black acrylic paint and then dabbed at Santa's forehead with quick, precise strokes. "See?" she said, stretching out her arm and showing the newly adorned Santa to everyone else in the room. "Not too difficult."

Miss Hannah was an old friend of Camille's who had recently started a business selling Christmas figurines. She brought the unpainted ceramic Santas and Mrs. Santa Clauses, reindeer, elves, and gift packages to us by the box load and spent every Tuesday evening from 7:00 to 8:30 or sometimes 9:00 showing us how to properly paint the white figures so that they looked "neat" and "professionally done." The figures that came out looking the best, Miss Hannah promised, would be sold through her online store and in her sister's boutique, and the residents would receive 40 percent of the profits. Alysha mandated that the residents who weren't working or in evening classes attend Miss Hannah's workshops, which turned out to provide an odd combination of instructions on art, money management, and small business entrepreneurship.

"She a little crazy, but I like her," Terri said about Miss Hannah, and made a point to attend every class when she wasn't working the closing shift at Claire's Boutique. Some of the other residents were less convinced.

"That bullshit?!" Angel refused to stop cursing and, in fact, seemed to derive lots of pleasure out of following a long string of obscenities with a flurry of Fresh Start dollars. "Y'all look real special sitting up in there painting ornaments and shit. Truly like some mental patients."

"I don't even care if I see the money," Terri confessed. "Something about painting is just mad relaxing."

Miss Hannah's program continued for six weeks. Like Terri, I found painting with the seven or so other residents, listening to Miss Hannah's ridiculous and irrelevant business advice, and focusing intently on the details of the figures' brows, bows, hooves, and buckles oddly soothing. Alysha participated by wincing whenever Miss Hannah offered budgeting advice that conflicted with her employment seminars and by cynically encouraging the girls with comments like "Okay, Terri, those black boots are looking good. Maybe you should add one more coat of paint, though." Charlene walked by the open door to the art room, shaking her head and laughing, but a few minutes later she was sitting next to me and asking me to pass her more white paint for Santa's moustache.

"Now, I don't care if you make Santa a little browner than usual . . . I mean you can make some Black Santas, of course." Miss Hannah was nervous and searching for words. "But we do need some white ones, too. Remember how we talked about knowing our customer?"

"So, what color is the white Santa supposed to be, because his mous-tache is very white so . . ." At the back of the room, Kendra sounded genu-inely interested in the right artistic choice.

"Well . . ." Miss Hannah began, her face flushed.

"You can just mix some white and red and make 'em pink," Terri suggested.

"But then he be a funny pink. I don't like that," Kendra said.

"Mix a little yellow and brown into it then. I don't know," Terri countered.

Miss Hannah handed the reindeer she was trying to rescue from an overindulgence of brown paint back to one of the residents and walked over to the table where Terri and Kendra were working. On the newspaper in front of them were puddles of muddy water and paint, attempts at finding the right shade.

"Oh, dear." It was clear that Miss Hannah hadn't meant to comment out loud, but Terri and Kendra didn't seem to mind as they surveyed their Santas of indeterminate hues.

"You can't make this up. This dumbness that be going on here. I promise you can't make this up." Charlene stopped working on her brown elf and was fully engaged in the Santa affair.

"Let's just name him Santa Carlos and call it a day." It was hard to tell if Terri was serious. "You gotta have some Mexican customers, right, Miss Hannah?"

"Black, Hispanic, white . . . nobody's buying this mess. I mean, just look at this sloppy shit." Kendra paused to give us all a chance to take in the figurines around the room in various states of distress. Paint congealed on the side of one Santa's face, too-thin coats made most of the reindeer look like they were suffering from alopecia, and elves on every table were drowning in paint. "Just so y'all know. I am keeping all my Santas black since, apparently, don't nobody know the color for white, and I doubt painting Santas will get any of our Black asses out of this shelter any damn way."

"That'll be $10," Charlene said, holding out her hand and only half joking.

Miss Hannah facilitated the remaining two weeks of her six-week young entrepreneurs program without, as far as I know, mentioning the color of the Santas again. As the residents had suspected before they ever picked up a paintbrush, none of the figures appeared professional enough for the market. Nonetheless, Miss Hannah kept her commitment to hold a small graduation ceremony at her home for the residents who completed the program. Each young woman received an envelope containing a handmade certificate and a check for $200 as compensation for their "effort and time." Within fifteen minutes of the first workshop, Alysha and I had known that Miss Hannah's vision for the residents' financial success was a losing proposition. The only thing to be gained, we surmised, was the guaranteed $200 stipend at the end of the program. "A little more than $30 for one and a half hours of painting and listening to Miss Hannah really isn't that bad, "Alysha said. "I mean, to be honest, most of them don't have any better options right now."

As the six graduates, Alysha, Camille, and I sat in Miss Hannah's backyard drinking lemonade and enjoying a day together, I thought about the desperation and hope that had brought us to that point. All ten of us knew the likely outcome of the six weeks would be this graduation ceremony and the envelopes that acknowledged the limits of our current capacities to imagine and implement a "productive, prosperous, and fulfilling career pathway" with and for these young women. I was also reminded of Poetess and her ability to dream differently.

Poetess

Poetess was eighteen years old when she came to Fresh Start. Although her birth name was Cynthia, she called herself Poetess because her career goal was to become a professional spoken-word artist and English teacher. From the day she entered the shelter, Poetess was like a sharp thorn in the side of the other residents and the staff. She spontaneously broke into her latest poem while the other girls were trying to watch TV and kept canceling meetings with her caseworker because she "wasn't feelin' the vibe and needed to be alone with her thoughts." While Poetess could be infuriating, she was also undeniably endearing. Her small size, huge brown eyes, and indefatigable personality made her like the younger sister we all wished we had. After she had had three months of job searching with no result, regularly canceled appointments, and missed workshop sessions, the RAs and caseworkers said that something needed to be done about Poetess and that I should be the one to talk to her. Poetess's caseworker told me that she had overheard Poetess telling the other girls that instead of job searching she would hang out at the park with her friends. "I'm done with her. Maybe you can talk to her," she said, walking out of my office after literally throwing her hands up in the air.

Poetess talked to me for over two hours about her experience being shuffled among different foster homes and her tumultuous relationship with her biological mother. In the midst of the emotional journey that her oral history was taking us both on, I remembered that I was actually supposed to be imposing some discipline on her life. Poetess seemed shocked to hear that the staff thought she was trying to "get over" in the program and cited the poetry workshop she had tried to initiate among the residents as evidence of her commitment to the curriculum. She also told me that she wasn't focused on finding a job because she planned to attend Columbia College in Chicago in the fall. I had many questions. How could she be attending college in the fall when it was already June and no one on staff seemed to know anything about these plans? When did she apply? Had she been accepted?

Poetess had mailed her application months before but had not shared this news with anyone at Fresh Start because she feared the influence of "negative energy." I asked to see Poetess's copy of the application materials she had sent in and found that most of the forms were incomplete, she had not followed several mandatory guidelines such as typing essays instead of writing them out by hand and including three letters of recommendation. The one letter she had was from her estranged aunt, a self-proclaimed actress who lived in the northern suburbs with her boyfriend in between the times she wasn't ordered by the court to be in a drug rehabilitation program. The letter was beautifully and powerfully written on Poetess's behalf. I pointed out these problems to Poetess, along with the fact that the application had been due on January 15. I was inspired by Poetess's commitment to developing her art and her ability to identify an educational institution in line with her goals. But I was annoyed with her refusal to move toward what I felt, at the time, to be the reality she faced. By the end of an hour-long battle with Poetess, feeling completely frustrated, I gave her two weeks to turn around her participation in the program. If she failed, she would be put on a conditional stay.[15] A few days later, Poetess went job searching with a group of four other new shelter residents who had heard that the new open-air baseball stadium and home of the Detroit Tigers, Comerica Park, was hiring at least a hundred employees over the next few days. At the end of the day, the four young women returned with a packet of "new employee information" and crisply folded uniforms.

"Where is Cynthia?" I asked. The girls looked at each other, apparently trying to figure out who should be the one to give me the news. One of them finally told me, "Um, she said that she didn't need to serve hotdogs since she is going to school in a few months."

I stayed at the shelter until 9:00 PM waiting for Poetess to come home. When she did, I let her have it in a way that I have never spoken to a girl before or since. Poetess slammed her bedroom door and screamed at me from the other side, "You just hatin' but you gonna see when I get my acceptance letter." I felt out of order and defeated. I had never before felt the need to raise my voice to one of the residents, which was the primary reason why caseworkers or RAs came to me when they felt emotionally out of control or needed someone to talk to the girls before they felt compelled to "put their hands on them." But more than my own reaction, I felt terrible witnessing a break in Poetess's perpetual optimism.

The conflict between school and work was something that all residents of the shelter, along with the shelter staff, found difficult to negotiate. On the one hand, education held the key to social mobility. On the other hand, a paycheck, no matter how small, was the first practical step to moving out of the shelter and becoming self-sufficient. Although some young women were able to do both—working part-time and pursuing a GED or attending college or vocational school—most had to make a choice, and a steady job usually won out. Part-time work, even with assistance from the Family Independence Agency, rarely covered monthly expenses. Thus, the prioritization of education more often than not meant that a young woman would focus on getting a job in the present and make the commitment to pursue her educational goals at some point in the future. The future inevitably became more and more distant as the need to eat, pay bills, find transportation, and obtain child care became more pressing.

My desire as a middle-class Black woman reaping the rewards of a good education was to be able to, in some way, at least provide access to the same educational opportunities for young women without the benefit of family support or pressure and the cultural capital that allows one to navigate opaque social systems. However, being able to crack the codes or superficially penetrate the boundaries of exclusionary systems on an individual level does not change how these systems continue to operate in the collective lives of Black women. Beyond the issue of not being able to affect enduring or systematic change, middle-class Black women often unwittingly find themselves endorsing behavior and aspirational standards that are complicit with hegemonic structures that constrain the possibilities for all Black women to live and work as they choose. This feeling of powerlessness binds middle-class and poor Black women together in what can often be a volatile and self-sabotaging dynamic. It becomes easier and seemingly more efficacious to place blame on those closest to you in social status (other Black women) than to attack the larger, faceless ideologies and structures that truly constrain the movement of Black girls and women across the boundaries of race, class, and gender.

Poetess avoided me for a few days after our argument. At the end of the week, she slid a single sheet of paper under my office door. I had to read it over four times before it registered: Columbia College had accepted

Poetess and was offering her a full scholarship. I was elated and incredulous. I called the contact number for the financial aid administrator listed on the bottom of the page and spoke to a Mr. Thompson, who verified Poetess's acceptance and put me in touch with a Professor Dreyer who—after obtaining permission from Poetess—spoke to me for a half-hour about "the passion in her letter" and her "potential as an artist." News of Poetess's acceptance moved through the agency, and Poetess kept a copy of the letter on her person at all times so she could pull it out to silence the disbelievers. Motivated by her impending move to Chicago, Poetess found a job within a week, so that she could start saving money for the transition.

By the time Poetess left Fresh Start, our disagreement was long buried. I drove her to the Greyhound bus station and left her with the numbers of several friends I had in the Chicago area. Poetess kept in touch with me for the first year of her time in Chicago, giving me regular updates on the difficulty of her classes and her job working at a downtown CVS. For the first four months she stayed in a youth-serving transitional shelter that was much like Fresh Start, but then moved into an apartment with one of the other young women from the shelter. By all accounts, Poetess is a GGC success story even though it is hard for me not to think that she "made it" in spite of us.

Swinging Pendulum

A week after what the residents called the "Black Santa Graduation," my relationship with Charlene took an irreparable turn for the worst. Charlene had started classes at Wayne County Community College that disrupted her usual shift schedule. I and the other RAs made accommodations to the regular schedule, such as allowing Charlene to work split and double shifts. There wasn't a way for any further changes to be made on Charlene's behalf without imposing on the other staff, so I gave Charlene three weeks to transition out of her RA position and find another job. Charlene was furious and managed to rally the majority of the staff around her, telling them that I was trying to block her from moving up and wanted to be the only "educated Negro in the building," even though the scheduling changes she requested made the RAs' work lives even more challenging. Charlene fought hard and long to keep her job, even though she refused the shift schedule I created for her out of the only feasible options, instead demanding a schedule that was already covered by an

RA with seniority. Essentially, Charlene believed that her decision to go back to school should override all other considerations, even if it meant her friend and co-worker would lose her job. Charlene demanded to meet with Camille, which was a bad strategic move since from Camille's perspective Charlene represented "the worst of the resident advisors."

A little over a year after losing her bid to receive unemployment, Charlene was taking the agency to unemployment court.[16] Even though I was no longer working at the agency, Camille called me back to represent the agency at the hearing. I met with the overly anxious human resources (HR) team a few days before the proceedings to review what had happened and, more importantly, how I was going to frame what had happened. I dreaded coming back to deal with this tired issue and was suspicious of the tone of the meeting with HR. Although because of their job responsibilities they knew all the details that had led up to and followed Charlene's departure and, at the time, they had expressed nothing but support for the decision, they were now framing the issue as if it were a petty disagreement between two women who could not get along. What should have been a very simple, cut-and-dried supervisory matter was now personalized, not only by the shelter staff, but also by the administration. Coded in the language of "difficult personalities" (used to describe both myself and the staff), "ongoing drama," and "street behaviors"[17] was racialized subtext that any and all problems in the shelter could be traced back to the problem of Blackness.

The hearing in the judge's chambers was the first time I had seen Charlene since her last day of work. Charlene sat next to her lawyer, and I sat by myself at an adjacent table in front of the judge's oversize desk. The HR team sat together on the folding chairs behind us. I was intimidated at first by the fact that Charlene had a lawyer, but I quickly started to feel sorry for her as the judge started to ask questions that revealed the inconsistencies in her claim. Although I should have felt secured of a positive outcome when Charlene had to answer questions like "Is it true that you initiated a change to your schedule that made it impossible for you to work shifts in the shelter?" and "Did Ms. Cox ever make accommodations to your schedule when possible prior to this event?," the entire event ensured that there would be no winners.

It was clear from the pieces of the affidavit the judge read that Charlene's anger was directed at me, not GGC. She tried to attack my job performance by making up incidents that never happened and discussed everything that upset her in her job regardless of its relevancy to her claim. As the judge read her statement aloud (emphasizing the grammatical errors), his disregard and condescension for Charlene was clear. The hearing lasted an hour and a half. At its end, Charlene stormed out of the room, leaving her lawyer to gather the papers and scribbled notes they had been passing back and forth each time I answered a question. A month later, the HR team notified me that the court had found in the agency's favor and Charlene would not be getting unemployment.

Time away from the agency enabled me to see Charlene's frustration more clearly. There was a strong emphasis in the Fresh Start program on education as the most practical way to reach economic success and social mobility. All staff members, especially the RAs, were expected to support this ideology and promote it in their work with the girls, regardless of its incongruence with actual opportunities and outcomes. Camille rarely introduced me to a potential donor or volunteer without mentioning that I had graduated from Vassar and was working on my doctorate. Shelter staff members were usually in earshot of these comments and were able to witness, along with me, the immediate transformation that the voicing of my credentials had on the way I was received. When Charlene decided to go back to school, she was ostensibly providing the appropriate modeling of educational values. There were concessions made for me at GGC based on my educational status. My level of education overshadowed my lack of experience working in a managerial capacity. In addition, I was allowed to work and collect a paycheck at the same site where I was conducting fieldwork. My educational history was often talked about by GGC staff in ways that made my work as a program director seem ancillary and beside the point. It is understandable, then, why Charlene would feel justified in waging her year-long battle; her actions were motivated more by what she perceived as hypocrisy than by a desire for monetary gain.[18]

Before I left the shelter, Lynnette developed a self-empowerment class for the Fresh Start residents called the Inner Circle. She used the Inner Circle to create a setting where the girls could speak openly with and support each other as they worked through their individual problems, roadblocks, anger, and concerns. No topic or expression of emotion was off-limits. Lynnette had a loose lesson plan for the series of classes but usually let the mood in the room dictate the flow of the class and determine the "lesson" for the week. A parent by the age of fifteen and abandoned by parents who both struggled with substance abuse, Lynnette had learned quickly how to care for herself and her child. She also learned that part of being young, Black, poor, and parenting meant that you needed to demand respect and continually reclaim your subjectivity. When Lynnette returned to the shelter, she reinstated the practice of leaving "love notes" in the young women's rooms at the end of each day. After completing their chores, they would find slips of paper with "you are divine and wise," "your smile shines like the sun," "walk in your beauty," and "you are loved" written with Crayola markers on scraps of paper placed on top of their pillows.

The Inner Circle was always full. Current residents reorganized their work schedules so their Tuesday evenings were free. Former residents who had left the shelter as long as a year earlier still returned faithfully to be a part of the Inner Circle. In addition, residents were allowed to bring their friends and family members as long as they had permission from the group, and Lynnette always kept the group guessing which one of her eclectic friends she would invite to share their unique brand of knowledge based on personal experience, empathy, and intuition. They called themselves poets, massage therapists, relationship counselors, "diviners," and "goddesses," and they mesmerized the girls with their open spirits and genuine desire to connect with the residents. One day, Lynnette's friend Sa'at came to talk to the girls about the power of thought and the importance of having an open heart to receive blessings and experience self-transformation. Initially the conversation was lively, as the girls talked over each other, offering stories about times when they changed their luck through prayer or "felt" a troubling situation brewing before it occurred. But the conversation stopped when Sa'at pulled out her crystal pendulum and explained that she was going to test the openness of our hearts. If the pendulum swung energetically it would signal an open heart; if it moved lethargically or barely at all it would mean the opposite.

Sa'at first started with the infants in the room to demonstrate that we are all born with open hearts. They become closed as we develop defense mechanisms to shield ourselves from the threat of pain. We all watched, captivated, as the pendulum swung wildly in a wide circle when Sa'at placed it close to Shannon's baby's heart. "See," Sa'at said, "she has yet to experience any reason to close herself off."

"Oooh, do me! Do me!" the young women were springing out of their seats and raising their hands like excited schoolgirls for a chance to reveal the nature of their hearts.

"Okay, okay," Sa'at said. "Let me go around the room, one at a time. Now remember, an open heart chakra will show a swinging pendulum. If your heart is closed, there will be very little or no movement. But, ladies, if your heart is closed, this is just a temporary thing. You can always do the work necessary to open your heart."

Sa'at started around the room, testing the girls one by one. As she placed the pendulum in front of the first young woman's heart, everyone in the room sucked in her breath in anticipation. The pendulum was as still as a rock, as dead as a stone. Shannon's eyes grew wide, and she reached out to touch the pendulum. "Do it again, Sa'at," she begged. "I wasn't paying attention, I wasn't concentrating."

Sa'at tried to calm Shannon down by saying, "Baby, it's okay. We all have a little self-work to do. This doesn't mean that you're a bad person. It just means that you have some things, some baggage in your life you need to let go of. There are some things weighing on you."

The rest of the room was completely silent. You would have thought Sa'at had just diagnosed Shannon with terminal cancer.

"But I don't want my heart to be closed," Shannon said, looking down at her daughter whose heart just minutes before made the pendulum go crazy. "I have a baby. I need an open heart to be a good mother."

Sa'at and Lynnette tried to encourage Shannon by letting her know that she was a good mother, and that the pendulum exercise was just about temporary flows of energy. But Shannon closed her eyes as tears ran down her face. Sa'at, unsure now, continued making her way around the room. She took great pains to emphasize the impermanence of a closed heart and said that the pendulum was not identifying the girls as good or bad. I held my breath as Sa'at's pendulum hung still in front of each of the fifteen girls' chests. There was a ceremonial silence in the room, so I didn't notice until I took my gaze off the hypnotic pendulum and looked up at the girls' faces that every one of them was crying. Lynnette was up next. The pendulum moved lethargically from side to side.

"See, y'all," Lynnette told the depressed group, "I got work to do too. We all got baggage. No big deal."

I was up next, the last one in the circle. I was surprised how much I cared about the outcome even as I remained unsure about how I felt about this whole exercise. The pendulum was a dead weight, with no motion what-soever. I didn't know what to say.

"There ain't no hope in this room," one of the girls to my left said under her breath.

"Listen, ladies," Sa'at began, "let me explain something to you. There is no reason to be upset and crying. You are all beautiful, strong, intelligent, amazing young women. Some of you are mothers, and I watch you do a great job with your babies. This was not meant to judge you or upset you. I was only trying to demonstrate how the power of energy works in our lives and how energy flows can get blocked in our bodies. When the pendulum doesn't move, it just means that the energy in that part of your body is blocked. It means that we all have to take a look at ourselves—that includes me, too—and see how we can free up some of that energy. We need to let go of some things and learn how to forgive and move on. I know it is hard, but it is in our own best interest. We can sometimes hold on to things from the past that will eventually make us physically and mentally sick."

Sa'at paused and looked around the room to read the faces. Most of the girls still had tears streaming down their faces and their heads bowed.

Sa'at cleared her throat. "Um, well . . . are there any questions?"

No one said a word for a few minutes. Then Shannon raised her hand.

"Yes, Shannon?" Sa'at seemed relieved to finally have a response.

Shannon looked at Sa'at and said, "Can you tell us how to forgive, so we can have open hearts?"

I believe that both Poetess's caseworker and I would have taken swifter and more decisive action in getting Poetess back on track with her program requirements had we not been afraid of appearing to squash her dream. Poetess was a young woman who, like both of us, dreamed of becoming an artist. The distinct difference was, however, that the caseworker and I had the financial support of our parents, who were able to indulge us with ballet and music lessons and help us with the college tuition necessary to continue to realistically feed these dreams. Neither one of us really wanted to be the one to tell Poetess that she had to give up dreaming because she did not have these advantages. The fear of being insensitive to class inequalities and the blind belief that these inequalities would unilaterally determine Poetess's fate contributed to our hesitancy to present her with realistic options beyond saying, "Get a job!"

Both Charlene and Poetess were shapeshifters. Charlene held GGC accountable for living up to its mission of promoting education as part of a larger package of strategies for independent living and empowered citizenship. Even though this mission was reserved for the program participants and shelter residents, Charlene demanded that her educational aspirations be acknowledged and accommodated as an employee. What was evident to Charlene and many of the other shelter staff members was that educational attainment was more than a part of the residents' case plans; it was a foundational component of the value of and respect for adult staff members, as well. We flaunted education as the golden ticket for the residents' success and the legitimization of prestige among staff in the agency. Yet, while the RAs were devalued for their limited education, they were not expected to strive for more than a GED or high-school diploma. In Charlene's failure to comply with the terms of her revised schedule and the lawsuit she filed against the agency, she shifted the disingenuous terms of proposed success in the shelter whereby subjects were shaped discursively as free agents, "entrepreneurs of the self," while the limits of their social mobility was prefigured.

A healthy choice in the land of opportunity available to Poetess was chasing a low-wage service industry job at Comerica Park that would require her to find two other jobs to make a living wage. Desire, joy, and the satisfaction that comes from work that speaks to the fullness of who you are and a self-crafted life are values that are congruent with the organizational mission and upheld in theory by the support staff. However, it did not become a part of how we talked about life goals or developed case plans with the shelter residents. Dreaming, divining, and conjuring up a fulfilling life where work fueled young women holistically was fantasized as something that would come later after they had stable housing and could present themselves as employable through the service sector. I believed my real talk and tough love approach to Poetess was a way to protect her and ensure that Fresh Start did its best to transition her out of homelessness. Nonetheless, it matters less whether my intention was to protect Poetess or whether I genuinely believed a low-wage job was her destiny. Both sentiments are based on a paternalistic politics of care that denies Black girls the right to live outside of a market logic that sees them first and foremost as laborers in the service of everyone but themselves, as perpetually struggly, and as bodies that need to be disciplined or reshaped to begin to approach legibility as worthy citizens. Like Charlene, Poetess forced Fresh Start and me to confront the incongruencies between our values related to young women's empowerment and our actions in service of a status quo that kept the doors of the shelter open but that delineated inequitable boundaries around the ways the lives inside the institution could be led.[19]

But the story is more complicated than one-sided dramas of misunderstandings and betrayal, of class bias and cultural denial. There were no obvious villains or heroines at Fresh Start. The roles we all stepped into reflected our identities in the outside world but only to a certain extent, since the nature of our relationships often shifted when we left.

For example, caseworkers disparaged the RAs' work protocols and the RAs described the caseworkers as out of touch and snobby, but RAs and caseworkers hung out together after work, attended one another's baby and bridal showers, and went on vacations together. My relationships with the Browns shifted outside of the shelter, where our genuine concern for one another wasn't as compromised by institutional expectations about what these relationships should look like given our status within the agency. At Fresh Start identities were created, solidified, and reshaped relationally.

The direct service staff and administrators did not unilaterally pigeonhole residents into ill-fitting identities or see them only in terms of dichotomous narratives. The youth development philosophy and curriculum design used in the shelter was not entirely dismissive of the experiences, skills and knowledge that these young women walked in the door with. In fact, former residents spoke often and fondly of the positive aspects of the program, such as the genuine friendships they made with the staff members and the sense of belonging, acceptance, and encouragement that many of them felt for the first time in their lives at Fresh Start. Sensing that I was holding onto some animosity toward the agency and Camille triggered by the court hearing, Lynnette asked me to join her for coffee after the Inner Circle.

"You know, when you first asked me to come back to Fresh Start, I heard all these things about Camille," Lynnette said. "Before I could even get in the door good the RAs were like, 'That Camille is evil. Watch your back.' Now, you know me, I am thinking evil is some pretty strong terminology to be using to talk about a fellow human being."

"Uh-huh," I was tired and only half-interested in what Lynnette was saying.

"Well, you know after you left, Camille and I got close." Lynnette paused, expecting a response. I had a strong one internally, but I kept my eyes on my coffee. She continued: "Anyway it happened one day after our shelter evaluation meeting with her. Miriam gave this presentation, and when she was done Camille just went after her. I mean really let loose on her. It was hard to watch. You know, 'you are unprepared,' 'you made no sense.' It was bad. You should have seen Miriam's face."

"What happened?" I was looking at Lynnette now and interested in where the story was going.

"Well, after the meeting I pulled Camille aside because she looked confused by how the meeting ended and why everyone seemed so down,"

Lynnette said. "So, I told her, 'You can't talk to people like that, Camille. Did you see her face? She was really hurt by what you said.' And she looked at me right dead in my eyes, girl, and I thought she was about to cry. She looked at me and said, 'What should I do?'"

"Yeah, I'm sorry, Lynnette," I said, "If I am supposed to be moved by this . . ."

"Let me finish," Lynnette said firmly. "She told me she started this spiritual journey through General Motors and that it opened her up to where she realized that we all the same. She said she wanted to do away with titles because we treat people according to titles and she wanted everyone to be treated with respect. And then she said [Lynnette paused here for emphasis] she said she wanted to be different—she just didn't know how."

Lynnette's anecdote did not make me feel sorry for Camille, but it did make me consider the cost of not being able to see Black girls and the inherent value in their cultural and community-making practices. Camille, like the rest of us at Fresh Start, acted from what she understood and was able to perceive. Her assessment of the shelter as unproductive was based on her perception of the physical space of the shelter and the physical bodies of the residents, along with the actions and interactions that she was both able and allowed to see. The time Camille spent in the shelter felt like voyeurism to the staff and residents, even though her intention was to cross affective barriers and make genuine connections. Camille was, thus, unable to witness the practices of self- and community care the residents enacted on a daily basis, and the ways in which they were productively engaged in solving their own problems, whether related to employment, familial tensions, or personal safety and protection. The literature on Black girls emphasizes the ways in which they disrupt community through competition and physically fighting one another as opposed to the strategies they use to support and care for one another. The group counsel that Terri sought before drafting a letter to her boss so she could improve working conditions for herself and her peers; the steps the residents took to ensure one another's safety and provide child care when a mother was in desperate need of rest; the way young women provided levity and peace, especially when it was the staff members who were causing disruption—all these mundane yet significant shapeshifting techniques that could be missed if you didn't know where to look or how to see past bodies. For the residents, a home space was not antithetical to a productive space. This was evident in the young women's request that the staff and administration encourage more realistic longer-term residencies and in-house internships that would support their transition out of homelessness through the more intentional making of home at Fresh Start. Camille was not evil or even ill-intentioned. In light of her wish to "do away with titles," "treat everyone with respect," and "be different" herself, her compromised vision reflects the limits of our will to transform ourselves in the face of persistent socioeconomic inequities that our empathetic desires alone cannot undo.[20]

Unlikely Cowgirls

Bessie's back porch was not an ideal place to have a conversation. The door out of the kitchen was constantly being flung open, barely missing people on the porch before it banged against the porch wall and rebounded closed. The younger grandchildren were almost always underfoot or spilling out onto the driveway, where they tossed dusty pebbles and ran from each other, screaming in mock terror. Nonetheless, this is where we often migrated to talk, especially when the story was long and required multiple tellers. Since there was no phone at the Browns', I would stop by in the mornings to remind them of a workshop happening at Give Girls a Chance (GGC) later that day or of an appointment that was scheduled for the end of the week, and I often ended up there for hours longer than I had anticipated. Janice, Crystal, and Tina were the only three of the eight Brown sisters and cousins staying at their grandmother's house on this particular day. Tina's little twin boys, nearly two years old, punctuated our conversation with excited squeals as they slapped the hard wood of the porch floor with their hands and played peekaboo between our legs that were dangling over the steps.

Janice was always outspoken, but Crystal and Tina were typically more reserved. It took nearly a year before they warmed up to me and freely initiated conversations. At first, Crystal only spoke to me when she was mad or wanted me to do something for her, and Tina hardly ever spoke to anybody, keeping her eyes on the ground whenever she did. But now—six years, two babies, and countless experiences later—hours passed without a single pause in the conversation. It seems that in addition to music, neighborhood gossip, and the latest family drama, the Browns' favorite topic of conversation was GGC "back in the day." *Back in the day* refers to, as Janice puts it, the times before I "got moved up," meaning the time before I became the Fresh Start program director and was no longer categorized, in the Browns' minds, as part of the staff.

On this day, the "back in the day" story was the infamous week-long camping excursion that the Browns, ten other young women, and I embarked on in a small rural town eighty miles outside of Cincinnati, Ohio. Six days, thirteen preteen and teenage girls who had never slept outdoors, two chaperones unskilled in outdoor adventures, and a rural community that had only a vague understanding of what Detroit was like, made for many compelling stories. Over the years, the stories were passed down to the younger generation of Brown cousins and sisters who were not old enough at the time to go on the trip, as well as to newer GGC program participants who were told the stories as part of their informal peer orientation to the outreach program. At the time of the trip, the Browns made up the younger group of girls in the program. Tina and Crystal had just turned thirteen and Janice was fourteen, while the other young women were juniors and seniors in high school.

There was some debate among the after-school program staff about whether or not to take the Browns on the trip because of their age and the fact that they were, for the most part, considered behavioral problems. Although the outreach program serves girls and young women considered to be "high risk," the Browns fit that definition in ways that made some of the outreach staff uncomfortable. Unlike the older girls who had been associated with the agency since they were young girls in the Early Start Program, the Browns seemed rootless and unpredictable. When I first started working as an outreach coordinator, it was made very clear to me that the Browns were not thought of by the other coordinators and the program director as typical GGC girls and possibly signified a crisis in the already high-risk population and the family structure of the surrounding community. I was told on more than one occasion that the Browns were not what people were "used to." At the same time, however, the Browns started to symbolize a challenge to the outreach staff, a kind of testing of our integrity and dedication. Unlike many of the longer-term participants in the Community Outreach Program, whose employed parents picked them up from program activities, knew the names of all the outreach staff, and demonstrated concerns when workshops conflicted with the completion of homework assignments, the Browns appeared to have no such adult interventions.

The program driver whose job it was to pick up and drop off program participants for workshops and other agency events continually bypassed their home the first couple of weeks they were added to his route because he refused to believe that the building at the address was not condemned. Saran wrap hanging from deteriorating window frames and a front porch that looked like a human booby trap made the outreach staff believe that there must have been, or soon would be, as one of them said to me, "some type of outside, city, legal type of intervention to prevent occupancy in such a dangerous location." When the Browns acted up by cussing out the driver, stealing something from the office, getting into fights with each other during workshops, or threatening other girls, there seemed to be no checks and balances between the agency and the home. There was no home phone, and no one felt comfortable trying to reach the girls' mothers, Gwen and JoJo, at their jobs. Notes sent home were like releasing scraps of paper in a high wind; they probably landed nowhere of any consequence. The Browns showed each of the outreach staff their own weaknesses and revealed the heart of our collective hypocrisy. Here were, in front of our faces in almost textbook-like clarity, the very girls described in the GGC mission statement.[1] Yet we needed them to make the journey to self-improvement and personal transformation that we hoped for them less encumbered, less difficult to travel.

The Browns called the week-long trip the "Black camping trip" because, from their perspective, Black people do not hike, sleep in tents, go canoeing, or do any of the things that could fit in the categories of outdoor activities or adventures. Thus, it made sense to them that the Outdoor Adventure Team was the brainchild of Pam, the Community Outreach Program director, who felt—like many youth workers in the inner city before and since then—that one way to expand the leadership potential and skill development of urban youth is to provide them with challenges outside of the familiar environment of the city.[2]

"You know I wasn't even trying to go on no camping trip. Please. Like I'mma be in the tent with some bugs and stuff like that. I looked at them like, you musta lost your mind, but then when I found out that Pam wasn't coming and Aimee and Nikki was going I was like, bet I'mma be there." Crystal was talking to her cousin, Tina, who had joined us on the porch after calling down to us from the second-floor window above. Apparently, she had been trying to take a nap but had given up.

"Damn, y'all. I heard this story before. How many times you gonna tell the same damn story?" Tina rubbed her eyes, pulled up her pajama bottoms, and sat down next to me on the porch.

Crystal continued, undeterred. "Well, like I said. You remember, Janice, right? Like I was like, okay, we should go cause Nikki is cool and— I'mma be honest—we knew that you would be trying to make us do some ol' crazy, active mountain man-type stuff, but we knew it wouldn't be too crazy cause you still Black."

It broke Pam's heart not to able to participate in the trip, but the date conflicted with her honeymoon. She was anxious because four of the thirteen girls attending were from the Brown family, and Nikki, another program coordinator in the Community Outreach Program, and I (with zero camping experience between the two of us) would be the adults in charge. I liked Nikki, enjoyed her company, and was looking forward to sharing responsibilities with an adult who as a peer and—I assumed—less experienced than me in this particular arena, would not be overly critical about the outcome. However, I suspected not having a more experienced person along would mean more work for me in terms of making sure that the trip focused on the goals of skill acquisition and team building that were supposed to be of primary importance. My first clue that this might be more of a challenging proposition than I had anticipated occurred during a shopping trip with Nikki to purchase supplies. She bought a small TV and air mattress for her tent, thus reinforcing the girls' view that "camping is not a Black thing."

Since I was responsible for planning the details of the trip, I chose a campsite in Ohio that was just a little over an hour's drive from my parents' home in Cincinnati. I thought the proximity to the familiar would somehow make this venture less daunting. We left on a Sunday morning and returned the following Saturday afternoon. Six days is a long time to fill with active, adventure-type activities for thirteen girls who are suspicious of camping in the first place. The crammed agenda I eventually came up with included a canoeing trip, kayaking, low and high ropes courses, horseback riding, and an obstacle course on the campgrounds. We arrived in two fifteen-passenger vans, one driven by Nikki with all of the girls and the other driven by me and filled with all of our bags and equipment.

"'Member how scared we was, Tina, when we stopped for gas at that one station and everybody was lookin' at us like we was straight crazy? I was like, okay is it gonna straight up be some KKK type stuff going on here?" Crystal stood up as she imitated how the gas station owner and the other customers had stared at them when they walked into the convenience store. "I mean, I am like y'all have got to have seen Blacks before. I know you have TV at home. I know you get BET. So we started messing with them and like turning the tables on them, and then we felt less scared . . . for a minute."

"What did you do?" I asked.

"We just was fucking with them, so like when they asked, 'Where y'all from?,' we was like, 'Detroit, Compton, Watts, the Bronx, Harlem.' Like, it was so funny. Each one of us said something different and like really hardcore. And then Monica—y'all remember Monica? She was like talking to these dudes who came up to the van when Nikki was pumping gas, and she was like talking out the window like. 'Please step away from the van' in this real serious voice. And they was asking Nikki if we were from a girls' home, and they was like asking what we did and saying like, 'Y'all some bad girls, right?' And I could tell Nikki was getting pissed and she was trying to hurry up and pump the gas. I don't think she wanted to go off on them out in front of us. But Monica was so funny—she was like, 'Yes, you are right. These are very, very bad girls who have done things I can't even speak about. So, sirs, please step away from the van and please do not talk to my girls. They can't talk to people from the outside.[3] We can't be held responsible for what they might do.'"

"What happened then?" I had heard the story before but still wanted Crystal to continue.

"Well, they started backing up, like actually walking backwards like they was scared. And then one of 'em tripped over a pop can and fell. That shit was so dope. Funny, man. Just straight up funny."

This chapter considers how young Black women construct and use narrative and the performance of memory through storytelling to talk about themselves for and to one another. In the story of their experience at a dude ranch during a camping trip in Ohio and the contradictory narrative of a protest in the Fresh Start shelter that some question even actually happened, Black girls enact oral history as a reflection of what I call Black girl genealogies. These stories reflect and protest young Black women's placement at the nexus of various points of social erasure and degradation, but by no means are they solely concerned with forms of resistance that generally, in literature and practice concerned with the expressions of the dispossessed, have been cast as speaking back or giving voice. Storytelling, recalling, and renarrating involve, at their core, creative play, artistry, performative skill, trickery, and wit. The nature of young women's storytelling in this chapter suggests the concept of storying that Kevin Young uses to ground his exploration of Black cultural practices and productions. Young writes that he is "interested in the ways in which black folks use fiction in its various forms to free themselves from the bounds of fact" (2012, 19). The storying tradition that Young explores across Black life is one of "counterfeit and fiction," and one that he brilliantly demonstrates "has just as much place in African-American letters as our rituals of church or prayer or music" (ibid., 25). The stories that the Browns and the other young women in this chapter tell, remember, misremember, and perform allow them to learn from history as they retell and shapeshift it, to simultaneously critique and reimagine the present, and to propose the possibilities for protest and play in the future.

Horseplay

The dude ranch brochure listed scenic horseback riding, an authentic cowboy-style lunch, a tour of the ranch facilities, storytelling time, three-legged horse races, and team building exercises as options that could be combined to make "the perfect day at the ranch for the experienced or novice cowboy or cowgirl." Some of the activities sounded a bit hokey and not really age appropriate for young women in high school, but the prices were cheap and the girls who helped plan the trip were adamant about including horseback riding. The dude ranch had the most stringent rules of the local recreational facilities for groups. When we arrived, we were told that even though I had selected only horseback riding, the tour, and lunch as our activities for the day, we would have to participate in the full range of options because "they created the full ranch experience and could not be separated." Randy, the director of the ranch and our tour guide for the day, also informed us that he had assigned all the ranch staff to take care of our large group, so we should take advantage of the resources made available to us. Since we had decided to spend most of the day at the ranch anyway, Nikki and I agreed to go ahead with the suggested "full cowgirl treatment."

Randy and his staff met our van after we pulled up on the gravel road at the side of the ranch. Every time I think about our first appearance and what we looked like to Randy and his staff, I picture the gravel dust our wheels kicked up when we parked first swirling around and obscuring us and then dramatically fading to reveal unlikely cowgirls. Randy was overly friendly when he walked over to welcome us, and he shook each of our hands so furiously that he had to grab his cowboy hat in his other hand to keep it from falling to the ground. The rest of his staff stood back, looking as if they were stifling laughter. I couldn't tell if Randy was usually this enthusiastic or if he was trying to make up for his reserved staff. The bemused looks continued as we made our way through the tour of the ranch and eventually to the stables, where we were to be assisted in mounting our horses.

Through all of this, the girls were talking excitedly and making jokes, and it was difficult for me to tell at the time if they felt the tension that Nikki and I did. By the time we were on the trail, I heard some of the girls talking to the staff cowboy helpers, who rode back and forth to make sure that no one got lost or injured. Crystal recalled:

Them dudes was pretty cool. We just thought that they was like the quiet type, like real cowboys, like all silent and proud and manly—you know. So we started messing with them to get them to talk and making them laugh, like asking questions like and just making it seem like we was scared like, "How many people have died on this trail?" And then Janice was like, "Have you ever had a horse burger?" and trippin' like she thought they were going to try to feed us horse burgers. But they was cool, to me. They was like laughing with us and making jokes, too. They said we was like the most fun group that came there so far that summer.

"They just said that because you was acting hella foolish," Janice laughed. "That dude who was up front riding with us was like not even trying to hear it. He was acting like, 'if I don't look at them or talk to them maybe they'll go away.'"

I asked Janice what she thought that was about. She said: "You know . . . just not used to Black people. Just scared of something different. They live in the country and don't see much. But it was like, okay, we don't sit up every day surrounded by people wearing cowboy boots and what not. I mean like what I am feeling is like, this ain't old hat to us. Like, okay, when have we ever seen a horse, let alone [been] ridin' on one? But we still open to it and like ready to be open to them . . ."

"Whatever," Tina had been pretty much silent up to this point, but now she cut Janice off. "Janice, you always trying to say some shit is racist. I had fun. It was cool to me until they made us make that damn horse. That's when I thought you know the only person not cool up in here is Randy. I mean, he really pissed me off with that mess." Everybody on the porch laughed at this, because the making of the horse was the highpoint of the story.

At the ranch the rule was that every group's day of activities culminated with the making of the horse under the tent canopy at the back of the main ranch house, where Randy lived with his family. There, under the canopy, we found a picnic table and all the tools we supposedly needed to make our horse replica: four two-by-fours, a manual saw, a hammer, nails, crazy glue, yarn, glitter, and two plastic eyeballs. Randy told us that we had an hour to make the horse and come up with a story about it. Every girl had to participate in creating the horse and making up the story, no adult help was allowed, no materials other than the ones provided could be used, and all the materials had to be used in some way. He was leaving us, he said, to check on his wife who was preparing dinner in the main house. By this time, it was after 6:00 PM and painfully apparent that everyone was tired, had had enough of each other and the entire experience, and more than ready to go home—even though home for us meant damp tents on rough ground.

Randy wasn't smiling anymore, and there were no more ironic jokes being made by the older girls. Nikki and I were just as uninterested as the girls in the oddly age inappropriate craft project,[4] but we tried to raise their spirits and offer some encouraging words. Slowly and deliberately, the girls started working on the horse. Because they were tired and annoyed by what they believed to be the pointlessness of the assignment, arguments began to break out. It didn't help matters that their raised voices caused Randy and his wife to stand in the doorway of the main house, observing us with their two children. The girl, who looked to be about seven years old, was pointing and laughing at Crystal who was chasing one of the other girls around the picnic table in semi-mock menace with the saw. By now, over an hour had passed, and the horse was no closer to materializing out of the wood, glue, and nails than before Randy left us. I could hear the girls mumbling "damn" under their breath and sucking their teeth as Randy approached the canopy. I think Janice tells this part of the story best:

We looked up like, damn, okay, so here he come again. And by now we like just more than a little tired of Randy. And this time, he came wit' his kids. And they was trip too—that little boy with his big hat and the girl was like missing her front teeth. But I like wanted to think they were cute and like couldn't even go there because Randy just brought them out to be like, "Look, kids . . . look at the Negroes. They are a new species you have not seen before." And like we was already frustrated and ready to go home and trying to not disrespect, but that was taking me to the edge—I mean, the fact that they was looking at us like entertainment or some shit.

Nikki and I felt the girls' frustration and were fed up with the fascination with our group that seemed to come to a head in this last assignment. Before Randy returned, we asked the girls if they wanted to leave and told them that they didn't have to finish the project. It had been a long day, and we still had to repitch our tents and make our dinner and complete other campsite chores before it got too dark.

At that point, Janice remembers, "there was no way in holy hell we were going to give up. It was like, 'Oh, hell naw. We 'bout to make a damn horse. Just because you think we can't.'"

Although "adult chaperones" were not supposed to participate or help in any way during this final assignment, Nikki and I took turns trying to help cut the two-by-fours with the dull saw and offered suggestions on how to manipulate the yarn to make the mane. Fed up, Monica grabbed a two-by-four and laid it on the picnic table bench so that half of it was on the seat and half hung over the edge. She asked Tina to stand on the half on the bench and then stomped on the other half until it broke off.

"I ain't know what she was about to do, but it worked and that stuff was mad funny and a good idea," Tina recalled. She chuckled as she reenacted Monica jumping down on the piece of wood with a grimace on her face. "Moni was like, unga bunga and making monkey sounds . . . she had us rolling. She was like, 'Yeah, okay, we're monkeys in the zoo, you can see monkeys in the zoo. Here we are.'" I asked Tina to clarify if this was before or after Randy came out with the kids.

"After," she said. "You don't remember? They came out the first time when they busted you helping us cut the wood and you was like, 'Whatever, Randy, these girls need to finish up so we can eat.'" Crystal and Janice cracked up at the way Tina made fun of the way I talked and nodded to show that they remembered this part of the story as well.

I do remember what happened next, however. Energized by Monica's innovative solution to our material challenges, the rest of the girls started going to work hammering and gluing on plastic eyes. It was getting darker, more difficult to see, and harder to work through the hunger and exhaustion. I started cleaning up the scraps around the canopy and encouraged the girls to start thinking about their story so that they would be ready when Randy returned and we could get back on the road to camp. I tried not to notice that the horse had only three legs and generally looked a mess. When Randy returned, he brought his entire clan with him: his wife, two children, an older brother, and his father. They had already eaten dinner and seemed ready for a show as they stood back and watched the girls put the finishing touches on the horse. By now it was nearly 8:30, and the lights had come on around the backyard area where we were gathered. Randy's wife and children looked wide-eyed and were pretty much speechless, aside from the whispered remarks they made to each other behind their hands. The children did a lot of pointing and giggling, even though they were much closer to us than is usually considered pointing distance. The grandfather kept clearing his throat, making us all look over to see if he was about to say something or if he wanted to get our attention. When I looked over, he was exchanging curious looks with Randy.

After fifteen or so minutes of this awkward watchfulness, Randy asked the girls to present their horse and tell its story. I think I heard a gasp when Janice stepped forward to place the wobbly horse on the table and it promptly fell on its side. The ends of the horse's three legs were rough and splintery where they had been broken off instead of sawed. Each leg was a different length. The brown yarn that was meant to be a mane was not securely glued on and hung down over what, based on proximity, would have been the horse's face. One eye swung precariously off the side of the face, and the other was unfortunately stuck to the bottom of one of the splintery legs. The poor horse was almost too sad to be hilarious—but not quite. Nikki's eyes were watering as she tried to hold back tears. I could only briefly glance at the girls because the looks on their faces threatened to send me over the edge. Only silence came from Randy's group. There was no more throat clearing or giggling.

"I know they thought we was like some slow kids or like mentally retarded when they saw that horse." Janice moved to the other side of the porch to swat at a fly that had landed near one of the twins. Tina, Crystal, and I were doubled over in laughter, picturing the wooden horse in our minds and redescribing the worst parts.

Randy took off his hat, which was the first time I had seen him without it, and placed it on the table next to the fallen horse. He took the horse in his hands with an odd gentleness that made it seem as if he was preparing to perform some type of healing surgical procedure. He looked the horse over, turning it upside down, and then tried to place it back on the table. But a piece of gluey yarn stuck to his hand, and in the process of trying to free himself he took off what was left of the pitiful mane, except for a small scrap of yarn that clung to the horse's forehead. I wanted to laugh so badly that I felt my head might explode, and Nikki reached over to squeeze my hand. Randy blushed with what seemed to be a combination of amusement and embarrassment and cleared his throat like his father. "Well, ladies," he said. "Why don't you tell us what you have done here. I mean, tell us this horse's story."

Since this was Janice's favorite part of the story, we let her initiate the retelling. She said that they were all "just basically beyond pissed at this point" and felt humiliated by Randy and his family: "We wasn't mad 'bout the way the horse looked 'cause that was like the funniest part, so we wasn't mad that everybody was trying not to laugh 'cause we were laughing ourselves. But we didn't appreciate being looked at like we were in a zoo or like—you know, the way they played us, it was like they thought we were crazy or stupid. That is the part that made me really angry. So we just made up a story on the spot like, 'Okay . . . this is probably what you want to hear.'"

The girls did not have time to come up with a story together beforehand, so they improvised a story with each girl adding to the mythical life of the horse before turning the narrative over to the next girl. They were standing in a straight line that was perpendicular to the edge of the picnic table, which made them look like soldiers standing at attention.

The story started with Monica. "This is our horse, Swoop," she said. "We call her Swoop because as you can see her bangs are swooped to one side, a popular hairstyle where I come from." The one thin piece of yarn meant to be the horse's mane actually did look like the swoop bangs that were common among teenage girls in Detroit that year.[5] Monica's name for the horse sent chuckles down the line of girls.

Janice, next in line, grabbed Swoop from Monica's hands and continued the story in the same matter-of-fact, academic tone that Monica had used. "Well, as you can see, Swoop's hair is very important to her. Like most horses that grow up in the city, she puts a lot of time and effort into her hair and spends her hard-earned money working late nights at the Chicken Shack on her hair."

Nikki closed her eyes and shook her head back and forth, and then hit me on the hand. "Can you believe them? They are *really* trippin'. Umm, those girls." Her tone was that of a mother talking to another parent about her mischievous child, trying to appear stern and in control but secretly proud of her child's creativity and spunk.

Janice was prepared to go on, but Sharon took Swoop out of her hands and took over the story: "Yes, working late nights at the Chicken Shack is not always easy for Swoop. Sometimes she is tired and afraid to walk home on 6 Mile Road by herself. The Livernois bus doesn't run that late and she doesn't have a car, so she must gallop home through the dark streets alone."

On the porch at the Browns' house, I had already pulled out my tape recorder. This was at least the third time I had witnessed Janice telling the Swoop story, complete with each girl's addition to the plot, and I was determined to finally get it on tape. The Brown girls had become so accustomed to my tape recorder that they already set it up and tested the voice volume for me before I realized it. The recorder encouraged Janice's theatrics as she told the Swoop story in the voice and demeanor of each girl.

"Tina, you were next, right?" Janice got ready to offer her best impersonation of her cousin: "There is no rest for horses like Swoop growing up in the harsh ghetto. They try to escape the drugs, the crime, the risks of—."

Tina cut Janice off at this point. "I didn't say that. I said 'the at-risk, the high-risk, the drugs, the crime, [her voice got low and pseudo-emotional] the tragedy.'"

Janice continued: "Whatev. Then that one girl what was her name? Karen, or something like that—was like, 'As you may have noticed by now, Swoop only has three legs. I hate to say it but, yes, Swoop lost one of her legs in a tragic drive-by shooting. The police say they are still looking for the suspects but . . . we all know what that means.'"

Crystal, who had been leaning back against my legs from her seat on the step in front of mine sat up. "Okay. This was my part now. Okay. I was like, 'Yes. Let's take a moment to say a prayer for poor Swoop.'" Crystal deepened her voice to re-create the preacher-like cadence she had used during her performance at the ranch: "'My people. Bow your heads and raise your right hand above the head of this poor horse. Let this horse know that you are with her through her pain and want to see her raise up to a new life in the Lord. Can I get an Amen?' I remember everybody was like all serious and like amen, amen—now that was like the true funniness. And then a couple of them other girls, the more quiet ones, was like laughing and trying to add something in. Like, what? What'd they say, Tina?"

Crystal seemed unsure of how the story finally ended, but she went on: "They was just like, 'Let's try to help poor Swoop get to the Derby so she can finally take home the trophy.[6] Help her get out of the ghetto.'"

By the time Swoop had been passed down through all of the girls' hands and placed back on the picnic table, she was completely bald and threatening to become two-legged. For some reason, I will always remember the end of the story being punctuated by the pop of Swoop's plastic eye as it landed on the floor after Monica flicked it off her shoulder.

"Do you remember what Randy and his family did after the story?" I asked the girls.

"They was just standing there looking straight crazy as far as I remember. They was like trying to be all nice but they was straight shook. You know, they ain't know what to say or do. But damn, it felt good like to be like, okay, this is what you think, this is what you asked for, this is like, what you really been thinking 'bout us since we got here." Janice moved over on the step so she could get closer to the tape recorder.

"Right," Tina jumped in:

You know, it was like you want to stand around and point fingers like you ain't never seen nothing like us, and then you want to hear a nice—I mean, I'm sure they was expecting to hear a nice story like, "Okay. Our horse's name is Meadow, and she is a friendly horse that likes to eat hay, blah, blah, and whatnot whatever." But we was like all tired. I mean tired, like really tired. It ain't to me—I mean, to me it didn't matter at that point in time what ol' boy at the ranch or his jankety family thought. I was like, "Look, you think we stupid and the horse we made looks jacked up, so here is a jacked-up story to go along with it."

"But you can't even really trip on the dude ranch like that is the only place and time where you felt like that." Janice seemed to be thoughtfully considering what Tina had just said. She continued:

"I mean, I been in the GGC van in Detroit before where peeps be like, "What'd y'all do? Y'all some bad girls, right?" But I don't understand that, like, why they just assume that we did something bad in order to end up in GGC. Because when I talk about I'm at GGC they're like, "Why, what'd you do? Why your momma put you in there?" I'm like, "Nothing, why do you think that?" And it ain't just because people don't know what GGC is or associate it with a home, 'cause I'm sure don't nobody be asking those white girls from Girls, Inc.[7] if they did something bad cause they see Girls, Inc. as like a spin-off of the Girl Scouts and think them girls is like winning awards and badges and stuff and getting good grades. Like it is an honor to be in that program, and like even at GGC we might be doing some of the same stuff and, I mean, good stuff—but it is just like assumed that we are troubled.

"Right, but it was like the last straw at the ranch 'cause I felt that was supposed to be like a vacation." The exasperation was clear in Tina's voice. "It was like, 'Okay, show time' when that piece of crap horse came up and dude was like, you know, talking to us like we was ignorant: 'Tell us what your horse did.' Please. I'm thinking, 'My horse ain't do shit but sit up here and look crazier 'n hell, and if it did you really didn't care 'cause you really just trying to figure all us out.'"

"I don't know." Crystal added her commentary in what had gone from light-hearted reminiscing to an emotionally charged debate. "Like when you said we should just go"—Crystal was looking at me now and talking about my suggestion that we leave in lieu of completing the horse assignment—"I was like happy and agreeing at first 'cause it was like some ridiculous shit that was about to go down. I could feel it. But now I ain't mad we stayed 'cause I think we was able to show them that we got it. That we get what they think."

After Crystal's last comment, Tina turned off the tape recorder and went inside with a twin on each hip. She said she needed to check their diapers. Janice and Crystal decided they wanted to walk to the beauty supply store on Michigan Avenue and asked what time I would be back to pick them up for the dance workshop later that evening. They were getting on with their day and also signaling to me that they had had enough of the current conversation. Driving home, I thought about how the girls talked about the Swoop story in the van on the way home from the ranch, how they now assessed the time at the ranch, and why the story was so important to them that it was retold so often and in such great detail.

The younger Brown cousins were too young at the time to go with us on the trip, but they added their two cents to the story because they had heard it so many times. Sometimes I still get confused about which girls were actually on the trip because they all speak about that time in Ohio with so much clarity and emotion—especially the ones who weren't there. The incident at the gas station before the girls reached the campsite foreshadowed what was to happen at the dude ranch while also encapsulating in the young men's taunting sarcasm and the young women's witty response the game of identity presentation that these young women play in less obvious ways in their daily encounters. As Janice points out toward the end of the story, these types of misreadings of who they are and of value judgments placed on their identity occur in their own communities in Detroit and are, thus, not a new negotiation specific to rural Ohio.

At the start of the forty-five-minute ride back to the campsite from the dude ranch, the van was vibrating with the girls' energy. There was a lot of repeated "Did you see their faces?" and "See what happens the next time they get a call from a group from the D. They'll be like, 'Oh, hell naw!'" The overall tone of the girls was one of victory and pride, and there was a distinct feeling that they had proved a point long in the making. But as I heard the Browns retell the story in the years since, I began to see another angle to the story and the significance it held as it was passed down and variously performed. The oral documentation of the event and the story's place in the historical record for the GGC participants was just as important as the actual Swoop event—perhaps even more so. The playfully subversive content at the heart of the story certainly mattered for how the Black girls at GGC understood the possibilities for shifting the shape of contexts as foreign as a dude ranch in Ohio. However, it also contributed to their expanding Black girl archive.

They were both constructing and referring to a road map, a set of choreographed steps used to upset the prevailing narratives of their lives. In the moment that the story was told, each girl took her turn to draw from and then add to the collective plot in a spontaneous revision and satire of the trope of Black girls from the Detroit ghetto. Over the years, Swoop's collaborative biography became a concrete example of the power of self-authored narratives as a key shapeshifting strategy. Swoop's story made transparent how the girls were read as out of place in real time at the dude ranch while tethered to other geographically and psychically plotted places, such as Detroit and Blackness, that were imagined through their bodies. They performed a version of fish-out-of-water comedy embedded with critical social commentary to both highlight and challenge this mapping of their bodies' space. In the Fresh Start shelter, the Swoop story, most often retold by Janice during her time as a resident, became part of a protest history that included a school walkout staged by Detroit students on the city streets in 1999 and the elusive shelter protest.

Schoolgirl Rapes

In November 1999, three hundred students from Denby High School staged a walkout. They left their classes and walked from their school on Kelly Avenue on the east side of Detroit to the school administration building. Since the start of the school year in early September, eight young women had been raped and another twenty young women had been victims of attempted abduction while trying to make their way to school. Frustrated by the underplaying of these sexual attacks in the media and the slow response of city administrators and law enforcement officials, the group of students, most of whom were Black girls, decided to march as a protest against their invisibility and their lack of protection. When I first heard about the schoolgirl rapes, as they were officially and sensationally called in televised and print news reports, it was at the height of student outrage. The media reports seemed to focus more on the brewing conflict between the students and the school administrators than on the disturbing reality of sexual violence that was making their everyday walk to school a matter of life and death for several hundred Black girls living in Detroit.

Eventually, Mayor Dennis Archer entered the conversation and tried to address the troubling situation by holding a series of town meetings to which parents, students, and concerned community members were invited. Disappointingly, however, the 300,000 flyers distributed to announce the meetings netted only fifty attendees. While the mayor worked to motivate the citizens of Detroit with statements like, "Now is the time for every Detroiter to do what he or she can do to make sure our streets are safer," the young women expressed their own feelings of abandonment and lack of adult accountability. One sixteen-year-old young woman told reporters, "I'm really, really mad about it." She wondered, "What is wrong with the parents? They're all out there blaming the mayor. What about everybody sitting at home right now?"[8] After several more months of attempted and successful assaults on young women, one man was finally apprehended, and the events swirling around the schoolgirl rapes started to slowly fade from public view and concern.

The Shelter Protest

While I was still employed as a program coordinator in the Community Outreach Program and trying to decide if I should accept the executive director's invitation to direct the shelter, I started to hear snatches of stories and vague anecdotes about a protest staged by the residents of the Fresh Start shelter the year before I came to GGC. Curious about what had really happened, I asked longtime GGC staff members what they remembered about the protest. At first, their individual accounts were clear and coherent, but as time passed and I compared the stories to one another, the details became muddled and the storytellers were rarely able to defend their original narratives with any degree of confidence. Some of the staff members called the event the shelter strike, others termed it a boycott, and still others referred to a time when the shelter residents were "acting out" or "looking for attention." All of the responses, however, were similar in that the event was discussed a year later as an urban legend—a mythical story about the shelter that, once told as truth, had become a tale of what could have happened. The story I first heard was that on one hot summer day, fed up with what they believed to be the unfair and overly punitive shelter rules, the residents boycotted the shelter by staging a sit-in on the front lawn of the church where the shelter was then housed. Apparently, this boycott even included hand-crafted signs and marching in an orderly circle. I was told this story by Ms. Germaine, a Black woman in her late fifties who worked in the Early Start Program, when I started as a volunteer dance instructor at GGC. She talked to me a few months after the shelter strike as a way of warning me against working with the girls and staff in the shelter:

> Um, you can work over there if you want to, but note that those girls over there are a trip. It ain't like in Early Start. I mean, how you gonna protest your living environment when you live in a shelter? Come on, you are homeless! Those girls are rough, and they don't care about nothing having to do with common sense or order. I had to drive down Michigan Avenue myself that night to see it. Girl, they had signs and everything. Can you believe it? Striking and you don't even have a job? Folks trying to help your Black butt. What kind of nonsense is that? Nah, you better off here. That shelter is a trip.

By the time I started classes with the shelter residents, nearly fourteen months had passed since the so-called strike, and none of the current residents had been living in the shelter at the time of the protest, although they had all heard about it. The comments they made included:

> "Yeah, I heard that was crazy. I wish I had been there. Them girls must have been trippin'."

"I mean, there are rules that get on your nerves, but come on. I ain't a little kid. I have a job and trying to get my own apartment. I couldn't be risking getting thrown out like that."

"I think that is good what happened because it probably made things different. I think most of the rules that I see now make sense to me, but they wasn't—I mean, I don't think they was like this until recently."

When I pressed those newer residents[9] to think about what things about Fresh Start could have been so bad before, they all agreed that it probably had to do with the way the previous residents were talked to and treated by the resident advisors (RAs) and was less about the actual program guidelines and expectations. One resident said: "You can tell most of the staff is strugglin' with niceness. They first instinct is to talk to you like you stupid, and then they usually try to clean it up later when they think you are going to go above they heads and say something or go off real bad."

The idea of RAs "cleaning it up" is something that many of the residents mention as a way of explaining what they see as the direct service staff's compulsion to treat them with respect only when there is the threat of disciplinary action from a supervisor. This is just one of the many ways that the residents demonstrated their perception of the RAs as powerless within the organization. The contradictory statements the residents made regarding the RAs were emblematic of the complicated nature of their relationship, and the oral history tied to the shelter protest reflected these tensions. Out of the fifteen RAs who worked full- or part-time shifts in the shelter while I was the director, three were former residents of Fresh Start and five more had spent some time in other residential facilities while they transitioned out of homelessness or sought refuge from an abusive relationship.[10] The RAs provided the residents with a sense of how power dynamics worked for and against them at Fresh Start and in the world outside of the building.

In some accounts of the shelter protest, the residents were said to be protesting against being overly policed by the RAs. In other accounts, the residents and RAs were portrayed as protesting together in solidarity against the disrespect both groups received within GGC. The residents were frustrated with the task of constant self-improvement in an organizational structure where their older age and perceived lack of familial connections automatically framed them as delinquent. The RAs were protesting their economic and social marginalization in GGC. The story of the residents protesting against the organization and the RAs as the most punitive aspect of the organization and the story of the residents and RAs mobilizing together against their status never truly cohered in one narrative told by multiple people.

The two accounts did, however, make sense as parts of the same concern. If the RAs—half of them at any given time former shelter residents— were reflections of the residents' future selves, then was working for hourly wages in jobs that held little possibility for advancement or respect the future that the young women had to look forward to after obediently and conscientiously "working the program"? This not improbable outcome undoubtedly fed resentment between the residents (who recognized themselves in the RAs and resisted that future) and the RAs (who often wanted the residents to have more than they themselves did, in terms of economic capital and social status). Thus, the protest may have emerged from both the residents' and the RAs' refusal to believe the promise of social mobility offered through Fresh Start. More interesting than the question of the mythical or real nature of the shelter protest is the salience of the narrative at Fresh Start as a cautionary tale—meant not to warn potential shelter employees about the out-of-control nature of the residents, as Ms. Germaine intended, but as an indictment of another narrative: that of the traditional path to financial stability, occupational security, and respect for low-income Black girls and women.

In spite of the contradictory stories attached to the real or imaginary (as some staff members persistently claimed) shelter protest, one particular story resonated with me. Andrea had been an RA during the time of the alleged protest, although by the time of our conversation she had moved on to an administrative job with the city. She was eager to talk about what she called the "sit-in" and began, with intense animation, by offering details she recalled from the event:

> Well believe it or not, a few of them started making signs like "unfair treatment," "we are people too"—stuff like that. Girl, it was so funny to me. I mean, it was more like by the time we had got to that point, it was like we were really already over it. But it was like, okay, we went this far—why not go all the way? But I mean by that time we had all vented and were just taking it as a joke. We was playing by that point, but at the same time the reason behind it all was serious. I don't know if you know what I mean, but it was like they were like doin' it tongue in cheek. And to be honest, I didn't think it lasted more than a few hours. I called

Christine to come down to the shelter because she was always on call, supposedly, and—well, maybe the other girl called her, but I know it wasn't because we couldn't handle the girls. We thought she should see what was going on. But, you know, by the time she came down the girls was mainly just chillin' on the front steps—just hanging out like any other summer night.

What interests me in Andrea's story more than the fact that her clear and specific details, earnest narration, and distance from the organization lent her memory credibility is the way she told the story. Her description of the play within the protest aligned with the events that occurred at the dude ranch, along with its endless retelling in the Brown family and throughout the organization. Both the shelter protest and the dude ranch stories acted as part of a larger narrative genealogy that provided the residents with performative, shapeshifting texts useful within and beyond institutions like Fresh Start. The schoolgirl rapes protest of 1999 was important as the example from recent historical memory that the young women could draw on as representative of courageous collective action publicly taken in defense of the brutal violation of Black girls' bodies. The student protest in response to the sexual assaults was a bold statement of the value of Black girls' lives within a social context where their right to reside in cities that afford them safety and protection is denied. Although the young women at the dude ranch and the residents sitting in on the front lawn of the church were not necessarily in imminent danger of the type of life-threatening brutality that spawned the 1999 protest, the telling of the Swoop story at the dude ranch and the shelter protest were responding to the same sentiment of unprotected and denigrated Black girlhood the schoolgirl rapes represented.

Protesting and playing are interconnected practices used by both the young women in the shelter and its staff members in very well planned and overt ways as well as in ways that appear unconscious and spontaneous. I use *play* in this context to refer to the joy in working collectively to confront the most subtle and difficult to define aspects of institutionalized injustice and everyday instances in which Black girls find themselves dismissed and/or violated. The indignity felt on an individual level becomes a source of power and a catalyst for inspiring feelings of freedom and control, when young Black women realize that they do not have to emotionally process their experiences alone. Andrea explains this feeling in her account of the shelter protest, which—from her perspective—was able to become a "tongue in cheek" reaction to perceived agency injustice after the young women were able to verbalize their common frustration. The shelter became a tenable space from which the play in protest could be performed, once it was clear that the residents and the RAs were of like mind in addition to being of like background and recipients of like treatment. The play in the protest is a sense of temporary freedom from and control over structural constraints. Politically charged anger and resentment erupted in this communal home space of shared cultural and life experiences. Barbara Myerhoff describes these shifts from political to cultural protests as "subtle and gradual but distinct and frequent" (1971, 115). This is a useful way to capture the nature of the many overt and hidden acts of protest (by the staff and residents) in the agency in which politics and culture become mutually definitive.

In adult responses to the schoolgirl rape protest, the focus was mostly on the boldness demonstrated by the girls in deciding to skip classes and confront school administrators. The incredulous tone of their reactions made the adults appear more aggrieved at the young women's act of speaking out against the violence enacted on them than at the idea that girls were being raped in broad daylight on their way to school. We see this same disdain in the staff members' commentaries on the shelter protest: all of the statements, except for Andrea's, seemed to be most concerned with the perceived audacity of the residents' believing that they had a right to complain about anything, given their circumstances as homeless young women with presumably no other support or options outside of GGC. The events (both those that were clear and known and those that were vague and hypothesized) that ignited the protests in both situations were lost in the overreaction to the fact that young women felt entitled to challenge institutional authority. I compare these two scenarios to get at how rights and protections are directly connected to the value placed on certain bodies (Crenshaw 1991). The abduction and rapes of the high-school students received the most sustained attention only after young Black women demonstrated their defiance by leaving the supposed safety of the school environment and marching in the very streets that threatened them.

It is through the daily acts of play and protest (not all of which are as remarkable as the shelter protest) that take place in the context of the agency that the contours of class- and race-based expectations and boundaries are alternately reinforced and threatened, and the instruments of power are revealed.[11] The conscious employment of these acts—along with their interpretations, correct or not—influences perceptions of what it means to be considered appropriate and acceptable, or out of control and ghetto.

This, in turn, shapes the basis for the tensions between residents, staff members, and board members related to attributions of cultural capital and personal worth invested in specific bodies. Through her creative and political work with Black girls and women, Ruth Nicole Brown has come to understand the seriousness with which Black girls approach play and with which we need to read their practices. In the creative ciphers and games played in Saving Our Lives, Hearing Our Truths (SOLHOT), it is clear to all participants that what they were up to before, and what they "will return to after the game, is not play" (2009, 100). At the dude ranch and on the church lawn, the playfulness in the protests acknowledged the seriousness of what was at stake in the girls' lives before the break marked by each event and of what may or may not be changed by their play. Brown is also clear about what does not constitute play. She uses what occurs during the game called Little Sally Walker to articulate how the rules of play are collectively established and sometimes broken by a girl who substitutes discipline for play:

> But the real culprit of unraveling the cipher typically manifests in those overly disciplined bodies that don't have much play practice. Through the chanting, we can distinguish and facilitate the healing of a Black woman girl child whose youth was stolen. Little Sally Walker, after all, is ritual. However, what cannot be tolerated is someone whose disciplined indoctrination shows up when they become Sally and, for example, take "too long" to teach us a move, confirming that what they are about to dance is over-choreographed to the point of leaving no surprise. This translates as domination. Why, Black girl, can't you move the way you want to move on a whim? Why, Black girl, can you not think for a moment about yourself, what you want to say and how you want to say it? Why, Black girl, are you still seeking someone's permission and/or approval to dance? This is domination. The game is over. This is not playing. (2009, 101)

During what was alternately called Camille's reign or the shelter takeover, the matter of approving of Black girls' bodies and the ways in which their bodies occupied space critically influenced the perception of what was needed to renovate Fresh Start beyond changing the color of the walls or the fabric on the couches. Black girls' bodies were seen as sites to be reworked, and their biographies were also significant factors in determining the girls' ability to receive resources from the institution and be seen as primed for the various stages of transition through the shelter—from initial intake as a worthy resident, through program milestones, to eventually moving out on their own. Thus, the ways in which the residents talked about their personal histories and the biographies that garnered salience in the agency were directly tied to the limited ways Black girls and women are able to gain legibility and validity as proper residents, workers, and citizens. Black girls and women at Fresh Start who appeared to be seeking permission from upper-level white administrators by working within standards of normative social acceptability—who managed their bodies and reframed their personal narratives—had lost the ability to play, even if they appeared to be mastering the game. Terri's comment to Sharita[12] at the end of the house meeting about the shelter renovations demonstrated that Terri suspected Sharita might be losing the game in her attempts to please everyone but herself. The two narratives that were the most common in the shelter were those of redemption and of exception.

Narratives of Redemption and Exception

Three months after I finished my fieldwork at Fresh Start, I pulled up at the McDonald's drive-through in midtown Detroit and found Sharita Daniels ready to take my money at the first window. Sharita had been a resident of Fresh Start for a little over a year, which was six months longer than the average woman's stay. After she discharged herself from the shelter,[13] Sharita continued to be a regular fixture at the agency, acting as a tour guide for donors on site visits, speaking to current residents in workshops, and generally being the face of Fresh Start until there were others who could fill her shoes.

I don't know which of us was more shocked to see the other. Sharita had endured many of my long lectures on the dangers of fast food, and the last few times I had heard from Sharita, she was on her way to Lansing to study at Michigan State University. I guess we both wondered what had happened since then. Sharita asked me if I was still at Fresh Start. I told her I was doing some research there and joined the residents on recreational outings from time to time.

"Well, be careful," she said. "I can't stand that place."

I didn't know what would be appropriate to say to her in the short time I had as one car in a long line of customers. I think I said "umm" and nodded my head to show I understood. "So, you still writing that book about Fresh Start?" Sharita asked. "Do you want to talk to me?" We exchanged phone numbers and made tentative plans to meet up later that week.

The McDonald's exchange was not the first time I heard Sharita criticize Fresh Start. She and I had spent a fair amount of time together, especially toward the end of her term when she was an official Fresh Start resident. Although I no longer worked at GGC and Sharita was no longer a resident at the time, we were both frequently called on to represent and speak on behalf of the shelter. For Sharita, this meant talking to board members, donors, and staff from other collaborating agencies about her life prior to Fresh Start and how the program was helping her achieve her goals. On one occasion, Sharita and I even traveled together to the state capital to testify to the state legislative committee on youth and families. Our goal was to convince these policy makers that programs in Detroit for high-risk and homeless teens were worth supporting; that they were making the types of differences in young people's lives that challenged negative views of poor, urban youth.

Sharita had shared an apartment with her mother, five-year-old twin brothers, and a twenty-two-year-old brother, but the building burned down. Sharita's mother and brothers moved in with an aunt of Sharita's and her two young daughters. When the overcrowded living situation became overwhelming for the combined families, her mother decided that Sharita would be the one to find a new place to stay. Even though she had a brother who was five years older, her family thought that Sharita would have better luck in the search for housing, since she was young, attractive, and female.

During the ninety-minute drive from Detroit to Lansing to testify to the legislature, Sharita talked a lot about her feelings about GGC. Her words flowed seamlessly as she discussed what she believed to be the dishonest and self-serving way she was "used as a poster child." She understood that what made her a Fresh Start success story were her articulateness, wit, fair skin, ultrafeminine appearance ("I definitely am a girly-girly," was one of her favorite ways to describe herself), and ability to say the types of things that older, conservative adults with money and self-defined altruistic leanings liked to hear. At the same time, Sharita's personal history, along with the circumstances that brought her to the shelter, were tragic enough to guarantee that she fit the mold of Fresh Start's target population.

Much of who Sharita was in these public and presentation settings, she said, was based on information she had gathered early on, as a girl in elementary and middle school.

"As long as you act nice and polite and can speak well, you have one up on everybody else. You get 'let in' in a way." Sharita said she felt good about the positive attention she received in school at the time but now, looking back, it was clear that she could see how unfair this particular brand of attention was to those who were unable to perform appropriately. Sharita talked at length about the friends she had who she felt were smarter than she was or worked harder but were ignored because they didn't know how to "talk right" to the teachers or chose to hang out with "thugs" and "juvenile delinquents."

"You know whenever I am about to go to one of those board meetings or something like this with you, I always tell the girls that I am getting ready to do my whiteface routine?" I could feel Sharita's eyes on me as I drove. "What do you think about that? Are you in whiteface, too?" she asked.

Less than a month after this conversation, Sharita discharged herself from the shelter. It was the climax of her success story at Fresh Start. She had been accepted at Michigan State and was going off to begin her first semester as a college student. Or, at least, this is how it appeared at the time. However, the truth that I learned during an informal interview with Sharita after her morning shift at McDonald's was that even though she had gotten into Michigan State, she wasn't able to enroll because she had no place to stay and no way of paying her portion of the tuition. Sharita knew it would be difficult to iron these things out, but she assumed that GGC "had her back," that they would cover these details and make sure she was okay. After all, her case worker knew her circumstances, and she had even had several conversations with the executive director of the agency about these hurdles in the way of her success. In the middle of replaying for me one of the conversations she had had with the executive director prior to a board meeting, she stopped herself.

"She didn't hear a word I was saying." Sharita gave a short, bitter laugh as she thought about this. "She was so caught up in whether or not I was prepared for the presentation to the board." In the end, Sharita left the agency covered with accolades and followed by numerous false stories of her immediate future. She was too embarrassed at the time to reveal to anyone that she had no idea where she was really going or how she would take care of herself: "It felt so good to be on top, to be seen as a type of hero. I played along so well, I didn't even know how mad I was about to be." Sharita could still smile when recalling that feeling—one that still felt good in retrospect, even as she exposed the lies and betrayal that surrounded it.

Sharita had no choice but to figure out how to make it on her own. Getting support from her family was out of the question; there was too much pain left from their abandonment of her. Even though they reached out to her when they started to get wind of her successes at Fresh Start and the possibility that she would be the first in their family to attend college, Sharita was not ready to forgive them. She was also too ashamed and too angry to go back to Fresh Start for help. She felt that the agency had an obligation to her that it had not fulfilled and that she had been used like a show pony to mask and prettify the shortcomings of both the shelter program and the young women who resided at Fresh Start. But Sharita was also determined not to tarnish the image of herself that she performed for the administration, a segment of the staff, and even some of the girls. It seemed difficult for her to untangle her own complicity in creating the façade. The cab that she was put in when leaving Fresh Start with much fanfare and ceremony drove her directly to another shelter. Sharita stayed there for a few weeks and then moved into an apartment with her current boyfriend. She contributed part of her small check to their shared household expenses, even though his income from selling weed and crack cocaine made this unnecessary.

"It is more about principle," Sharita told me. "I was always taught to make money and to be a contributor. Nobody will put up with a gold digger for very long. Plus, it just isn't my style."

Sharita had to move forward, and so did GGC. There were others like Sharita who came and went after serving their time as role models and superficial representations of the agency's success and the possibilities for homeless and high-risk young women if they were just "given a chance."[14]

The circumstances that brought Sharita to the shelter and the ways in which her attitude was read as good-natured and proactive made her story a narrative of both redemption and exception in the context of Fresh Start. Rebecca Wanzo's incisive work on the affective agency of Black women illuminates the difficulties Black women face in being seen as sympathetic objects worthy of media and political concern. Wanzo's term "sentimental political storytelling" (2009, 19) refers to the practice of narrating sympathetic stories for the purposes of political mobilization. However, Black women have a limited range of affective narrative tropes that they can access to tell stories about themselves that move a populace and produce institutional effects. Narratives that involve a transformation from tragedy or degradation to uplift allow Black women to become legible in the larger society and, possibly, to be considered subjects worthy of sympathy and concern. Sentimental political storytelling, as well as neo-confessional narratives that overpopulate the self-help phenomena of the late twentieth and early twenty-first centuries, eliminates the larger social and historical context so that the individual is charged with her own transformation.

These transformations are legible, then, through optimistic stories of overcoming. Histories of racist oppression and structural inequalities disappear in these narratives, to be replaced by tales of individual ascendency through tenacity, self-revelation, and often humility. Although race, gender, and geographic location shape a woman's current circumstances, she must talk about unfortunate events as intensified, instead of remedied, by the choices individual actors (usually also poor and Black) made after the events. In Sharita's case, the event was the fire in her apartment building that could have been prevented had the landlord in her low-income community been held to the same safety codes and legal obligations of landlords in wealthier neighborhoods. The choice was her family's dismissal of her after the fire. The question of accountability in terms of who or what is actually to blame for a shelter resident's current state of homelessness and the corresponding acts of neglect, abuse, and abandonment is asked in the context of family members and partners, whose actions or nonactions are recounted as separate from the larger political and economic context in which they occur. In this way, individual relationships can also become sites for redemption by being repaired through counseling and monitoring by the state. But most often these relationships are severed, allowing the young woman to move forward unfettered and isolated, a lone agent expected to be able to choose healthier bonds of care and attachment in the future. Sharita's family was the villain in her story of redemption, and her biography gained traction from the narrative of familial betrayal, her physical appearance (light-skinned, attractive, and overtly feminine), and her demeanor of competence and resiliency. Sharita had fallen (or was tripped) but, apparently, had the strength of character to care for herself and set off on a track of academic success that would secure her rise from the ashes. All of these factors enabled Sharita to embody proper victim status.

At Fresh Start redemption is ultimately a lonely endeavor, despite the number of staff members officially responsible for assisting young women out of homelessness and into new independent living situations. This is primarily why Sharita felt so isolated both while she lived in the shelter and after she had discharged herself. Redemption narratives require the subject of the story to agree to hold no one but her- or himself accountable for what happens after the tragedy and before the transformation. In this way, redemption narratives are in direct opposition to the sense of entitlement that Janice exhibits. Emerging like a phoenix from the ashes, the redeemed Black girl is expected to fly without seeking redress or leveling accusations. Entitled young Black women, who understand the contradictions in being asked to climb a ladder of success built on their exclusion, rummage through the ashes to find the source of what must surely be arson. Redemption narratives, on the other hand, require both faith in the interlocking social systems that made the subject worthy of redemption in the first place and silence about the culpability of the neoliberal state. Sharita's redemption narrative was so powerfully persuasive as a success story in the shelter, and, in part, as a source of her own identity that even with the possibility of financial support and a new plan for success through Fresh Start's counseling services, she would rather not disrupt the false coherence of the narrative arc. Sharita also suspected that the agency would be less likely to assist her, given what would be seen as her failed attempt at redemption.

In any given year, the Fresh Start shelter took in as many as 150 new residents whose histories prior to coming to the shelter were as complicated and diverse as they were. Yet the narratives that were apparently seen as most credible and were best understood by the shelter staff were those that appeared to require redemption or present young women as exceptions. Sharita's circumstances meant that she fit in both categories. Narratives of exception at Fresh Start imply an exception to the rules of what it means to be a young woman who is Black and also homeless in Detroit. In other words, exception refers to Black girls who have achieved a remarkable measure of normative success. But, as is evidenced in Sharita's story, exceptionalism can also be performed. In fact, it is always performed regardless of the credibility of the actual story. Style of dress, speech patterns and comfort in communicating with adults and white people, how little or much space you take up, and knowing when and how to do this are examples of how narratives of exception were validated through the performance of success in the shelter. Young women whose lives seemed to make them likely prospects for successful redemption through the shelter or who came to the shelter in ways that appeared incredible due to their status as undergraduate students or history of having a normative familial structure, for example, appeared to have an easy time in and beyond the shelter. They did not have to work as hard to be visible or to make the kinds of credible claims that motivated staff members and other residents to support them, whether emotionally or through material and social resources.

Some of the young women challenged these narrative tropes when others applied them to their biographies, but these residents found that it was hard to articulate their reality in ways that would be heard and receive a productive response. Stories staff members talked about as not making sense or sounding confusing were usually thought to be so because they not only didn't conform to the structure of the redemption or exception narrative, but they also confounded the usual strategies for the shelter to educate, train, discipline, or transform. What, for example, do you do with the young woman whose homelessness can't be tied to her lack of skills, drive, or education; or pinned on poor choices or unfortunate family circumstances, but who knows that her life is not an exception, that there are Black girls throughout Detroit and beyond—some homeless, some not—whose life stories will never cohere in a society that chooses to see and react to them as dichotomous tropes: victim or perpetrator, perpetual failure or incomprehensible success. In redemption narratives, race and structural oppression are absented from the discussion. In exception narratives, race shows up but only as a way to explain why a Black girl's apparent success is so unexpected and exceptional. The obstacle in the case of the exception narrative is her inferiority and inadequate aptitude due to her Blackness, not the institutional racism to which she is subjected.

Redemption and exception are susceptible to being read through the dichotomous lens of authenticity or respectability. Redemption stories appeared authentic—the true and believable life paths of homeless Black girls—while also validating the shelter as savior and transformer. And even though the real work of transforming was believed to occur through individual determination and self-reliance, these individual acts constituted the larger institutional narrative of assisting many individual girls in pulling themselves up by their bootstraps. Exceptions or exceptional girls and women had already been branded with the respectability stamp of approval. The fact that Fresh Start provides services to girls and young women reflected an underlying gendered analysis of the unique needs and vulnerabilities of girls. GGC's gender-specific services included identifying the determinants of risky behavior as it related to girls and implementing curricula across the programs that spoke to these findings. This is why a mainstream white liberal girl-power feminism permeated the organization without a corresponding critique of how race necessarily shaped the lives of the young Black women Fresh Start served.

PART III Bodies

4 | Sex, Gender, and Scripted Bodies

Fucked

"Okay, next up is LaTonya. Show some love, y'all. Give it up for LaTonya." The MC stepped back and handed the microphone to LaTonya.

LaTonya turned to put the mic on the stand and turned back to face the small crowd with her hands on her hips. "Hello y'all, how you doing?" Several "Goods" and "All right, nows" echoed through the audience of spoken-word artists and enthusiasts.

"My poem is called 'He Fucked Me.'" LaTonya took a couple of steps forward as she spoke the title.

From the back of the room a female voice let out a slightly embarrassed "oop," and laughter rippled across the room.

In a strong, clear voice LaTonya recited her poem:

He fucked me
Oh, yes—He fucked me
He fucked me and it was good
He fucked me all night long, He fucked me hard and strong
And—it was good
He licked me from head to toe and my body was screamin'
    out for mo'
Our bodies were locked together in love, lust, and sweat
Oh my Lord he fucked me and I never been so wet

He fucked, He fucked, He fucked me and then we passed out asleep
I woke up the next day and said, this one I just might keep.

LaTonya paused after the last line of her poem and dramatically walked in a small circle around the stage. She was seven months pregnant, and her protruding belly seemed to carve out the space before she walked through it. There was some clapping and a low buzz in the crowd, as people whispered and looked to each other for some sign of how to respond appropriately. LaTonya now had her back to the audience. We all quieted down while we watched to see what she was about to do. She bent over, sticking her butt out toward the audience. Crystal, sitting to next to me, buried her head in my shoulder and said, "Oh, no, she's not. Please tell me she ain't about to . . ." But she did. LaTonya put her hands to her knees and started moving her backside in a dance called the booty clap.[1] She rolled her shoulder back in the same rhythm as her backside was moving, turned her head to look back at the audience, and smiled.

"I guess that was supposed to be her little dance to bring the poem to life?" Crystal said, still refusing to look at the stage. She covered her eyes with her hands and put her head down on the table.

"See, this is why you can't take shelter girls nowhere," Rachel was talking to Lynnette and trying not to laugh.

Lynnette, always calm and thoughtful, winked at me from across the café table but said nothing. When LaTonya returned to her seat at the table, Lynnette said, "Okay, girl. I liked your confidence up there. You are a natural."

Rachel, playing instigator, said, "What'd you think, Ms. Aimee? How would you rate that performance?"

"LaT, you are fearless. I'm just relieved that you didn't go into labor on stage." I had already read LaT's poem and knew that she was planning to read it at poetry night. The booty clap dance, however, was a surprise ending.

On certain Friday nights when there were three resident advisors (RAs) on duty, Lynnette and I would take a group of girls down to the Brown Bean café for open mic night. Most of the girls would already be out of the shelter, getting a jump on their weekend activities, so two RAs could easily hold down the fort. Before making our way to the Brown Bean, we would usually stop by Borders to browse the books, get ice cream, and walk around downtown. Usually three to five girls would join us, even though they would all claim to have big plans for Friday night. When the boyfriend, girlfriend, or unreliable family member forgot them, they ended up in the Give Girls a Chance (GGC) van with us. Lynnette, the girls, and I liked listening to the original poetry and rating the singers and comedians.

Two weeks prior to LaT's performance, the girls had been beside themselves after a particularly handsome Black man in his mid-twenties read a poem about making love to his girlfriend. The poem was full of metaphoric references to nature and food and painted a very saccharine portrait of sex. On the way home the girls were still swooning. They reread his verses that they had copied down in their pocket notebooks, pretending to woo each other. LaTonya, however, did not seem so impressed and let everybody know that she felt his performance was fake and not masculine enough for her. "Now you know he ain't talking that shit when it is really time to throw down—'your eyes are like deep pools,' and what not and whatever. I bet he is at home right now just straight up fuckin' somebody."

The other girls in the van, including Janice, Rachel, and Crystal, laughed LaTonya off and kept on with their romantic rereadings. So LaTonya turned her attention to me and Lynnette. "Y'all think I can get on the mic next time? I want to read the real version. Let 'em know what is really up."

Rachel, the shelter's resident poet, read one of her poems each time we went to the Brown Bean, and a few of the other residents had read once or twice. The hope was that the girls who wanted to read would feel comfortable sharing their work and begin to consider themselves on the same plane as the spoken-word artists they admired. Because the Fresh Start girls were a bit younger than the average person who took the mic, they were always well received and encouraged throughout their reading. As soon as we walked through the door, Big Mike, the café manager, always greeted us the same way: "Hello, little sisters."

"Of course you can read," Lynnette said. "I been dying to hear you share some wisdom. What you think you going to call your piece?"

"He Fucked Me," LaTonya said, without missing a beat.

The events in this chapter complicate the more prevalent discourses employed to talk about Black women as gendered bodies and sexual actors. Discussions of gender conformity and disruption and of expressions of sexual pleasure and desire in enduring contexts of violence and exploitation rarely include how these critical inquiries differ for Black girls and young women. The young women at Fresh Start wrestle with the ability to deliberately act in their own bodies in ways that honor their wants and needs beyond sexual fulfillment or the most efficacious presentations of self. The stories here combine questions of sexuality, sexual preference, gendered identity, and gender performance not to conflate them but to highlight the ways in which Black girls most frequently attain legibility and, therefore, arouse concern. In a published roundtable discussion on queer studies, materialism, and crisis, Heather Love states that she wants "to recall a queer tradition that focuses on the lived experience of structural inequality" and is invested in a dialogue that takes seriously the processes of "making do and getting by" (2011, 131). Following Love, I am seeking to enliven conversations about the intimate lives as well as the sexual and gendered experiences of Black girls that consider their particular vulnerability to the state. I am asking for a dialogue, a practice, and a politic that provide space for Black girls to love and care for themselves, knowing that they are loved and cared for in ways that honor their rights to safety, protection, self-exploration, self-defined happiness, and home.

In an article on the representation of the Black womanhood in music videos, Rana Emerson is able to show that although some videos were clearly degrading to Black women (she calls this hegemonic) and some videos consciously portrayed a positive and empowering image of Black womanhood (counterhegemonic), most presented hegemonic and counterhegemonic themes side by side, offering an "interconnected, . . . complex, often contradictory and multifaceted representation of Black womanhood" (2002, 117). As an example of this type of complex representation, she looks at a video by En Vogue in which the female singers in the group act as seductresses who are in control of their sexuality. As the women sing a rendition of Aretha Franklin's "Giving Him Something He Can Feel," the camera scans their bodies, showing them as objects of temptation and sexual desire. The camera also scans the bodies in the all-male audience, portraying them as desirable to the members of En Vogue and potentially to the viewing public watching the video. This display of mutual and consensual desire is missing from the historical narrative and current media representations of Black women's sexuality, especially within relationships defined as heterosexual. In the En Vogue video the Black male body becomes the object of pleasure and arousal, allowing the women singers to express their sexual subjectivity. Although the concept behind the En Vogue video can be seen as liberating in many ways, expressions of sexual desire are not so easily negotiated by young Black women, the professional adult care providers in their lives, and the larger society.

Black feminist scholars have asserted that the Black female body becomes visible "when it is synonymous with accessibility, availability, when it is sexually deviant" (hooks 1992, 66). This is especially true in the context of Black popular cultural forms, where the Black woman's body is primarily currency, an object whose value exists in its ability to be traded. The refusal of sexual commodification by Black women through claims to fulfillment of their own pleasure and desire has the possibility of creating more accurate and nuanced representations of Black women's sexual subjectivity. These questions of agency, pleasure, power, and counternarrative performance surround LaT's spoken-word reading and dance. In addition, we should be attuned to the ways in which LaT was less concerned with the reception her body and performance received than with her investment in commenting on the space of artificial sexual desire constructed through traditional Brown Bean performances and the corresponding exclusion of the bodies, styles, and expressions of desire that fail to replicate this tradition. LaT was also committed to shifting the normative shape of the modes of expression that were valued at the café, to privilege play and irreverence over a respectability that masquerades as creativity.

Both Patricia Hill Collins (2005) and Paul Gilroy (1991) have discussed the interconnected historical development of sexuality and racial discourse in Western culture. Collins, in fact, uses the metaphor of a prison (race) and a closet (sexuality) to address the mutually defining character of race and sexuality. Sexuality is undoubtedly read differently on different bodies, and thus the implication of its expression depends on the positionality of the individual. For young Black women this means being included among the category of women who "represent subjectivities outside of marriage—prostitutes, single mothers, women involved with multiple partners, and particularly black single mothers" (Weitz 1984, as quoted in Fine 1992, 47), and are, therefore, seen as deviant.

Jezebel is a significant cautionary figure in the tale of Black female sexuality. Jezebel is the representation that all Black women fight against as part of the journey toward respectability and social acceptance. In Black feminist literature (Collins 2000 and 2004; Higginbotham 1992; E. White 2001), it appears that there are two primary options: resist the Jezebel image and become a lady who is constrained by rules of propriety to prim and proper asexuality, or attempt to rework the image and reclaim your sexual autonomy. Performances of sexuality and articulations of sexual identities at Fresh Start demonstrate that neither of these options is particularly useful for young Black women. The way they choose to define and act out their sexuality reveals that there are other critical factors at stake beyond social status and mobility. In addition, the Jezebel image does not function in the same way for Black girls and teenagers as it does for Black women. The dangerous agency of the Jezebel is never fully available to Black girls—who, because of their age, do not fulfill the status of ultimate blameworthiness attributed to the image. Black girls can be fast or promiscuous, but their youth or minor status requires that the state be accountable for their behavior to some degree, which usually translates to the surveillance and disciplining of their bodies and sexual expression. Yet state policing of the intimate and sexual lives of Black girls may look no different from the same policing of the lives of Black women, thus contributing to the conflation of Black girlhood and womanhood in much of the data collected, policies enacted, and scholarship produced on Black women.

Why did LaT's performance make some of us feel so uncomfortable? Crystal immediately covered her face in shame, Rachel felt the need to make a joke to break the awkwardness at our table, and I was unable to put together a meaningful response. All the way home, Crystal kept muttering under her breath, "You is so nasty, just nasty." Finally, LaT told her to either "speak up or shut the fuck up."

I told Crystal, "You know, you don't have to like LaT's poem, but she has just as much of a right to express herself as the guy you were in love with last week."

"Um, okay. Respect differences, whatever," Crystal said.

Rachel, still playing the instigator, piped up with, "GGC 101."

"But answer me this: how is it in any way okay to get up in a public space, unless it is a strip club, and do the booty clap? We all know that was triflin'."[2] Through the rearview mirror I could see Crystal turned around in her seat and talking to LaT.

"T, that was kinda off the chain," Rachel said, seeming serious now. "I mean, you about to drop a baby like any second now."

"So," LaT oddly seemed to be getting more resolute the more she was challenged by Rachel and Crystal. "Y'all worried about them fake, tryin'-to-be-bourgie motherfuckers think about you? They ain't thinking about nar[y] one of us. I thoroughly enjoyed myself. End of discussion."

"I bet if Mel was there he would have been ready to beat your ass." Rachel was referring to the father of LaT's yet-to-be-born son.

"Please, that Negro would be happy as hell to be getting a shout-out. And ain't no ass beatin' happenin' round here." LaT laughed at the idea.

"You know what, Ms. Aimee?" Rachel turned to me, only half joking. "You getting soft. When you really worked here you wouldn't even let the girls leave the shelter in Daisy Dukes—right, Ms. Lynnette? And now we got the booty clap going on in public . . ."

Lynnette had seemed lighthearted and amused at the Brown Bean, but when I talked to her in the GGC parking lot after the girls had gone inside, she reacted differently.

"Girl, did you have any idea it was going to be like that? Did you see my face? I think I was blushing, and I'm grown,"[3] Lynnette said.

"It's not like we hadn't heard it before she went on stage, but it was shocking to actually see it," I said. "Her pregnant belly and all—it was too much!"

"Should we have stopped her?" Lynnette asked.

"She is almost twenty-two years old, and aren't we supposed to be teaching them that they own their sexuality?" Jokingly, I added: "Or should I say, 'Aren't *you* supposed to be teaching that?' I technically don't work here anymore, remember?" But my conclusion was that "I told her what the possible responses could be. She wanted to do it."

"Oh, that is how you are going to try to get out of this one?" Lynnette laughed. "That was probably why Big Mike was asking you if you were still the shelter director. He probably like, 'What the hell is going on over at GGC?'"

Ain't Got No Class, But Can Shake That Ass!

The crowd of regulars at the café had tried hard to appear neutral during LaT's reading, offering the usual respectful signs of engagement. But when the poem morphed into the booty clap dance, you could feel discomfort spreading across the room. There were a few nervous laughs, but during the dance most people acted as if LaT's time was up, resuming conversations with their friends and getting up to order a drink or go to the bathroom. No one wanted to look at LaT's Black, pregnant, barely adult body bent over, butt to the audience. It should be emphasized, however, that the shock of LaT's performance was partly the shock of seeing any body of any shape, size, color, age, or gender perform the booty clap dance in the coffeehouse setting. The crowd at the Brown Bean was a combination of college students, young professionals in their mid-twenties to early thirties, and students from the nearby public high school. The audience was always overwhelmingly Black, a mix of middle- and working-class people, with about one man to every four women. Big Mike, the manager, knew that we were from GGC only because Lynnette made a deal with him so that we didn't have to pay the cover charge. We never overtly made our affiliation known, but neither did we try to conceal it from any of the other patrons or employees. But after our third time at the Brown Bean, we were considered regulars, and—treating us like all the other regulars—the staff let us know that they knew our business.

The most scandalous verses spoken to this crowd before LaT read her poem included mentions of "chocolate nipples" and "silky smooth thighs." No one had ever said *fuck*, although people had used every sanitized word in the dictionary to convey the same meaning. Although patronized by a relatively mixed group in terms of class, the Brown Bean was definitely marked as a middle-class space. The enforcing of a dress code and the assessment of a cover charge help protect these classed boundaries, along with specials offered to members of sororities and fraternities, corporate groups, and small business owners. In the brief time that LaT was on stage, she was able to reveal the intersection of race, class, and gendered sexuality there.[4]

In the context of the welfare system and social service care institutions, the sexual lives of poor adolescent women receive an inordinate amount of attention. The fear of future pregnancies out of wedlock and the belief that the state has the right to mandate the family structures of poor women lead caseworkers to violate the privacy of young women's sexual and domestic lives. These workers seek information to assure them that the single, poor young women for whom they are responsible are not engaging in deviant sex. More positive attitudes toward sex, often in a hip-hop feminist framework, challenge Black feminists to consider the sexual lives of Black women outside of the "enduring legacy that frames black women as hypersexual" in favor of "an equally important history of black women asserting sexual autonomy and self-defining their sexual desires and realities" (Lindsey 2013, 63). Sex positivism makes room for Black women to move through, but not necessarily past, histories of bodily degradation and sexual violence that undoubtedly shape the ways in which they explore and experience their sexuality. The healthy sense of freedom and self-reclaiming implied through sex positivism has the potential to, as Lindsey claims, support more nuanced approaches to understanding the ways in which a younger generation of Black women think about sex and sexuality. Within this sex-positive framing, however, it is important to remain mindful of the privilege inherent in the ability to foreground pleasure and desire, for Black girls in their everyday lives as well as for Black women theorizing and speculating on the ways in which sexual identities and orientations may be read as positive. The autonomy on which sex positivism depends is, like all sovereignty, embedded in relations of power.

On the way back to GGC, Rachel and Crystal attempted to police LaT, citing as inappropriate the context, her pregnant body, and the sexual expression it had performed. When that didn't seem to sway LaT, Rachel evoked LaT's boyfriend, Mel, to see if either his gender or the place of significance he occupied in her life would rein her in. Often in the shelter I would hear girls use "Imma tell [insert the boyfriend's name here]" in the same way that children threaten to tell on their siblings to their parents. And the phrase was said in varied situations, not just ones relevant to the couple's commitment to each other as exclusive partners. Although it was used in a joking fashion, even in play, maleness was afforded supreme authority. LaT's response to Rachel seemed to imply that her boyfriend approved of and shared in her sexual enjoyment and did not necessarily have a place of authority in their relationship.

As I listened to the girls' conversation in the back of the van, I was not convinced by LaT's overconfident attitude and wondered if we had left her unprotected. She must have felt the discomfort in the room and been affected by it to some degree. Or perhaps I was limited by my indoctrination in a society that believes there must be some negative consequence for sexual enjoyment and that a young single pregnant woman must internalize the social shame thrown at her. LaT continued to come to the Brown Bean up until Mel Jr.'s birth, and she continued to be just as critical of the "fake poets" as ever, although she never read again. Although I discussed the "He Fucked Me" incident with her on various occasions, she never demonstrated regret or even slight embarrassment. It was not that I wished to shame her; I was just suspicious that the re-working of the Jezebel image by a thrown-back-in-our-faces enactment of sexual vitality could be enacted without harming the actor. But just as LaT need not internalize shame for others to continue to try to shame her, and for this shame to be reflected in very real and concrete ways,[5] her lack of legible regret does not mean that her sexual expression is entirely free. Like her young, pregnant Black body, LaT's public performance of sexuality—regardless of her feelings of esteem or power related to it—can be used against her in making and enforcing of social welfare policies, program guidelines, resource allocations, and employment practices. "He fucked me" in this context takes on a new and larger meaning.

> "You know, you're too pretty for me to leave you on the couch like that,"
> he said, pulling me toward him. I didn't know that, but I did understand
> then that there was no such thing as safe, only safer; that this, if it didn't
> happen now, would happen later but not better.
> —*Danielle Evans,* Before You Suffocate Your Own Fool Self

> To tell the truth is to become beautiful to begin to love yourself, value
> yourself, and that's political in its most profound way.
> —*June Jordan*

Agencies like GGC that work with youth populations often bump up
against the philosophies and practices of government-run welfare agencies, school systems, and training programs that work with the same population. For example, GGC's mission of providing a safe, nonjudgmental
space where young women could make informed choices about their lives
was not always congruent with the messages that the young women received from their caseworkers at the Family Independence Agency (FIA,
the local welfare office) and their teachers in training programs like the
Job Corps. For example, shelter residents often complained that their FIA
caseworkers were judgmental and chastised them for being single parents, often assuming that they were not able to live at home because they
didn't know how to obey their parents. Several of the FIA workers that I
came into contact with while I was a GGC employee had a fundamentally
antagonistic attitude toward young people in general and young women
in particular. In training sessions and community advocacy meetings
with these women workers, the sentiments they expressed most often
were about not wanting to work with girls because they are difficult and
hardheaded, not as compliant as boys. It was also generally assumed that
young women, particularly pregnant or parenting ones, were promiscuous and had, as one worker stated, "low moral standards." The challenge
that faced the staff at Fresh Start was finding a way to empower young
women while also providing a structure that did not demean, underesti-
mate, or stereotype them in the way they often experienced what was called
education and guidance in other institutional environments. The issue of
sexuality and sex education is probably the most difficult subject to tackle
in this regard.

Michelle Fine's description of the three most prevalent discourses of
female sexuality in public schools also applies to other settings such as

the welfare office, the homes of extended family members, the street, and well-meaning agencies like GGC. These three discourses are sexuality as violence, sexuality as victimization, and sexuality as individual morality. There is a fourth discourse, the discourse of desire, that has been silenced in this setting. Fine demonstrates how outside of the classroom setting, young women actively and openly discuss desire and pleasure as an essential aspect of the conversation about sex. By ignoring desire, Fine asserts, young women are not allowed to "explore what feels good and bad, desirable and undesirable, grounded in experiences, needs and limits" and thus are unable to be released from a "position of receptivity" (1992, 35). Carissa Froyum's work (2010) offers additional insight on the discourses that frame young women's sexuality as always on the verge of impending violence and danger, or as moral failure. Froyum conducted research on a sex education curriculum for low-income Black girls that essentially proposed waiting until monogamous marriage to engage in sexual activity. The race and class identities of the young women were significant in how the adult facilitators thought about and taught sexual restraint. The adult Black women running the program believed that if the girls not only abstained from sex but dressed conservatively, they could challenge racialized stereotypes regarding Black girls' promiscuity.

In this program, sexual restraint was presented as a "positive social and identity resource" (Froyum 2010, 70). Froyum pushes feminist theorists to take into account the race and class dimensions of sexual scripts for girls and the ways in which they may be recast and reworked to address the social and structural challenges that Black girls face, as defined by Black women and the girls themselves. For example, the Black youth whom Cathy Cohen interviewed regarding their ideas on Black love, deviance, and the sexual politics of morality expressed conservative viewpoints that did not align with their actions, demonstrating the "contradictory nature of their decision making" (2010, 56). The way young Black women talk about sex (in terms of personal responsibility, not of structural constraints) reveals their hyperawareness of the representation of Black women as sexually deviant. We can assume, then, that sexual scripts are often used by Black girls, in ways similar to how they were used by the Fresh Start residents, at least as much to counter these negative stereotypes and protect their self-image as to describe the events they experience.

When I left the Community Outreach Program to work in the Fresh Start shelter, I was shocked to find that the shelter had no consistent program or workshop devoted to sex education and healthy relationships like the one for the teens in the street outreach. The closest thing to this was a program called Healthy Moms, which was only for the pregnant and parenting clients and which focused mostly on the physical health of mother and child and the development of parenting skills. Working midnight RA shifts in my first few months of employment allowed me to be included in many casual conversations about sex and intimate relationships. In these conversations, residents spoke candidly about what they enjoyed about sex, including different positions and techniques they had tried to increase their partner's and their own pleasure. Some girls talked about their frustrations with male lovers who failed to understand that they wanted only a sexual relationship with them.

One eighteen-year-old woman who identified herself as bisexual said: "They act like only guys want to hit it and run. We can save a lot of time if we just come out up front and [be] honest and admit what we want. If me and my last boyfriend would have done that, I wouldn't of wasted a whole year with him."

A big theme among the young women who had recently given birth was self-respect, a topic they preached to other girls: "Okay, you may say it is just sex, but in the back of your head you thinking that it could be more. So you need to be honest with yourself, ask for what you want, and if he ain't going to give it to you have enough self-respect to move on to the next."

One new mother who had just finished pumping milk on the couch next to me commented: "I saw this painting once where they had a pregnant woman's body and they showed it like her breast and her stomach were like a landscape. It was drawn right on her, like she was the earth. That kept coming to me when I was pregnant. I mean, y'all don't understand how a woman's body is like the earth. We are second only to God because we can create life. You should tell that to the fools you mess with and be like, 'Bow down!'"

Some young women were less sure of the attitude they wanted to take regarding sex, their bodies, and the individuals they chose to share or not share those bodies with. One resident said: "I only done it once and I am like, 'What is the big whoop?' I mean, I ain't saying it is off limits to me, but you won't see me running, chasing after no guy. And if a guy is chasing after you, he want something. I don't care if it's sex, money, food, a place to stay—he trying to get something from you."

Young women who identified themselves as lesbians also shared their experiences in what was mostly a heterosexually oriented conversation, and they talked about similar issues related to trust and intimacy: "Girls is just the same. You find some that want something from you and try to use you for sex, just like men. You can't let people get in too close. That's when you start trippin' an' forgettin' yourself, and a girl can do that to you too."

I was sometimes asked for my opinion on whether or not I thought they were being played by their boyfriends and about how to handle difficult interpersonal conversations like breaking up or confronting a suspected cheater. Although the sexually explicit conversations were never censored for me, I was rarely actively brought into these parts of the discussion. When I was, it was generally when I was asked to respond to a concrete question like "You can't get HIV from giving head, can you?" and "Is there sperm in pre-cum?" The day after working these shifts, I would review the notes I scrawled about the residents' comments and questions. I pulled together a small team that included two RAs and the curriculum coordinator to design a workshop the residents named Sex, Love, and Lies.

I didn't know if I should be a part of the workshop. Technically, workshop facilitation fell under the responsibilities of the curriculum coordinator and caseworkers, but I was always involved in a good deal of direct service because we were often short-staffed, and I found it the most enjoyable part of working in the shelter. And for the RAs, this was another way to gain recognition, in a formalized, official setting, for their knowledge that was usually undervalued within the shelter. In an anonymous vote, the residents all agreed that they wanted me to stay. However, I soon got the sense that some of the staff felt otherwise.

One of the RAs and, in some cases, the curriculum coordinator didn't feel at ease with practicing nonjudgmental facilitation, which I felt was essential for this workshop to be effective. They weren't fully comfortable with the fact that they couldn't just "tell them the facts about what they should do" instead of taking the time to let the young women walk through the process of interrogating their feelings and helping each other come up with the healthiest and most viable answers in each situation. I decided to stay for the first two sessions and then just meet with the staff afterward to help them work through any challenges they had encountered and prepare for the next session.

The Sex, Love, and Lies participants included all the young women in the shelter at that time: ten adults, two minors, four pregnant adults, and two adult women with one child each. In the first session they were asked to fill out an anonymous[6] questionnaire designed by the staff. Some of the results are below.

All of the eighteen young women claimed to be sexually active. Only two reported that they used condoms at least some of the time; the other sixteen revealed that they never used condoms. Some of the alternative methods of birth control the residents listed were "pulling out," "have sex right after my period," "take it in the ass," and "we see what happens." Every young woman said that there had been a time when she was forced to have sex. Fourteen of the eighteen said that they often had sex even though they didn't want to because they wanted to "please their man," "keep their man," "or just get it over with."

Only four young women (perhaps the ones who had been in the activity room the night I was asked about this) knew that you could transmit HIV by having oral sex. Fifteen young women stated that they had previously been diagnosed and treated for a sexually transmitted infection, the most common one being chlamydia. Yet all of the women stated that they were not worried about getting such an infection and rated their chances of contracting one as "very low."

The questionnaire was not just about the negative consequences or aspects of sexual activity. However, I present this aspect of the questionnaire to show the stark distinction between the young women's active physical participation in sex with their lack of knowledge, pleasure, and emotional engagement. Although seventeen of the eighteen young women claimed that they had been in love (these were unsolicited comments), none of them stated that they were in love with their current sexual partners. I am not implying that there should be a direct correlation between love and sex, but I am seeking to demonstrate what the young women identified as significant in their experience. It is important to consider what it means when seventeen out of eighteen young women spontaneously admit that they have been in love, would like to be in love again, and are not being emotionally fulfilled by their current sexual partners, whom they variously describe as "a way to get extra money," "just for now, not to be bored," "a boy too young to be a man to me and his child," someone who "helps me when I'm horny," "he can lay pipe,"[7] and "transportation." Aside from the two comments "helps me when I'm horny" and "he can lay pipe," none of the other young women mentioned desire anywhere in the survey as a part of their decision to engage in sex. However, sex can have material benefits even when it does not provide emotional or physical ones. Money and regular access to transportation can be exchanged for sexual favors even if the exchange is not explicitly discussed or negotiated.

We used the information from the questionnaires to decide how to proceed with the second session. I urged the three staff facilitators not to plan too far in advance since, as we had seen, revelations would occur at each meeting and should guide the structure of subsequent sessions. The young women's responses were not a moral issue. Their ignorance about the transmission of disease and their own bodies along with their matter-of-fact attitudes toward their own experiences of sexual abuse were issues related to their health and safety. The performance of uninhibited sexuality late at night in the activity room was not the full picture of what the young women had experienced and how they felt about it. They bragged about sexual conquests and unapologetically indulging in the pleasure of sex. Stories of sexual skill and the ability to experience orgasmic pleasure were offered to top ones previously told, and rather than dividing the girls, they created an environment of solidarity. Yet I didn't want to assume that the narratives told in the activity room were any less real than the words anonymously scrawled on the workshop questionnaire. One in three Fresh Start residents report at intake that they have been sexually abused, with the vast majority of this abuse perpetrated by adult males in their families or communities.[8] Given the silence about sexual abuse in Black communities and the fact that for every act of sexual violence reported, fifteen instances go unreported, it is safe to assume that the number of young women at the shelter who have experienced sexual violence was much higher than we knew. The young women's sexuality, consensual sexual experiences, and sexual abuse cannot be disengaged from their experience of poverty. Living in circumstances marked by dire economic stress means that sex is not just or only about pleasure or unfettered agency, since relationships are often complicated by the bartering and trade used to survive and meet basic material needs. Sex is frequently part of these exchanges for young Black women, and the narratives they tell about their sexual desires and experiences often conceal or deceptively appear to revel in the dangers inherent in this dynamic.

In the second session we dispensed with any games and extraneous team-building exercises and got straight to the point. We addressed our concerns with the residents' lack of safe sex practices and broached the topic of sexual abuse. We also asked the residents how they thought Sex, Love, and Lies could benefit them most. You could almost hear a collective exhalation from the young women in the room. Margaret, one of the RAs involved in planning the sessions, said she felt like the girls "finally felt relieved that they could take off their armor." The group collectively decided that they wanted staff members to just give them the facts about safe sex and the spread of sexually transmitted infections. In addition, although the mothers in the group seemed embarrassed to admit it, they wanted to review how their menstrual cycles worked and get an "overall breakdown of the female and male genitalia."

The shelter staff made fun of the plastic penises that were used in the Community Outreach Program and the condom relay races they used to teach the girls how to put on a condom (in record time, no less). Sex was discussed in this program freely, without self-consciousness or moral undertones. It was just another conversation. Condoms, lubricant packets, and dental dams were posted with tacks on the walls of staff cubicles. The girls in the program, who were a bit younger than shelter residents, could talk about the process of ovulation and recite all the symptoms of gonorrhea. But in the shelter it seemed the focus on employment and working the program overshadowed the larger issues of the residents' physical and emotional health.

Although the residents made it clear that they wanted to just be given information about safe sex and their bodies, there were other things that they identified as issues they wanted to process as a group and openly discuss. The things that they said they wanted to "find answers to" revolved around figuring out how to trust without getting hurt and learning how to develop respectful, reciprocal relationships. In this discussion sex was framed as something that was currently a prerequisite—something that had to be done to, as one of the residents put it, "get some of the basics covered." These basics, they told us, were not confined to the material, but included desire and the pleasure of having "a body next to yours." Through our discussion, the sexual dramas in the activity room were revealed to be the performance of feelings the residents had experienced but that were by no means repeated with any regularity. When the curriculum coordinator asked the young women about the difference between the way they talked to each other about sex and the way they felt about sex, a twenty-year-old woman named Lisa offered this explanation:

> When we talk about sex it is just like when you telling somebody about your trip to Cedar Point.[9] Yeah, you went one time a long time ago as a kid and had fun, but then you go now and it's not the same. But everybody got you hyped up to believe that it is, and so you tell them when you get back, "Oh, it was the bomb, and we did this and that—it was off the hook!" It's not like it wasn't fun, but what you are telling is

from what you think you remember and what other people tell you it should be like. So it's not like you lying. You—.

Lisa's voice trailed off and another young woman, eighteen years old and pregnant, jumped in: "You just hoping it can be like that."

The other young women appeared to be thinking about what had just been said but didn't offer any other counter or supporting explanation. Such comments reveal that the talks in the activity room and the questionnaires are not inconsistent with one another. Questions of sex and sexuality for young Black women are not simply matters of desire, survival sex, victimization, or morality. These young women consciously try to figure out how they would like to experience sex as pleasure, as part of a loving healthy relationship, and as a form of self-expression. Social service agencies and public educational institutions are concerned with policing the sexual practices of poor young women, but these women show that we need to move beyond the sensationalized and voyeuristic aspects of their sexuality and consider how it intersects with their other needs, such as the need to establish loving interactions, to eat, to live in a safe home, and to exert control over their own lives.

Doing Masculinity

I was sitting in the newly constructed park in the middle of Detroit's main boulevard, Woodward Avenue, enjoying the free downtown wireless connection and trying to ignore the guy I could see in my peripheral vision who was walking toward me. The face looked familiar, but I was unable to put the young man in context. He reached out to hug me and greeted me by name, then laughed when it was obvious I wasn't even able to offer the pretense of knowing him.

"Miss Aimee, it's me, Summer." The only Summer I knew had been a resident at the Fresh Start shelter when I first started working there. She was in the first group of young women I had met over three years before. The Summer I knew was tiny, with small, delicate bones and an even tinier birdlike voice. At the time, her newborn son, although quite small himself, seemed to weigh her down when she carried him and made her look even more miniature and breakable. This Summer was also, according to the RAs, "boy crazy" and set the record for arguments about using the pay phone after the restricted hours so she could check up on the whereabouts of whichever young man with whom she was currently involved.

The Summer I knew was extremely proud of her "good hair" and taunted the other girls in the shelter with claims that their "short nappy heads" were the reason that they couldn't "catch a man." The Summer I thought I knew wore her hair long, in corkscrew curls, and would be caught dead before leaving the shelter looking anything but fly. Her clothing choices were a source of aggravation for many of the RAs, who felt her close-fitting dresses and hot pants were "ho-ish" and trashy.

The Summer who stood in front of me, laughing at my inability to hide my surprise and close my gaping mouth, was unrecognizable to me. This Summer wore long, baggy denim shorts that hit her at her shins, almost meeting the stark white athletic socks that she wore on her small feet inside Adidas slides. Her striped polo shirt hung down past her behind and seemed weighted down by the huge gold medallion around her neck that swung low, near her belly, and looked like it could take her out for the count if she moved too quickly. This Summer had a close-cropped fade haircut with deep-ridged waves, signaling her still very meticulous grooming practices. This Summer looked like a preteen male rapper. But Summer was still Summer, even though she appeared new to me.

I got up to return Summer's hug and confessed, "Girl, I can't even lie. I had no idea who you were."

"Yeah, I saw you play the 'I don't know who this dude is, and he better not step to me' role." I was relieved that she broke the ice and allowed me to laugh through my disorientation and shock.

"Well, how are you? How is your son? What has been going on with you since I last saw you? Where are you living? Are things okay?" I delivered the questions rapid fire, and she doubled over in exaggerated laughter, holding her belly and hitting me in the back—even her mannerisms had changed. She seemed to be working hard to give me the full masculine effect of her new (to me) self.

"You still asking a lot of questions! I been good. You know, I went to the Job Corps and got me a trade. I got into carpentry and been even doing some furniture making. I was working for this ol' dude, but I been talking to some of my dogs about leaving and starting my own business. I can get a small business loan and branch out and do my own. 'Cause in a few years I wanna start thinking about buying my own house." Summer's update flowed seamlessly, as if she had gotten used to telling lots of people in a short period of time about the changes she was initiating in her life.

"Wow. That's fantastic, Summer." Buying a house seemed so far away from my graduate student possibilities. "I have heard mixed things about the Job Corps, but you liked your experience there?"

"I mean, I could complain, but I won't. Like with anything, you have to find a way to make it work for you. Mugs need to just learn how to get dey hustle on. I saw that it could work for me, and I wasn't about to come up out of there without a job making money. Otherwise I could just work the street—there's always paper there."

"Right. Well, you look good. I'm happy for you," I told her.

"Yeah, just staying away from those girls—you know, they get you all twisted. I don't mess around with those girls. You know, they get you into trouble, so I am just living the single life right now." Summer took a deep breath and paused after she said this. She seemed to be waiting for me to ask her a question. I didn't.

"Well, yeah," I said. "Relationships can sometimes take your focus away from the goals that you are working on if you let them become a distraction."

Summer kept on. "Me? I don't get distracted. I'm different from when I was at the shelter. I am trying to own some property and get my own thing started. That is the only way we are ever going to get ahead. You got to own something and you got to work for yourself. Otherwise you just a slave."

"I'm happy for you, Summer. It sounds like you have figured out what you want for yourself. That is a huge accomplishment."

Summer grabbed my hand to shake it, then pulled me in for a quick hug goodbye.

Summer had found a way to work the the Job Corps system and get out of it what she felt would make her ultimately successful and truly independent. Whether she was the ultrafeminine young woman of the past or the current more masculine version in b-boy attire, one thing that remained discernibly consistent about Summer was her self-determination and confidence. She always gave the impression that anything she was doing at the time made sense and was the right thing to do. I imagine the Job Corps instructors and administration being just as challenged and inspired by Summer's tenacious self-protective tendencies as the Fresh Start staff had been. It is difficult to say if those qualities alone were what got her into the coveted carpentry track. In the estimation of the young women I spoke with about the Job Corps process, getting what you felt you deserved in the program meant being overly aggressive, strategically charming, or simply "boyish"—a term much used by all of the young women. The options for getting ahead that these young women identified for themselves were not confined to the Job Corps setting or to the current historical moment. The angry Black bitch; the cunning seductress; and the asexual, overpowering thug are tropes that have been used to define the ways of thinking about and potentially being a Black woman. Even when the stereotype has somewhat positive connotations, like the image of the superwoman, it is still a representation that requires a subjugation of the self to the interests of others and a strength that is presented as more combative and aggressive than empowering. Conscious performances and skilled navigation of strategies for social mobility are how young Black girls try to bridge the gap of the missing middle.

My bumping into Summer and facing my inability to directly inquire about the obvious changes in her self-representation, and even the fact that I found these changes so deeply curious, came at a very interesting time. Over the years that I worked as shelter director, there were five young women who openly identified themselves as gay. The sexual identity of a resident did not appear to be a significant or noteworthy issue to the staff or to the other young women in the shelter. In the Sex, Love, and Lies workshop, it came as second nature to staff members to alter game scenarios and questionnaires to make sure that they included the possibilities of same-sex attraction, bisexuality, and young women who chose not to define their sexuality through any of our available categories. Although shelter staff members were not without flaw in this regard, they strove to be conscious of the potential presence of youth who might be questioning their sexual identity or engaging in practices that they preferred to keep private. I knew that some of the staff members had personal beliefs that anything other than monogamous heterosexual unions were sinful, wrong, or just odd, but they were also aware that their personal beliefs directly opposed the GGC philosophy of acceptance, and thus they kept their feelings to themselves. This all changed, however, when a young woman named Dominique came into the shelter a few months before my encounter with Summer. I was no longer working in the shelter, but I was still at GGC regularly, doing volunteer work in the after-school program and working on call as an RA in the shelter.

Dominique grew up in a middle-class, predominantly Black suburb of Detroit with her mother. Her parents got divorced when she was four years old, and her father had moved to Tampa, Florida, shortly thereafter. Dominique had seen him only three times since then. When she was a sophomore in high school, Dominique knew that she was attracted to other girls, even though she had a boyfriend who became the father of her son later that year. Dominique came out to her mother when she was a junior. She said that her mother was "cool with it" at first but then couldn't live with the reality of seeing Dominique actually involved with and displaying affection toward other young women. Fighting became a routine interaction between Dominique and her mother soon after she expressed her sexual preferences. The police were called to their house more times than Dominique could count by neighbors troubled by their loud arguments, which started to turn to physical aggression around the time Dominique was approaching graduation from high school. Dominique entered the shelter on a Saturday night after her mother pulled a knife on her and demanded that she leave. She did so, taking only her son with her before the police could come. With no other family in the area and not wanting to stay with friends who were already overtaxed or dealing with precarious situations in their own homes, Dominique called her baby's father from a pay phone and told him to drive her to Fresh Start. She had heard about the shelter from a friend whose cousin had stayed there years ago, when it was still located in a church.

Dominique was stocky and muscular and seemed much taller than her five feet and three inches. She told me that because of her build, the way she dressed, and her low-cut fade, girls always flirted with her, mistaking her for a young man. This apparently happened at the shelter on her first day when she was standing outside smoking by the dumpster, and two of the residents thought she was a boy from the neighborhood. Dominique also possessed a low-key confidence that was magnetic. The minute she came into the shelter, the entire plane of interpersonal dynamics shifted dramatically. Dominique was completely out and had just as many female visitors as the other residents had boyfriends—if not more. "Mackin' hos"[10] and her overall powers of seduction were common topics of conversation when she was in the room. It did not take more than a week before the other residents started calling Dominique "Pimp," "Pimp Daddy," and "Big Dom." It was quite evident that the RAs responded to Dominique differently than they did to the other residents. Although she was always finding some way to get out of a chore—eventually managing to convince the other residents to do it for her—she was hardly ever reprimanded. The conversations I overheard between Dominique and the shelter staff regarding rule violations and missed appointments sounded playful and flirtatious. Dominique was strategic and charming, and she quickly learned how to "mack" the shelter.

Within a month, there was a noticeable change in at least five other young women in the shelter. These young women made a physical and behavioral transformation similar to the shift I saw in Summer. They traded in fitted jeans and baby T-shirts for baggy jeans that hung off their behinds and oversize sweat- and T-shirts, and sneakers or Timberland boots replaced their high-heeled sandals and wedges. The caseworkers and RAs responded to all of this as if it were a joke. "Please, they just try-ing to copy Dom," was what one RA said, which seemed to be the general consensus. However, once the change moved from attire to language and mannerisms, it stopped being treated as a joke and became a problem. The Dominique wannabes had boyfriends before they came into the shel-ter who now stopped dropping by for visits in the evening, and the wan-nabes all made attempts to change the way they walked by moving slower and with a wider gait. Watching the forced hypermasculine hand move-ments and body carriage usually reserved for male rappers (and usually only when they are in the context of a choreographed music video), the question at the forefront of the mind of almost everyone on the shelter staff was, is this for real?

We categorized Dominique, whose performances were perhaps the most dramatic of all, as sincere because she came into the shelter iden-tifying herself as a lesbian and never gave any indication that she wavered in this identity. The wannabes, by their very name, symbolized insincerity. The assumptions we made about these young women were a reflection of our acceptance of hegemonic notions of gender and its viable and, there-fore, authentic performance. Dominique was "real" because her perfor-mance was consistent, implying a permanency that made her masculine identification appear innate. The "wannabes" were not able to pull off their performances, failing to convince us. And what were we trying to be con-vinced of? That they were no longer sexually attracted to males? That they were questioning their sexual identity? Why was it so important to us that their intentions be apparent in their self-presentations?

Wannabes are nothing new in the residential single-sex setting. Case studies by Rose Giallombardo (1974) and Alice Propper (1981) talk about how butch and fem gendered roles were taken on by girls in juvenile jus-tice settings as a way to fulfill needs that were normally met differently in the outside world. In some cases girls re-created the roles of husband and wife to establish a fictive kin network in which they provided mutual aid, emotional reciprocity, and security and protection to everyone in the family (Giallombardo 1974, 81). In other cases, there was not such a strong sense of solidarity, and young women were looking to fulfill their emotional and sexual needs without making a commitment to a large network of people and relationships. Girls who, like Dominique, entered the facility identified as lesbian were called Trues, and the girls who got "turned out" after being in the institution were called "wanna-bes." *Turned out* was a phrase still very much in use among the young women in the shelter as well as those in other GGC programs who had some experience with the Job Corps and other similar vocational programs.

The way *turned out* is used by these girls conveys more of a blurriness and sense of complication than the concern expressed by staff members about the reality or fiction of the wannabes' gender performances. Dominique, as well as Janice and Crystal, used *turned out* to mean that a girl who identifies herself as heterosexual develops a relationship with another girl, which can be either "just sexual or both sexual and emotional," Dominique told me. When the relationship has ended or the young woman leaves the residential setting, she may continue to be involved with the other young woman, become involved with men, or decide that she will be undecided and "do whatever she is feeling with whoever she is feeling at the time." Getting turned out does not necessarily mean that a young woman has "shed" her heterosexual identity; instead, it means that she has, in Dominique's words, "become open to the possibilities."

Dominique discussed the nature of being turned out in a way that revealed she viewed gender and sexuality as somewhat arbitrary and unstable. Talking with Dominique, I learned that the Fresh Start wannabes were not necessarily being turned out. Their performances were about transgressing gender categories by seeing if they could play with the social consequences of being masculine or feminine. The catalyst for all of this was the effect produced by Dominique that they witnessed not only in the shelter but also outside of GGC. When the other Fresh Start residents hung out with Dominique, both males and females responded to them in ways the young women found appealing. For example, one of the wannabes told me that she didn't feel like she needed to be "in petty competition with other girls to see who is like the prettiest or who has the best clothes. You don't deal with that, and it's like you out of the game . . . you don't even have to play."

Another young woman labeled a wannabe said that she liked being able to walk down the street or go to the mall without "having to fuck with dudes" since "they don't even be paying me no mind, and I don't have to fight off all that bullshit." Dominique added that "some girls don't even care about dudes thinking they are gay. They would rather be labeled gay for a minute and get some respect than be treated like a bubblehead." Our curiosity as shelter staff members was grounded in a conflation of sex and gender that made us focus on what the wannabes' behaviors and stylized appearance said about the nature of their sexual lives more than on the implications for their social, economic, and political lives.

Within several weeks, tension developed between Dominique and the wannabes. During the last few shifts I worked on call in the shelter, Dominique ignored them or made jokes under her breath whenever one of the wannabes made a comment. On one late Saturday night, I convinced most of the girls to stay up to watch back-to-back movies with me. I hated it when they all ran to their rooms, because when I was left alone with just the TV it was all too easy to nod off. Although I kept telling myself that I had officially completed my fieldwork, I always brought the tools of the trade with me when I was called in to work shifts. There was always so much going on that seemed to connect directly to whatever theme I was currently trying to work through in my writing. I brought my tape recorder and laptop with me, but I rarely had a chance to use them. Most of the time I was too busy holding babies, making elaborate late night snacks with the insomniacs, or just too engrossed in the present conversation to remember how good it would be to have it on tape. In these cases, I would get a cramp in my hand from attempting to quickly jot down just enough key information to elaborate on later with the help of my computer. This night, a half-hour after the second movie was over, Dominique was the only resident who was still up and in the activity room. She said she was bored and couldn't sleep. The baby room monitor for her son, Imani, was by her side in case he woke up. I used the opportunity to talk about the wannabes.

"Can you record me?" Dominique asked. I generally asked the residents if I could record them, so I was taken aback by Dominique's request.

"Want to make sure you hear me." Dominique set up the recorder and turned off the TV while I headed to the kitchen to get something for us to eat. To honor Dominique's request to be taped and documented in a very specific way, I offer here the full transcript of our conversation.

AIMEE: It seems like there is some tension in the shelter between you and some of the other girls. I noticed it when I worked last week and again tonight.

DOMINIQUE: I really feel annoyed with them, the followers. That is all they really are to me. I am tired of them. It is just been going on for too long, and I feel myself being about to go off but I don't want to be kicked out of the shelter.

AIMEE: What happened in particular?

DOMINIQUE: I wish people would learn how to just be true to themselves. It is so annoying when you get up in a place around females around this age who don't know who they are yet 'cause they will just cling to anything. I came up in here, and you had girls who all they had to converse about was guys this and a dude said that and what Imma do 'bout this one who is not calling me back and how about this one who is sleeping with my best friend. I mean, it was nonsense; complete and utter nonsense, and I listen to this shit for like two weeks. Okay. Flash forward a week after these conversations. Stacey and them think that I am dykey but don't really think I am gay because I have Imani. So when they find out I am gay, they start acting like they are into women too.

AIMEE: But how do you know they aren't? [long dramatic pause from Dominique to emphasize the look on her face that says, "Are you really that stupid?"] I mean really, what do they tell you?

DOMINIQUE: These girls came in here wearing hoochie mama skirts, hair weaved all out, nails done up, the whole nine. Now they look harder 'n Lil Jon[11] and talking about liking pussy. Okay, key word here is, and I will spell it out . . . t-a-l-k-i-n-g. I mean, if you going get turned out, get turned out, but don't perp[12] like you are a butch dyke. I don't even know why staff was tripping so hard to ask like, "Are they really gay?" I heard Erica [one of the caseworkers] asking Stacey like [imitating Erica's clinical voice], "So Stacey, um, not to intrude, but do you think you might be questioning your sexuality? I mean, it is okay if you are, but I just want to know if I can support you in any way." She seemed so dumb to me.

AIMEE: Erica or Stacey?

DOMINIQUE: I was actually thinking about Stacey, but I guess you could throw Erica on up in there too.

AIMEE: What did Stacey say?

DOMINIQUE: I probably shouldn't be saying this 'cause I was eavesdropping by her cubicle, but she was like, "No! No! No!," acting all shocked and offended.

AIMEE: Is that why you are upset with her?

DOMINIQUE: I guess my real reason for being pissed is that I am tired of the bullshit. The only reason they trying to even think about acting gay is because of me. So I was just having this fantasy over and over again these past couple days. Imagine this: what if I walked up in the activity room one day with a weave down to my butt, a miniskirt, heels on, and talking about, "Damn! I met this fine ass dude at the bus stop." What do you think they would do? [long pause] No, Ms. Aimee, I am seriously asking you what you think they would do.

AIMEE: I don't know. I think it could be different for each of the girls. I don't really know how important it is to each of them what you do at this point. I mean, even if it started with you—even if you were their inspiration, they have been in this mode for several months now. They have probably found some other meaning in it now.

DOMINIQUE: That's deep. I'll be honest. That is real deep. But [short pause] wrong. I know they would be confused, running around like chickens with they heads off. And then, in like one day, they would be back to they old selves.

AIMEE: So you think that you are the only reason why they have seemed to change?

DOMINIQUE: No. I know that I am the *only* reason what initiated it.

AIMEE: What would be some other reasons?

DOMINIQUE: First and foremost, the man issue. Most of these girls get caught up in the wrong men and make all the wrong decisions in their lives because they are looking for that male stamp of approval. To the point where like they wouldn't even mind acting like a man if that means they get respect from a man.

AIMEE: Umm. I understand what you are saying. But respect is a major thing to have and not easy for everyone to earn.

DOMINIQUE: Exactly. That's why you can't fake it.

In this exchange, Dominique expresses anger over her perception that the wannabes do not wannabe identified as gay but do wannabe identified with the masculine presentation of a butch lesbian identity that will let them pass as hard and earn them respect. Unfortunately, none of the young women labeled wannabes would agree to talk with me. The only information I could squeeze out directly from one of them was the comment I noted above about not wanting to be in competition with other young women for both male and female attention and approval based on appearance. Dominique did not have a problem with the wannabes' performance of masculinity, just with their attempted performance of homosexuality. To Dominique, the masculine performance was a caricature of Black masculinity as portrayed in popular culture and given traction through the media's obsession with the Black urban thug. The high visibility of this image is, Dominique implies, what allows it to be easily appropriated through dress and mannerisms.

From Dominique's perspective, sexuality, on the other hand, is rooted in desire and the acting on this desire. Dominique was hurt by Stacey's immediate rejection of a lesbian identity when questioned by Erica, her caseworker; she took offense at Stacey's incredulous "No!" Through her frustration, Dominique is still able to consider possibilities for the wannabes' behavior and, in this reflection, extends her discussion to include young women beyond the wannabes, like the majority of the young women at Fresh Start—including Dominique—who seemed to be striving to reach a comfortable balance between garnering respect from others and not losing their self-respect in the process. Although performing respectability is ultimately about approval and validation, it can never guarantee a satisfactory outcome.

Gender, like respectability, is about performances and readings of those performances.[13] When someone is illegible to another through the lens of normative gender categories, this is disconcerting primarily for what it means for disturbing the first person's understanding of his or her own behavior, presentation, and knowledge of self. As Betsy Lucal is able to demonstrate through an exploration of responses to her own ambiguous gender display, gender labels enable us to interact (1999, 783). In the case of the wannabes, it was their sexuality—not their gender—that raised questions; their practices—not their displays—were matters of the utmost curiosity and concern for the staff. However, the wannabes were using a gender display to gain the benefits of what the male gender symbolizes. They knew that they were not being mistaken for men in the way that Dominique was, so they were not gaining the prestige of men but the prestige of girls bold enough to present themselves as male. Lucal writes that "bending gender rules does not erode but rather preserves gender roles" (ibid., 785), a statement that is supported in the work of Peggy Phelan (1998), Rosalind Morris (1995), and Judith Butler (1990). According to this understanding, any subversive intent by the wannabes would appear impotent. But the wannabes were not cross-dressing and using masculine behaviors to erode gender roles. Their goal was to uphold those roles and, instead, erode their presentation of self as gendered female in terms of all of the negative social associations with being female. The wannabes don't have the option of choosing not to do gender, but they can choose not to do femininity.

The shelter as a space and the developmental range of the young women involved may also provide insights into why the wannabes were able to make a place for themselves to "try on gender."[14] In transitional periods of life, such as the transition from girlhood to adulthood, or transitional spaces such as college or a new workplace, individuals may try on new gender roles. Trying on allows us to consider the gendered nature of specific spaces as well as "social contexts, such as race and class, and contingencies, such as control over adolescents, that shape gendered experiences" (L. Williams 2002, 31). Looking at gender displays in this way creates the possibility that the wannabes saw the shelter as a transitional space where new roles and new ways of being were possible without necessarily making a commitment to or identifying themselves through these roles. The status of the wannabes as poor Black girls offers another way to consider why trying on was appealing. The maleness they attempted to embody through dress, language, and mannerisms had the potential to elevate their social status both in the shelter (in the way that seemed to work for Dominique) and outside, where they were less objectified by the male gaze because of their rejection of the female performance. Of course, there is also the possibility that the wannabes had been "turned out" in the way described by Dominique and had decided that they had located an additional way of being and of expressing their sexuality. This is probably what occurred with Summer, and her masculine performance would thus have been a reflection of how she chose to display sexuality through gender. Nonetheless, it is important not to read any display or performance as final or wholly definitive. We are all wannabes to various degrees, and we demonstrate this through our own performances of gender; plays for prestige and respect; and attempts to locate spaces of love, care, and protection.

It is significant that the wannabes chose not to talk to me, the other staff members, or even the other residents about their visible shift. However, they did reveal that they felt less visible as female bodies in competition with other young women or as vulnerable female bodies always already the available target of the male gaze and potential verbal or physical assault. Their drag also, they believed, allowed them to appear more serious, not to be "fucked with," like "other bubbleheads." The lines of visibility and invisibility that the wannabes negotiated were embedded in their reading of where power is located, how it can be performed, and of the consequences of a believable performance. Their privileging of a visible masculinity afforded them freedom from unwanted attention from heterosexual males and confrontations with other young women. Visibility and power are not synonymous terms, however (Morris 1995, 570), as there is no surefire strategy for maneuvering or shapeshifting in public spaces that offers Black girls ultimate protection or ease of mobility.

The lives of young Black women living in poverty are scrutinized, evaluated, and policed through a rubric of sexuality rooted in perceptions of gender and its successful or failed performance. The young women at Fresh Start contended with a variety of confusing and contradictory scripts as they managed the intersection between Black girlhood and citizenship. Although it is possible to locate spaces of pushing back against the ways they shapeshifted the normative prescriptions for Black girls, it is vitally important that we heed Nicole Fleetwood's warning not to misread the "refusal of dominant scripts as emancipatory or radical positions, but ones that point to a considerable discrepancy between different generations and classes of blacks in terms of what are viable forms of loving, belonging, and attaching to others" (2013, 433). The stakes for Black girls are different from those for non-Black girls and for Black women. Trying on or playing with different ways of being and identifying invites consequences for Black girls' ability to take care of themselves, beyond those for their ability to experiment or explore in healthy ways. Black girls labor "in service of a survival project" (N. Jones 2009, 92) that requires that they "strategically choose from a variety of gender, race, and class displays depending on the situation" (ibid.). Locating Black girls' interaction with scripts that conflate sexuality and gender within a broader political economy that seeks to subjugate them on the basis of sex and gender does not undermine the transformative potential that forms the basis of their inherently political lives, but we still need to be attuned, as researchers and activists, to theoretically engaging in a "hasty search for resistance" (Morris 1995, 586).

Toward the end of Dominique's stay at Fresh Start, the residents who were on the cusp of graduating from the transitional living program were the same cohort of young women who had requested that the changes in the employment curriculum include an intentional focus on longer-term residential stays to meet their needs. The six young women who stayed in the shelter for over a year formed a strong bond that enabled them to support one another with child care; finances; and the emotional strain of their relationships with friends, lovers, and families outside of the shelter. Two of these young women were cast as wannabes. At that time, when residents moved out of the Fresh Start, they were eligible for assistance in the form of a first month's rent and deposit and the basic furnishings for a GGC-approved apartment if their living arrangements met the agency's criterion that they were moving into their own "independent living situation"—meaning that they would be living alone or only with their children. This group of long-term residents contested the terms of the relocation assistance by insisting that they be supported in living arrangements that included moving in together as roommate pairs or networks of three or four young women, so that they might be able to sustain the relationships they had cultivated at Fresh Start and that increased their earning potential, physical safety, and emotional health. Their demands illuminated the fact that they were able to transform the institutional social service agency into a home space where they privileged relationships of reciprocity and care over almost all other measures of success. Their commitment to homemaking also revealed that the organizational emphasis on independence was predicated on the belief that the relational worlds—and, implicitly, the intimate experiences and sexual lives—of most young Black women were liabilities to their civic and economic advancement. A comment by Jafari Allen is relevant here: "Consider that at least for Black same-gender loving persons to be lesbian, bisexual, trans, or gay, or more to the point, queer, is to build loving friendships and networks of friends and family outside not only symbolic discourse in which they are always already invisibilized or muted, but also outside of cultural institutions and often once removed from extended heteropatriarchal biological families, where the violences of traumatic racialized pasts very often resound, echo, and reproduce themselves in homes where protection cannot be assured" (2009, 319).

Amid the conversations about the relative privileges of owning desire and pleasure, exerting agency, and trying on, I urge us not to lose sight of the issues of protection, safety, care, and home as we consider the sexual lives, sexuality, and gendered possibilities for Black girls. LaTonya was able to play, offer satire, and express frustration at the paltry options for expressing sexual agency and desire in public, considering her bodily and social location. The other Fresh Start residents who chastised LaTonya and covered their heads felt the risk of simultaneously claiming bodily ownership, performing desire, and being a young Black single mother residing in a homeless shelter; thus, they experienced LaTonya's performance as audience members and unwilling coperforming bodies. The expectation of risk where "protection cannot be assured" is revealed in the Sex, Love, and Lies workshop and in the informal space of conversations in the shelter, when the young women realize that what they have done and what has happened to them and how they choose to talk about it or not can be equally harmful.[15]

The staff members' hyperattentiveness to Dominique and the wannabes was a concern with what bodies appeared to be and what they were assumed to be engaging in that was really not much different from Camille's investments in bodily renovations (see chapter 2) and from what self-presentation, self-fashioning, and corresponding external acts of fixing and reshaping might signal about productivity and the reproduction of families, social relationships, and earning potential. The long-term shelter residents—like LaTonya, Dominique, the participants in the sex education workshop, and the wannabes—were seeking ways to get the freedom to honor their needs and desires without being punished or prevented from continuing to explore, experiment, question, and creatively imagine themselves and other possible ways of life. How the young women of Fresh Start acted on "bodily limits" cannot be fully legible outside of these "local understandings of materiality" (Morris 1995, 575) that also encompass the possibilities for creative self-making among the girls and women in the Brown family.

Erica

The air smells like summer. Even though it is dark now, the thickness of sweat hangs heavy in my nostrils and the charcoal, still burning, from Miss Grundy's barbeque makes me hungry all over again. I am breathing it in—this life so active and urgent. Everything feels pressing. We start running. I dare them to beat me, knowing I am the fastest, and I feel first my sister and then Ricki fading behind my shoulder with the blur of passing houses. Grass turns to concrete under my feet. I close my eyes, extend my arms out to my sides, and imagine taking off in flight. The pull at my elbow arrests my upper body while my legs swing out in front of me, churning the air like I am riding an invisible bicycle. I scream—I think. And now I know I am screaming, because I hear Ricki matching my screams as he calls my name. The one who's not driving sits in the backseat holding me on his lap after he has covered my eyes. My body is shaking and his grip becomes slippery, but I am too terrified to cry. It is clear that their job is not to protect me, that they might mean me every harm, but I am still surprised that this grown man does not feel compelled to find the words to comfort me. They are careful not to say too much to one another, the driver and my backseat captor, but when they do speak, their voices sound like my body feels—shaken and quivery.

When we get to the where of this brief and sloppy journey, they remove the cloth from my eyes so I can see my way down the steps to the
basement. My legs are now limp as spaghetti, and my hands instinctively
grasp for this man I fear and, therefore, hate so as not to tumble head first
to the foot of the stairs. Moments later, I sit in dust, my sight blinded
again by a different cloth and my hands and feet bound together by the
sticky strength of duct tape. And now I am crying. Contracting and heav-
ing, my belly and shoulders dance like this for what seems like forever as I
wonder what will happen to me. I picture Ricki and my sister still running
behind me, just over my shoulder, and imagine them catching up to the
car, holding tight to the bumper, determined to make it here with me. They
are hiding underneath the car, waiting for just the right second to rescue
me. They are not, like me, crying and expecting the worst. I bring my wrists
to my mouth as comfort.

Grass, sugar, dirt, gasoline, and my sister's smell rise from my skin to
surround me and more than anything I have ever wished for in my life, I
want to be home, to be safe. I taste my tears as I chew through the tape,
freeing myself. Removing the blind, I peer into the darkness and realize I
am all alone—which, somehow, makes me both calmer and aware of how
much work I have to do. Within what feels like seconds, my feet are free. I
press my palms into the sooty floor, stand and feel eight feet tall. But my
wobbly legs remind me I am still terrified. Why am I here? Would these
men kill me—these men who look so much like my uncles and sound like
all the men on my block? Girls like me get hurt and go missing, I know.
And they are always forgotten. These thoughts make the floor solid, and
my body is returned to me with a force that propels me up the same stairs
I could barely walk down. I am flying. It is not the same as racing Ricki and
my sister. I don't feel free. But this other feeling is powerful in a different
way, surging through every part of my body to simultaneously ground
and levitate me. It sends my foot through the weak wooden panel at the
bottom of the door and guides the rest of my body through the space I
created. I don't know where I am, but I am here and there is more room
now, so I take it, running to the first place I see light.

It is dusk and darkening, but not as dark as when I was taken. How long
ago was that? The streetlight makes me feel better, makes me feel that there
must be someone who knows me, who cares about me, on the other side
of that window. As I run toward the yellowish light, it occurs to me that I
might not be alone after all. My head darts from side to side, but my feet
keep moving until I am close enough to the glass to put my fist through the

window. I feel nothing but the warm July air, barely a relief, on my skin. "Help! Help me! Who's there? Help!" I holler into the coming night, surprised at how normal the sounds of the street seem in between my screams.

Bleach Baths

The smell of bleach makes me sick. My eyes water, and I think of the shame we confuse with stains. The residents talked about bleach baths in the same matter-of-fact tones they used to talk about the best way to wash dishes or mop a floor. For some, a bleach bath was a remedy, the ultimate cure. For others, it was the ailment. Most agreed that the fumes tend to get caught in your throat. Jalisa's grandmother put bleach in her bathwater. She thought it was for her eczema but overheard her grandmother tell her sister, "Maybe it might lighten that child up, too." From that point on, even after her eczema cleared up, when Jalisa thought of her body she pictured it as "scaly, black, dirty and scarred" and said "things like that make you feel like you might never be clean."

As a little girl, Rhonda was fascinated by bleach's powers of erasure. Her mother would fill the tub with equal parts of water and bleach at night, and in the morning the sides of the bath gleamed the whitest white. To Rhonda, the smell of bleach was comforting and the prospect of "stripping off a shade or two" of her rich deep skin inspired her to add a few capfuls every now and then to her bath. Rising with the steam from the running water, the bleach smell filled the air of their one bedroom apartment. Her ten-year-old younger sister, Tiny, was the only person who ever questioned her. Cracking the bathroom door open, one eye and one small mouth filling the sliver of space, she would say with sincere concern, "What the hell is wrong with you?"

Everyone knew Yolanda's time in the shelter would be short. She had recently been placed at the top of the list for Section 8 housing[1] and would be moving with her two-year-old daughter to her own apartment in a few weeks. Although the caseworkers and resident advisors (RAs) told her it was her "own personal business and no one needed to know," by the end of her first day in the shelter, all of the residents knew that Yolanda was HIV-positive. In spite of her demands and obvious frustration, the other eighteen young women in the shelter started to treat Yolanda with what they felt was kindness but what she read as difference. Her chores were completed before she could get to them, and she frequently found paper bags filled with ten-cent candies on her bed. Yolanda suspected that these acts were meant to make up for the way she was quietly ignored when the girls took turns braiding each other's hair and greasing their scalps in the activity room, or for the way just being in close physical contact with her made some of the residents visibly uncomfortable. The hallway refrain of "You all right, Yo?" as she passed by was in no way a consolation.

After the first week, Yolanda spent most of her time in the parenting suite or the large bathroom that joined the two rooms reserved for mothers and their children. She was the only parenting resident at the time and was able to have the space to herself. Every evening, reporting as if providing dispatches from the field, one or two residents would come back to the activity room to confirm that they had completed their chores and to offer, "I hear her back there humming," "she sound like she already asleep," "her music is up real loud so I don't know . . . ," "she's reading to her baby," or "she said good night but didn't open the door." On the last night of Yolanda's stay, Jalisa walked into the activity room carrying Yolanda's daughter, Kiana.

"Come on, Kee-Kee, let's find something to play with while your mommy takes a bath." Jalisa put the child down and helped her walk to the colorfully carpeted toddler area. Then she said to me, "She said she hadn't been able to take a real bath in like a month."

The next day Yolanda's ride did not show up, so I volunteered to drive her and Kiana to their new home.

"You must be excited to be on your own again after two weeks at Fresh Start," I said. It came out sounding more like a question than a statement.

"Yeah, I guess." Yolanda's voice registered her uncertainty. "I don't know."

"Well, did you at least get to relax some last night with your bath?" I knew it was a silly question, but I asked it anyway, wanting to leave her with some fond memory of the shelter.

"Yeah, but y'all need to get some more bleach," Yolanda said.

"Okay," I said. "But there should have been plenty of other stuff to clean the tub with."

"Naw." Yolanda seemed confused by my response. "I need the bleach for the bath."

"Why are you bathing in bleach?" The question came out of my mouth before I could think of a better way of formulating it or think better of asking it at all.

"It kills everything." Yolanda was schooling me now. "You should know that."

Experiments in Movement

It was Saturday night and half of the residents were out, taking advantage of the later curfew than usual. I was in my office, trying to moderate a dispute between two of the residents over a missing twenty dollars. Even though the door was closed, every sound made in the shelter permeated the thin walls. *Boom. Boom. Clack. Boom. Boom. Clack.* The groove was subtle, though the bass was not. And I caught myself nodding my head to the rhythm pulsating through the carpeted floor. There was always music floating through the shelter, it seemed, so the beat was unremarkable but extremely distracting in the middle of our mediation session. I temporarily dismissed the feuding young women and walked down the short flight of stairs to the common room. The common room was on the first floor underneath the shelter and was used by all staff members and program participants at Give Girls a Chance (GGC) for daily craft activities, baby showers, graduation ceremonies from transitional living, dance workshops, guest speakers, all agency meetings, movie screenings, and family nights.

I walked in to find four young women scattered around the room. One of them was in the far corner, lying on her stomach and writing furiously in a composition book. Near the door I had just come through, two other young women were seated across from one another at one of the long plastic tables with metal collapsible legs. There was a CD player between them, but it was not the source of the driving beat. One young woman pushed play, and out came Alicia Keys's low and somewhat strained voice. After a few seconds, the other young woman pressed stop. They talked intently, jotted down notes, and repeated the process. Keys's ballads were no match for the hard steady beat vibrating from the built-in stereo system, but the only person in the room who seemed to be responsive to the rhythm carrying Usher's voice was Ashley—who, as if in a trance, stared at her image in the floor-to-ceiling mirror that lined an entire wall of the room. Her arms waved gracefully in front of her, in sync with Usher's voice; her lower body, knees bent and two-stepping, kept time to the infectious beat. When Lil Jon's growling rap came in, Ashley popped her chest forward and backward in the same rhythm as her staccato feet, while her arms, still rippling like waves, extended out to the mirror in front of her, floated down to her sides, and then lifted again, effortlessly. I stood in the doorway, watching for at least ten minutes. Although they were working in their own spaces, the room's occupants were viscerally aware of one another. The two young women at the table stopped talking when the quality of Ashley's movements changed, and the volume of the music, the added sonic texture emitting from the CD player, and Ashley's moving body seemed to encourage rather than frustrate the writer in the corner. I did not know what was going on, but I instinctively wanted in.

With the exception of one young woman who moved out of the shelter shortly after that evening, all of the young women creatively laboring in the common room on that Saturday were the beginning of the Move Experiment. In my last few months as the director of Fresh Start, the Move Experiment developed into a performance, class, workshop, and studio space primarily working out of the common room in the shelter. I was aware of how my presence would inevitably disrupt the sense of artistic flow and freedom among the girls, and, although my pull to the group was strong and immediate, at first I just tried to ensure that they had space where they could work together on a regular basis. It did not take long, however, before they asked me for assistance beyond scheduling the room, and I was transported back to my original entrée to Fresh Start as a volunteer dance instructor. The Move Experiment dominated the last five months of my official tenure as the Fresh Start director and, in many ways, charted a path that both invigorated and challenged the shapeshifting capacities of the young women. The Move Experiment confounded expectations we had and eluded assumptions we made regarding our positions as young and adult women variously located in this social service institution and the city of Detroit.

Camille was supportive of the Move Experiment from the time she heard about it and helped us secure a $50,000 grant from the Kellogg Foundation that gave the informal resident-led project the structure of other GGC community-based programs. Following the model of peer leadership in the Community Outreach Program, the Move Experiment was able to hire five young women as peer educators for a limited amount of time. I made flyers and promoted the program within the shelter to recruit two more peer educators in addition to the three original ones, interviewing candidates, and training all of the young women in the basics of workshop facilitation based on their self-identified talents in creative writing, movement and choreography, and performance poetry. The first phase of the Move Experiment was an in-house agencywide program that incorporated both shelter residents and young women living at home with strong ties to the other GGC programs. The original five participants (which included the four young women in the activity room with the addition of one resident who was a regular member of their informal creative team but not in the room on the day I entered) worked individually and collaboratively on creative projects of their choosing, most of which were related to the current conflicts in their lives and the ways in which they imagined themselves in the future. These young women also planned and facilitated writing, dance, meditation, and open dialogues to address interpersonal tensions in the shelter for other young women and staff within GGC. By the time the grant period was winding down and the funds for the program were dwindling (approximately seven months after its inception), I was transitioning out of my official duties in the shelter, though I was still very much connected to GGC and the young women in the shelter. In 2005–8, the years after I left the shelter and before I moved from Detroit, the Move Experiment changed membership, changed name, and shifted its focus from GGC to the entire city of Detroit. Janice and other members of the Brown family led this new, unfunded iteration of the Move Experiment. They called this project BlackLight.

I opened this chapter with an imaginative retelling of the Erica Pratt story and the intertwining narratives about bleach bathing at Fresh Start to provide the social context that made the Move Experiment and Black-Light necessary. On July 22, 2002, seven-year-old Erica Pratt was abducted close to 9:00 PM while playing outside of her home in Southwest Philadelphia. Throughout the rest of that night and into the next day, Erica worked to free herself from the basement of the abandoned building where she was kept captive by chewing through the duct tape that bound her wrists. Stumbling in the dark, she made her way up the basement stairs and managed to kick out a wooden panel blocking her exit. In her final act to free herself she punched out a window and shouted for help. Two young boys playing in the street heard Erica's screams and ran for help.[2]

Erica's abduction in July 2002 occurred in the midst of other extremely high-profile kidnappings of middle-class white girls in California and Utah. Another seven-year-old, Danielle Van Dam, was kidnapped from her bedroom on February 1, 2002, sexually abused, and then murdered by a male neighbor. Elizabeth Smart was fourteen when she was abducted from her bedroom in Salt Lake City, Utah, on June 5. Although Elizabeth was found nine months later, she was still missing during the time of Erica's kidnapping, and the unusual circumstances of her abduction were still being chronicled in various media and garnering widespread attention. And on July 15, just seven days prior to Erica's kidnapping, Samantha Runnion was taken by a male stranger who approached her in her front yard. Samantha's horrific fate was similar to Danielle's.

Certainly, disbelief, sadness, and anger are appropriate—if perhaps too reserved—responses to the unimaginable violence all of these young girls were forced to experience. Media reports led us to believe that, in addition to shock at the nature of the crimes and the innocence and helplessness of the victims, the public at large was also stunned not only by the how but also by the where of these crimes, essentially by the communities in which they occurred. A *Time* article that heralded Erica Pratt as the magazine's person of the week stated that Van Dam, Smart, and Runnion were "taken from neighborhoods where those kinds of things don't happen" (Coatney 2002). Erica's kidnapping, however ill-conceived by her captors, was depicted as a story of what happens when normalized violence meets the spunky determination of Black girlhood in the hood. Erica's story was made spectacular not by the fact that a child was subject to the violence and terror of being snatched from what should have been a safe and familiar setting—as was the case with the depictions of the abductions of Smart, Runnion, and Van Dam—but because she managed to escape.

What happened to Erica Pratt and the way that was publicly narrated in many ways reflects the limited social lexicon that makes violence against Black girls and young women legible to the broad public. Erica's kidnapping can be recounted as part of the story of drug- and gang-related kidnappings in an embattled neighborhood in Southwest (Black) Philadelphia, even though the stories of the actual Black girls who are the victims of these kidnappings are not commonly recounted.[3] We are then implored to respond to Erica's resiliency, her determination to fight for herself and demonstrate a unique pragmatism that belies her years. Admiring comments in the media about how Erica "kept her head and saved herself" and that ultimately surmise that the best way parents can protect their children is by "instilling self-assurance and presence of mind" (Coatney 2002) place Black children in a position where they are expected to defend and care for themselves, while the lack of protection and the various incarnations of violence they face are normalized. The public reaction to the schoolgirl rapes was replayed all over again in a different city where the girls are suspected of being the same.

In addition to the normalization of violence against Black girls that occurs through the narratization of Erica's kidnapping, an old trope of Black female superhuman strength and indefatigable resilience is reinforced and given intergenerational traction through her Black girl body. Erica acts. She patiently chews through the duct tape that binds her, kicks through a door, breaks a window, and screams for help. Her physicality is heightened as the primary active agent in a broader context of passivity and neglect in ensuring Black children's safety, health, and protection. Erica becomes a heroine primarily because she can be used as a distraction from the impact of interlocking forces of capital, white supremacy, industrial decline, and neighborhood speculation that contribute to the conditions that threaten the lives and livelihood of Erica and other Black girls in Southwest Philadelphia. Erica's admirable resiliency allows resiliency to be defined as an extraordinary individual act that erases the less newsworthy everyday ways in which Black girls are collectively forced to save their own lives.

To rewrite Erica's story with the information we have, I use a voice I imagine in a story that is a bricolage of the images from stories I have heard before from Black girls at Fresh Start and throughout other institutional and city spaces in the United States. The ways Black girls talk about their bodies and what it feels like to live in and through them is significant. The embodied knowledge that allows them to feel powerful and in control or degraded and unprotected can, in many cases, provide the information that keeps them alive. Young women talk about what "spaghetti" legs signal, and how they notice when their fear is matched body-to-body by those who they know intend to do them harm. They also talk about the sensation of energy that flows through them at that moment when it becomes clear they will have to come to their own rescue. I reconstruct Erica's abduction with the embodied themes and visceral images culled from Black girls because Erica's experience is painfully emblematic of the violence many Black girls experience on a daily basis, minus the grandiose media narratives after the fact.

It matters that this story begins with the sensory reflections of Erica's neighborhood, her friends and family, and her sense of the joy and freedom in her own body. Those sense memories, the felt and physically embedded stores of knowledge, are frequently what Black girls employ so that they can return their bodies to themselves as evidence to deny their valuelessness or failure. The contradictory evidence they receive from all manner of voices and locales often includes those close to home. Often unintentionally, or at least without the conscientious motivation to destroy, messages about their unfitness or unworthiness that is encapsulated in their bodies comes from family members, other Black girls, and themselves. Bleach appears in the many stories I witnessed as a home remedy for household dirt, skin conditions like eczema, general physical grime, the problem of the too Black body, and even perhaps viruses that are, in fact, incurable. If bleach bathing is passed down and across generations as something that Yolanda says "kills everything," we have to wonder what stays alive. In the Move Experiment and BlackLight, reclaiming oneself through the body, self-defined aesthetics, and choreographed movements that take up and shift space are practices that mirror Black girls' more mundane rituals of life affirmation and self-preservation. The ways in which the young women in these creative projects think about their health and well-being is magnified through the generational understanding of the elusive nature of Black girls' health as more than the capacity to "take it," be resilient, or settle for "struggly." And here, in these shapeshifting practices, almost everything has a chance to live.

Peer Educators

Rachel, Sonya, and Ashley posted job announcements for the Move Experiment peer educator positions all over GGC and asked the program coordinators and RAs to spread the word. Peer educators were to be paid $8 an hour to essentially learn the basics of various dance techniques[4] and relaxation strategies (including ballet, Horton,[5] jazz, hip-hop, and yoga) and lead workshops for other girls. The grant allowed us to hire five young women who could work up to twelve hours a week each.[6] I thought nearly a hundred dollars a week to learn how to dance and otherwise express yourself creatively would be at least a somewhat attractive offer to the residents, especially considering the bleak employment alternatives. We received five applications, but that number quickly dwindled down to zero after two of the residents moved out, two were hired as administrative assistants by a new consulting firm in the area, and one young woman's General Equivalency Diploma (GED) prep classes conflicted with the Move Experiment schedule. Two applicants from the Community Outreach Program brought our number back up to five when added to Rachel, Sonya, and Ashley.

The peer educators who were Fresh Start residents were Rachel, nineteen years old; Ashley, twenty-one; and Sonya, twenty. Rachel, the young woman who had been writing in her composition book in the corner of the room, was known in the shelter as a great poet and lyrical writer. Rachel was also full-figured and hyperconscious of her weight. Ashley, who had been dancing by the mirror, was the mother of two boys under the age of three and was nicknamed Lil Bit by the residents because of her small frame and short stature. At a glance she could pass for a fourteen-year-old. Ashley's habit of performing what she would later describe as "the helpless airhead" likely gave this moniker additional relevancy. Sonya was a young Italian American woman who came to the shelter after breaking up with her boyfriend and finding herself homeless. I first met Sonya when I was taking some trash out and startled her as she was smoking beside the dumpster. She had a pack-a-day habit when she first started in the Move Experiment. Sonya was very popular in the shelter, which was something she attributed to her "hard" personality and air of self-confidence.

The outreach participants included Janice's seventeen-year-old sister, Crystal Brown, who infuriated the other peer educators with her uncooperative attitude and volatile temper. I never heard the end of the complaining about Crystal, but to her face they all treated her like the little sister in the family, who they understood to need a bit more—or different kind of—care than the rest of the siblings. Izetta, also an outreach participant, was a young Mexican American woman whose father had passed away when she was ten years old. Izetta lived with her mother and six sisters in southwest Detroit. All of her older sisters had gone on to college, and Izetta was currently attending a private school she hated in the suburb of West Bloomfield. The Lopez sisters had been participants in the Early Start and Community Outreach Programs from the time they could walk.

At our first meeting, Rachel and I explained the basic premise of the Move Experiment project. Then I left the others alone for two hours to determine how to articulate the mission of the project and determine the actions needed to accomplish its goals. When I returned to the room, the young women were trying to decide where to put the poster board listing their eight-point plan of what the Move Experiment should include: (1) dance classes where peer educators could learn all different styles of dance, (2) peer educators' teaching classes to other girls at GGC and in the community, (3) learning how to eat better and be at the right weight, (4) making up their own dances, (5) writing poetry, (6) putting on a performance of their dances and poetry, (7) peer educators' being role models for the girls, and (8) loving and respecting themselves. In addition to this list of goals, the young women also came up with these personal statements about themselves:

I am Izetta Lopez, I am passionate . . . about life, about learning, about helping and dreaming . . . loving, trying, giving, I love my family. I want to be loved back by someone, by many. I want to leave legacies. I want to help others do the same. I want to "succeed" like the quote by Ralph Waldo Emerson. My age in years is sixteen. I don't know how old I really am in life. Sometimes I am old, sometimes I am young. When I walk past or look in a mirror, I have no face or body. I am just a person, whatever that looks like. I believe I am an artist and that somewhere inside everybody is another artist. I feel similarities to one another. We have to find them and help each other work with our differences. I dance because it makes me feel alive.

—*Izetta, sixteen*

I am a fairly pretty, heavyset African American female. I have a great smile. I'm sweet and giving. I am a positive role model and I feel that a challenge is only a challenge if you make it that. I am getting to know myself very well. I am also very smart and a quick learner. I love to be creative and express myself. I am wise beyond my years. Friends and family mean a lot to me. I want to lose weight and be healthier and show others how to do the same. I am more confident today than I have been in a while because I am dancing. People don't expect me to be able to dance.

—*Rachel, nineteen*

Well, my name is Crystal. I'm seventeen. I am 5'3" dark skinned. What a lot of people don't know about me is that I'm nice but I don't show people. They think that if I was asked to do something for them, I won't. I believe in myself and everything I do and I believe that anything is possible if I put my mind to it and that I've been through a lot and people think I'm mean 'cause I hide the real me. The real me is when I dance and when I write.

—*Crystal, seventeen*

Crystal also chose to write this poem:

I am a beautiful Black short-haired DIVA
In other words I'm just the me you wish you could be
I'm not trying to be some video ho no don't hate
Me because I'm breaking through all the bull shhh . . .
Don't you wish

You could be the me I choose to be
Y? R U mad?
It is because I don't follow the fads?
It is because I don't cry
For something I wish I had?
Do you want to know the reason?
It's because I am the me
You wish you could be
Now let's break it down
Those damn words that are used to describe me
Black, fat, thick,
Pretty, ugly, beautiful, brown skin
Shorty, baby, conceited/stuck up,
Smart, dumb . . . but not at all
All I can say is I choose to be ME
No . . . it is not sights and sounds that move me but feelings and
    colors . . . everything I choose to be.

I am Ashley. I am twenty-one with two beautiful boys that I love so
much. They are the reason why I get up in the morning. I am cheerful,
outgoing, loving. When I dance I can show people that I am really strong
because they don't see me that way.
—*Ashley, twenty-one*

My name is Sonya and I will be twenty in two months. I am very feminine, however I dislike sexism. I only have a few close friends but we love
each other a lot. I wish to be somebody, someday. One goal I have is to
stop smoking and find something to replace that feeling with. I dance
because I have a lot of stories to tell.
—*Sonya, nineteen*

These five peer educators created the Move Experiment and made it a
space in which they could directly confront the issues of identification
that framed their daily existence as young women discursively rendered
on the margins of society but fully centered in their own lives and their
communities. From the goals outlined by the peer educators, along with
the information they chose to include in their personal statements, several themes emerge that are central to ideas regarding the body, performance, and social identity.

The first is the idea of conscious, structured artistic performance and its relationship to the performance of self-presentation in everyday life. One thing that the peer educators made exceedingly clear was that they wanted the Move Experiment to conclude with a performance of their work in front of an audience. A performance was not a part of the plan that the three founding members discussed with me prior to the first meeting. We felt it important that young women who wanted the opportunity to learn how to dance and teach others not be turned off by the prospect of having to perform. But all five of the peer educators ultimately agreed in the first meeting that staging a performance would give meaning to all of their hard work, which they wanted to be seen and experienced outside of the training process or workshop setting. In this way, the young women were intent on bridging the gap between the continual performance of self in the sense of moving through daily life and performance as a means of intentional artistic expression aimed at a specific audience.

The desire to identify themselves underlay what all five young women hoped to accomplish through the Move Experiment. In the decision to write personal statements, without my prompting, the peer educators were proclaiming their right and need to define themselves. Self-definition was an implicit part of the process of defining the parameters of the Move Experiment. In defining who they are, all of the Black girls, except for Ashley, mention their bodies and/or a racial identifier such as skin color to identify themselves: Crystal states her height and that she is dark skinned. Rachel's full figure is central to her description of herself (perhaps calling it out and claiming it before others can). She calls herself pretty and heavyset. And then, in a stunning turn that practically belies the self-explanatory disclaimers and marked hesitancy in her prose, Crystal takes full advantage of her creative license in her poetic self-description. She defines herself as "a beautiful black short-haired DIVA" and then presents us with "those damn words that are used to describe" her—"black, fat, thick, pretty, ugly, beautiful, brown skin"[7]—words that sometimes contradict each other and thus reveal the arbitrariness and unreliability of external physical assessments.

In addition to physical characteristics, Crystal also identifies the assumptions made regarding her personality and abilities—"conceited/stuck up, smart, dumb"—and asserts that despite these assumptions, all she can say is that she chooses to be herself, a self that she perceives as actually inspiring envy in those who attempt to degrade or inaccurately identify her. Crystal also asks if we are mad because she doesn't follow the fads. Fads generated through the media; fed to youth populations and becoming altered in the process; and then exploited in their newer, fresher forms have the ability to limit people's possibilities for self-definition. In an earlier formal interview I conducted with Crystal at GGC, she talked about the fact that people are angry because young Black women are not buying into the commodified stereotypes sold to them as the only viable ways of being. Speaking back to the media and the narratives of young Black femininity formed in readings of hip-hop youth culture became a central objective of all Move Experiment peer educators. Crystal speaks to this directly when she directs us to not "hate" her because she is not trying to be some "video ho."[8] Sonya also addresses and challenges the contradictory and confusing ways femininity is represented to young women. Sonya tells us that she is feminine but, realizing the negative connotations that can be associated with this, also says that she dislikes sexism. It is almost as if she wants us to know that her positive gender identification and her decision to express her femininity do not make her complicit in the patriarchal degradation of femaleness.

Izetta rejects the image as identifier. When she walks past a mirror, the self she sees has "no face or body" and is "just a person, whatever that looks like." Izetta is challenging the ideas that her physicality defines who she is and that anyone can know her by looking at her. Izetta can't tell us what this person (herself) looks like. Perhaps it is a feeling that overrides the visual, the feeling that is brought to life through dance where she can create herself and "feel alive."

Sonya and Ashley discuss dance as the medium through which they can have essential conversations with an audience. Sonya dances because she has stories to tell, and Ashley wants to use dance as a way to reveal her real self and contradict the false image she is conscious of presenting (performing) as a survival mechanism in her everyday life.

Relationships are also significant in how all of the peer educators identify themselves and what is important in their lives. Especially significant are mentoring relationships and the idea of influencing other young women through serving as a positive role model, as Rachel says she is. Izetta believes that the way that she can help people is by encouraging them to develop the same things she would like to develop in herself—namely, the ability to leave behind a legacy and to learn how to work through differences. The stories that Sonya has to tell can be one way that she inspires and encourages other young women; her personal history is a lesson for navigating young womanhood. Crystal, always on the defense regarding perceptions that she has a bad attitude, offers a synopsis of her relationships with others in a negative voice. Hyperaware of her reputation, Crystal says not that she will help others but that people "think that if I was asked to do something for them, I won't." We are supposed to infer that this is actually not the case, and that she does help others and is a giving, compassionate person.

All of the young women include family and/or friends as people they love or who mean a lot to them. This seems significant in light of the nature of the Move Experiment and the fact that the act of writing a biography or personal statement in this context would not seem to call for this level of disclosure. In the first lines of her statement, Ashley identifies her role as a mother and her love for her sons as the inspiration that allows her to "get up in the morning." This role is central in defining who she is and how she sees herself, even in a setting where her primary responsibilities revolve around dancing and teaching others how to dance. Throughout the three months (July through September)[9] that I was able to pay these five young women to be a part of the Move Experiment, I saw how their relationships with their mothers, fathers, boyfriends, friends, lovers, grandmothers, aunts, and staff members at GGC helped them locate themselves in the world.

That Is So Ill!

"So, let's talk about how that went," I said, as we started gathering the chairs to form a circle in the middle of the room. We had just finished our first meditation workshop for the GGC staff.

"That was harder than I expected," Ashley spoke up first. "It seemed like they didn't want to relax."

"You mean, they didn't know how to relax," Sonya corrected.

"Yeah, like they were fighting their own bodies," Rachel added.

Crystal's eyes were fixed on the carpet. Izetta was nodding and looking intently at each young woman as she spoke.

"Why did you think it would be easy?" Izetta asked. "I mean, I was not surprised at all. When they first walked in they seemed uncomfortable, and during the guided visualization they kept opening their eyes to see what was going on. But I knew it was going to be a challenge with them when we first came up with the idea. Challenge is a good thing, though. So . . ."

"How did you know that from the beginning?" I asked.

"They have stressful jobs, and almost everybody seems to work long hours here," Izetta responded. "Even if we don't agree with or like some of the staff, it must be a lot to have to spend your whole day working to make sure children and teenagers are okay."

"I don't know about all that." Rachel was skeptical. "They seem to have plenty of ways to release their stress during the day—talking about the residents behind our backs, talking crazy and disrespectful to us, taking random smoke breaks all day long. They get their stress relief, believe me."

"That kinda just proves her point," Ashley said. "They do all of that stuff because they are stressed out. I mean, if it wasn't no big deal to them what happened to us or what happened at the agency, they would just be like 'La-di-damn-da' and go about they business."

"That's what they do anyway. At least that's how I see it," Crystal remarked.

"So, given all of this," I said, "can we talk about how it felt to lead this workshop for these women—to touch them and have to use your voice to get them centered? How did that feel to you?"

Izetta shifted from her chair to the floor so she could extend her legs in front of her. "Is this okay? My legs are a little crampy." She massaged one thigh and then worked her hands down toward her calf as she spoke. "It felt really powerful, like not good or bad, but really powerful. It was almost like I could feel the person's energy rising off of them and jumping into my hands."

Crystal, seated behind Izetta, raised one eyebrow, shook her head, and laughed to herself.

"No, I'm serious." Izetta turned to look at Crystal. "I could totally feel what they were feeling. Like at the end, when we had them check in about how they were feeling and Camille said she was feeling sad because of something that was going on with her family but felt better. I felt her sadness at first, and I felt when it came up off of her."

Rachel, Sonya, and Ashley looked at each other, at me, and then back at Izetta.

"I do think there was a point when I could feel something change in the room," Sonya said. "I mean, like I couldn't tell if it was coming from us or them, but when I started to do the image meditation, like I could hear people breathing heavy and I felt less stressed myself."

"Yes!" Ashley stood up. "That's what I want to talk about—our stress and how we are supposed to feel doing this. I mean, I am trying to make them feel relaxed, at ease, what have you, but I'm over here freaking out about what I have to do after this is over and where I have to be, and I'm looking at Paulette like, 'I am up here getting you all calm, but you'll be the first one to write me up if I come home late or don't do my chores right.' Why should I be making you feel good?"

Izetta hit Ashley playfully on the leg, and then everyone seemed to be nodding and mmhmming in agreement.

"Yeah, I feel you, Ash," Rachel said. "But that's the point. That's why we are here. That's why we are peer educators."

"What you mean?" Ashley asked.

"I mean we ain't perfect and you don't have to love or even like everybody, but the point of all of this writing and dancing and making up stuff and teaching people how to relax and meditate is for us." Rachel spread her arms wide when she said this, to indicate everyone in the room. "'Cause all that other stuff—like holding on to all that other stuff is not healthy."

"Oh my God! That is so it! That is it! We are not here to be perfect or like these ideal role models, but we are an example." Izetta was standing up next to Ashley now, and Crystal and Sonya were watching them as if they had finally reached the good part in a movie.

"We feel better when we make other people feel better," Sonya's support of Izetta's revelation wasn't very convincing.

"Y'all are really tripping," Crystal scooted her chair back from the circle and crossed her arms. "Don't nobody make me feel better so they can feel better. That just ain't happening—ever."

"I kind of agree," Ashley added.

I was absorbed in the intensity of the back-and-forth and struck by the conviction with which each young woman spoke or held her silence and her ground. "How do you feel better then?" I asked, curiously. "And what does that even mean? To feel better about what?"

"Okay." Sonya pressed her fingertips to her eyelids and let out a tired sigh. "If we want to feel better, we have a bunch a ways to do that. You don't have to cosign, but Imma keep it real." She looked directly at Izetta when she said this, and I noticed that Crystal sat up a little taller in her seat.

"I'll just speak for myself, then," Sonya continued. "I smoke. Y'all know I smoke, and on top of that shit I smoke menthols, which is supposed to be the worst shit out. But smoking keeps me from nuttin' up on somebody."

"So?" Rachel was looking for more.

"So?! So, I smoke, some of us eat too damn much, some shoot up, some get twisted."[10] Sonya stopped there, as if her point should have been clear.

"She's talking about self-medication," Izetta summarized. "That's how we compromise our health by doing things that we think are solving our problems but are actually making them worse."

"Right, but you didn't need to make people feel bad. I mean, none of us could be no damn Victoria's Secret models up in here." Ashley was reacting to Sonya's comment about overeating and what she perceived to be a jab at Rachel's weight.

"It's okay," Rachel said. "I get it. We all got issues and addictions. Some people are even addicted to other people. We all need to face and deal with our shit."

Everyone knew Rachel was talking about Sonya's boyfriend, Ed, whose contacts with Sonya over the last few weeks had decreased as her attempts to garner his attention had increased.

Sensing a moment that could turn volatile, Izetta and I started to speak at the same time. I let her have the floor.

"It shouldn't get this personal." Izetta sat back down on the floor and spoke calmly, looking up at Rachel and Sonya. "We all have stress and things we are trying to work out. Nobody is better than anybody else. We need each other."

"Kumbaya, my Lord, kumbaya," Crystal started singing.

"All I'm saying," Rachel said, "is we all got problems. Come on now! Three of us in this room is homeless. That ain't a problem, then I don't know what is. But we signed up for this, and even if we feel some kind of way about making other people feel better, we still have to hold it together. Think outside yourself."

"Hold it together. Think outside yourself," Ashley said. "Now that's that unhealthy shit."

The Fresh Start staff members had their own ideas regarding whether or not self-care should be considered a luxury or a necessity, not for the residents but for themselves as well. When the Move Experiment peer educators' names were announced in the shelter, the staff members hardly felt like celebrating. Although shelter residents had worked as peer educators in other outreach programs (conducting street outreach and working in the Free project) and had participated in unpaid training internships in GGC, the objectives of the Move Experiment seemed, from the staff perspective, to be "extra," auxiliary, and unnecessary.

It was one thing, in the minds of the RAs and caseworkers in the shelter, for residents to work in an office environment like the GGC's finance department, gaining "marketable skills" such as typing, filing, and phone etiquette, but quite another to get paid for learning how to "express yourself" and "eat right." The Move Experiment peer educators worked no more hours than the other shelter residents who were peer educators in other departments, nor did participation in the Move Experiment interfere with its peer educators' job searches, school hours, or responsibilities as shelter program participants. Still, the Move Experiment peer educators were given a hard time by the RAs and their caseworkers for spending too much time on an activity believed to be extracurricular. Rachel told me that several RAs and even her caseworker told her that they didn't understand why she was getting paid to dance, something that was just a "hobby." One RA even confronted me directly after rehearsals two days in a row made Sonya, Rachel, and Ashley a few minutes late in starting their evening chores in the shelter: "You need to help them get it in their heads that this is just a side-type thing. It may be something that is fun to them right now, but it is not going to do them any good in the long run. They need to think about what they need to do to find a job and get some skills they can carry out of here with them."

Some of the caseworkers shared their thoughts with me as well:

"I don't have a problem with Rachel doing something to work out because she is extremely overweight, but I don't want her to think that she can afford to spend a whole bunch of time focusing on that stuff. She needs to know that this will not have anything to do with what she will probably end up doing in the future."

"Can you please remind Sonya, Ashley, and Rachel that just because they are getting paid through your dance program does not mean they have a real job?"

"Um, yeah, about the Move Experiment—what exactly are they learning that is going to help them get out of this shelter and move on with their lives?"

These statements from the caseworkers who managed Rachel, Sonya, and Ashley's cases were spoken to directly to me with hostile, antagonistic overtones. In contrast, the comments I received from staff members who worked outside of the shelter were along the lines of:

"I am so impressed with the changes I see in those girls in your program. Has Rachel lost weight? She seems so much happier, like she has more energy. I think they need to do more of that in the shelter with all of the girls. It should be mandatory."

"I am so glad those girls are learning how to take care of themselves and express themselves. They have so much talent and probably don't even realize it. All they do in the shelter is get on them for what they do wrong. They don't have any space to be themselves."

My goal is not to belittle or dismiss the harsh reality that the RAs and other shelter staff members were responding to in their expressions of concern regarding the Move Experiment and the residents' involvement in the program. The basis for their concern is very real, given that the most immediate obstacles in these young women's lives is their homeless status and dearth of opportunities for moving out of homelessness. To the shelter staff members, whose job it was to help facilitate these young women's transition from homelessness to independent living, condoning participation in what they saw as just dance classes felt like rubber-stamping frivolity. It makes sense, then, that the shelter staff would be the most concerned with any program taking up time in the residents' lives that was not directly related to getting a job. The problem with paying undivided attention to goals and getting ahead economically is that it leaves the notion of self-care behind. For low-income and underemployed young women, especially young women of color, I contend that taking care of their emotional and physical health is not only a revolutionary act[11] but also the only way to sustain progress that can be measured materially. Overeating, depression, and forgetting or not having enough time or money to see a doctor may not appear as overtly dangerous to one's health and well-being as drug addiction or involvement in a physically abusive relationship, but they can be just as damaging in the long run to young women's abilities to live healthy, productive lives.

Rachel's weight was an issue beyond the question of problematic aesthetic ideals of body size. She talked about how her weight made it difficult to breathe and caused her physical discomfort. No real effort was made, however, to treat Rachel's weight and chronic overeating as a health concern. In fact, the prevalence of young women whose additional weight caused them health problems in the shelter was treated as a given[12] rather than a cause for concern or sign of deeper traumas. After participating in the Move Experiment for only one week, Rachel stated that she felt like she had more energy and was sleeping better. She also shared with the group in one of our daily wrap-up discussion sessions that expressing herself through dance and poetry was influencing her eating habits: she didn't eat as much and had stopped craving junk food.

These seemingly small steps are significant in the lives of young women like Rachel who have spent the majority of their young lives taking care of other family members (both elders and younger siblings and cousins) and have gotten used to putting their needs, desires, and hopes on the back burner. Growing up like Rachel, Janice, and Crystal in households where you are constantly told that you have to "be strong" and "hold it together" and set a stoic example for your brothers and sisters means that repression, displacement, and numbness are the ways you learn to disembody your emotions. Food becomes one very powerful form of comfort.

In many underresourced communities, cleaning your plate is not an option but a mandate, and constant snacking becomes a normative habit that takes the place of playing in the neighborhood or being part of extracurricular activities. Tamara Beauboeuf-Lafontant (2005) identifies the stereotype of the Black superwoman who takes on everyone else's problems and ignores her own needs as a primary factor in the development of compulsive overeating among Black women. In the case of Black women called by their families and communities to be pillars of strength under all circumstance, Beauboeuf-Lafontant states that "the 'body problem' of overeating may be productively viewed as a muted protest against the intense selflessness mandated of 'strong black women'" (2005, 105). We have to pay attention to how the value we place on various bodies in society affects how individuals experience living in those bodies.

In the midst of finding employment in an economically devastated city, fulfilling the many requirements of the transitional living program, developing an educational plan, and meeting with welfare caseworkers outside of the agency, shelter residents were silently coping with intersecting emotional traumas that got sidelined by the need to "make progress." Histories of sexual abuse, abandonment, and the indifference of parents (if they were even in the picture), and physically violent relationships often do not get the attention they deserve in programs like those at GGC, which are understaffed in the area of counseling and psychological care. The young women themselves put on a brave face and try to dismiss or downplay these traumas in an effort to move on and create a new life. Ironically, this new life, as captured in the name *independent living program*, is often one that compels them to rely too heavily on their own internal emotional resources and fails to adequately assist these young women in identifying social support systems outside of the social service care continuum. The consistency with which social service agencies are faced with lives marked by devastation leads many workers, out of an unconscious need to maintain their own emotional stability and ability to do their jobs, sometimes to miss the signs of these traumas. In fact, becoming homeless is a traumatic event, and one that is experienced by all shelter residents. However, the experience of actually being without a safe or livable residence was hardly ever overtly discussed at Fresh Start as an emotional, rather than a social or economic, event.

In programs that serve high-risk youth populations it is easy for terms like *acting out*, *having a bad attitude*, and *thinking she's grown* to take the place of more accurate assessments such as depression, anxiety, and fear that really define these young peoples' behaviors. The sisters Janice and Crystal were known to be somewhat difficult program participants, whose moods would swing with the wind. However, during the time that Crystal was a Move Experiment peer educator, Janice was preoccupied with extricating herself from the Job Corps and had less time and inclination to get into it with staff members and other participants. Therefore, I was somewhat taken off guard when one of the outreach coordinators brought Janice to me and told me that she had been asked to leave the outreach work area because she had been "short and disrespectful" to one of the volunteers. I had sensed something was wrong with Janice earlier that morning when she first arrived at the agency, but she had assured me that "she was tight." By the look on Janice's face, a look that most people mistook for anger, I knew she was about to cry. Since I had more than two hours before the peer educators would arrive to start preparing for the afternoon workshop, I took Janice out of the building for a drive.

I waited for Janice to tell me what was wrong, expecting her to drop a specific bombshell. Instead, the story I heard from Janice was one of sheer emotional exhaustion. She was tired of the constant fighting on her block, especially among other young women—most of whom were pregnant or parenting and were battling for the attention of the young men they shared as fathers of their children. She was tired of seeing that pathetic expression of desperation on behalf of the men who were hardly ever around to see the chaos they inspired. She said the constant hostility among the young women in her neighborhood, along with having to constantly worry about her younger nieces and nephews, was starting to make her physically sick. The night before, she had gotten into a physical altercation with her fifteen-year-old cousin as he was leaving the house to hang out with older guys Janice knew to be drug dealers. She said she had to literally "beat his ass" to keep him in the house. Afterward, she said, she felt so bad she stayed up the rest of the night, feeling sick to her stomach and throwing up. Bessie was getting more and more tired each day, taking care of her six great-grandchildren, and although Janice tried to do what should could to help, it wasn't appearing to make that much of a difference. As bad as all of this sounded to me, none of it really came as a shock or as anything out of the ordinary from what I knew of her life on Wesson Street. But the next thing Janice said did come as a surprise: "My psychiatrist made me write down all of the things I am worried about on these pieces of paper, and then she took them and put them on a plate. They didn't fit, and she took 'em one by one and showed me how most of them are things I can't control, so I need to just control myself."

"When—uh, who is your psychiatrist? When did you start seeing a psychiatrist?" I asked.

"Two weeks ago. I only been two times. I found her through Medicaid." Janice guessed that I was wondering how she was paying for the services. "She is a Black woman, which is good 'cause I told them that if they wasn't Black then there wan't no point in me going to see them 'cause they wouldn't be able to relate."

"What made you decide to look for counseling?" I asked, parking the car near Chene Park.

"Mental illness runs in my family. Like my aunt Ruby couldn't keep her job, because she was saying people were after her and she was starting to get all paranoid. She lost her job. And I know—like I can tell that some of the women in my family are depressed but they won't say anything, and like it seems like it is where if you Black you not supposed to get help or find someone to talk to. But I don't care 'cause I don't want to end up crazy. But I tell my friends like, 'Yeah, my psychiatrist said'—and you know, I tell them that I started going 'cause I don't see it as something bad."

Although Janice found some peace through therapy, and Rachel and the other peer educators found the forum for open expression in the Move Experiment one way to deal with trapped emotions and embodiments of them, these practices are not enough to make the kind of enduring changes in physical and mental health necessary for these young women to thrive. Experiences of living in urban poverty in bodies that are dismissed and undervalued, although televised for our viewing pleasure and rampant in our social service systems, should never become normalized.

The Show

"We want to put on a performance that shows people how we are all the same even though we are different. Each individual piece we have choreographed reflects who we are inside and out as individuals, and the group piece at the end shows how we all come together and work together through our differences. The poetry is also a way for us to show who we are and to be heard. We want the audience to see that we are strong and creative."

The concept for the show was fairly traditional in many aspects. Although the girls wanted to have the show on a theatre stage, we didn't have the money to rent a high-school theatre. We put hooks in the ceiling of the activity room and hung heavy black fabric on the back and side walls to create wings, and we went shopping as a group to pick out costumes for each dancer that fit within her allotted budget of $50. I worked with Rachel, Ashley, and Izetta to create the program. On the outside cover, they wanted to see the word *journey* in big block letters, to symbolize "the transformation that we all went through these past few months." The young women asked Lynnette, the beloved RA who facilitated the Inner Circle sessions, to be the MC for the event and to stand in as an audience member for the dress rehearsals. The preparation for the show felt much like any other performance I had participated in, from middle school through my brief professional career. Petty fights broke out the closer we got to the performance date, when nerves and anxiety were at a high, and there were many inexplicable tears and spontaneous bursts of misdirected anger. A day or two before the actual show, however, a joyful giddiness started to set in with the realization that the show was actually going to happen, whether we were ready or not.

A good deal of the heightened emotions related to the show could be attributed to what was at stake for each individual dancer. Each young woman had created a very personal piece that was directed to a specific person or people they invited to the show. The success of their individual performance therefore depended in large part on whether or not the intended audience members showed up and if they demonstrated the desired reaction. A half-hour before the show, the dancers could hardly maintain their focus and kept leaving the dressing room to see if "their people" had arrived yet. In the case of some of the girls, like Sonya, the appearance of a family member (in her case, her father) would mean the first time they had seen that person in several years. I tried not to place too much emphasis on the slowly increasing crowd and who was or was not among its members. I did not want them to be distracted before they even walked out on stage by the awareness of someone's absence.

I had seen and helped rehearse each of the girls' pieces as well as the group piece that they had made me responsible for choreographing. However, the show's opening was something that they had been working on in secret with Lynnette. Lynnette announced that there were fifteen minutes to curtain, and when the time came turned off the lights to signal the start of the show. I was seated by the sound system in a corner of the room. All eighty chairs we had placed in the room were occupied, and there were approximately twenty-five people standing up and sitting in the aisle. Before the room went black, I tried to see if I could pick out the people who the girls were hoping would come. In the semidarkness, the five young women entered from the back and took various poses on stage. When Lynnette turned the lights back on, I was surprised to see that they had taken off their individual costumes and were all wearing the practice clothes that they wore for classes and rehearsals.

Each dancer was frozen in some type of stretching or dance position. Rachel was the first to move. She walked to the front of the stage and shouted, "Move!" The other dancers broke out of their poses and started moving around the stage as if they were warming up. And then Rachel started talking. After her first few sentences, I realized that she was playing me and re-creating the first day we met. Only then did I notice that she had her sweatpants rolled up the way the girls made fun of me for wearing mine.

"Okay, girls," she said. "You are here to work together. I am going to leave you alone, and I want you to come up with an idea for what you want the Move Experiment to be. You have two and a half minutes to come up with a plan for the next three months."

The audience, composed of GGC staff members and participants and the family and friends of the peer educators, were laughing at Rachel's impersonation. While she was talking, the girls in the background were involved in some over-the-top acting. They were scratching their heads and making confused faces behind Rachel's back. The more the audience got into this opening act, the more improvised it became. My co-workers were pointing fingers at me from across the room, winking and laughing with me, while Rachel walked back and forth across the stage mimicking my mannerisms to perfection.

"All right, young women," she continued, "when I come back in thirty seconds I want to see a thirty-page business plan, a list of 150 things we need to do today, a diagram of how the stage would be set up, and the names and numbers of everyone you ever met." Rachel was on a roll. "Oh, and I want everything laminated."

The girls seemed a little thrown off by Rachel's improvisation and the intense audience response, so there was a little pause after she left the stage. The girls started performing an argument to show how difficult it was for them to reach a consensus about the vision for the Move Experiment. Each girl was playing a caricature of herself, taking her most identifiable qualities and blowing them out of proportion. I wondered how much of this self-reflection came out of their outspoken readings of each other. The behind-the-scenes look at the Move Experiment felt like reality TV to me. It was basically scripted but layered with improvisations based on outlined character types that played off one another. The exaggerated character sketches, I later found out from the girls, were planned to a certain extent because they wanted to show how much they had grown from the time they started working together to this final performance; growth would be exhibited in their individual pieces. They hadn't expected the audience to be so into the opening, and they added flourishes to their individual acts based on the audience reaction.

On the stage, they ultimately decided to work together, and by the time Rachel (as me) came back, they were ready to show their individual pieces. The lights went out on the dancers in motion, who were talking excitedly about the pieces they wanted to choreograph. From the wings, Rachel shouted, "Silence!," and they immediately stopped talking. Then Izetta started reciting the first stanza of a poem that they had written together. Each peer educator spoke the part that she had written until they got to the last sentence, which they recited in unison: "And together, but still individuals, we move and twirl, speak and breathe our strength, beauty, and intelligence." This was all spoken in the dark. The first dancer to come out after the group opening was Ashley. Her music started, and then she began dancing down the aisle through the crowd. As she passed her mother who was sitting in the second row in the aisle, her mother reached out to try to tap her on the arm and shouted out, "All right, now! Get it, girl!" I could see the outburst break Ashley's concentration for a split second when a smile crept across her face. It was extremely important to Ashley that she show strength and power in her performance, and she had chosen African dance and drumming music specifically because she felt it conveyed "seriousness" and "power from the ancestors." Ashley's performance was intended to speak to her mother and the father of her children. She felt that they treated her like a child and tried to intimidate her so that she would do what they wanted. The driving drum music was hypnotic, and Ashley's hips moved in perfect timing to the syncopated beat. Although her movements were sensual and fluid, they also displayed precision and enviable bodily control.

Ashley was definitely in charge and, from my perspective, proved her intended point, that as she was fond of saying, "she could run things and manage her own life." I scanned the audience for her boyfriend but could only see the top of his head bobbing to the beat. The longer she was on stage, the more confidence she seemed to gain, as the audience clapped to the beat and hooted each time she added a new step to her movement sequence. On her exit, when she passed by her mother again, she almost lost her balance when her mother slapped her on the behind. I don't think very many people in the audience noticed, but Ashley definitely did, and her face changed immediately to defeat. With that one gesture, Ashley's mother entered the performance space and altered the dynamic of the performance. Although Ashley had hoped to break through the fourth wall that separates performer from audience, with her performance by reaching out through her movements and speaking to her family, she hadn't anticipated it being a two-way conversation. The audience, oblivious to what changed for Ashley in that one instant, stood up and cheered her as she disappeared into the side wing.

Before the audience could quiet down, Sonya was winding her way down the aisle to the right of where Ashley had just exited. Noticing her presence, the audience became quiet, so that the only sound was the jangling metal hip shawl that dangled from her waist. Sonya began her dance, a creative combination of improvised belly dancing movement and steps taken from classical ballet. In rehearsals, Sonya kept telling us that she wanted to look "really pretty and feminine." The movements she had selected reflected her interpretation of a feminine body in motion. During constructive feedback sessions, the other peer educators told Sonya that they liked her dance and that she "looked good doing the movement," but they felt like she was "too worried about the steps" and was "not feeling the movement." There were a lot of kicks high up in the air and head rolls and undulations of the torso that, in practice, looked uncomfortable for Sonya. But in the performance in front of a real audience, Sonya seemed like a completely different person. She was committed to each movement and danced as if she were trying to put the audience in a trance. It may have helped that her musical choice was a "Sounds of Nature" CD that alternately played a babbling brook and quiet rainfall in the background. The jangling inter-woven coins that hung from her hips tinkled over these watery sounds. The spell she had over the audience didn't break until she left the stage. I noticed only when her music came to an end that the babies who had been screaming out during Ashley's dance had been silent throughout Sonya's two-minute routine.

The inspiration for Crystal's dance was Lauryn Hill's song "Zion." The peer educators and I were confused by this choice because Hill sings about finding joy in motherhood. Crystal did not have any children and was not pregnant. Although it was like pulling teeth, we finally got Crystal to tell us why she wanted to dance to this particular song: "I like how she sounds peaceful and calm. She sounds like someone who is like caring and has a lot of love." As it turned out, Crystal was tired of being thought of as the girl with the bad attitude and wanted to show her "true self" in her dance. By the time Crystal, the third of the five dancers, took the stage, I had gotten over my motherly pride at seeing "my girls" dancing on stage. I was moved by the effect that they seemed to be having on the audience and the fact that they all seemed to be dancing from a deep spirit-filled place. However, I could not help evaluating their performances on another level.

They were moving in the spirit and moving spirits, which should have been more than enough.[13] Yet unpointed feet, sloppy arms, and missteps kept attracting my attention. I was annoyed with myself for noticing these things, and even more annoyed that I was annoyed with the dancers for not being as compelling technically as they were theatrically. Since most of the girls had no or very little dance training before they started in the Move Experiment, I was not really expecting much in the way of technical expertise. The point of the project was to use dance as one vehicle for get-ting at more important considerations like self-confidence, self-respect, and peer mentoring. But the more we worked together, the more I started to see that some of the girls had technical skills that extended beyond the more therapeutic aspects of the program, and in the end I expected more from them as dancers, not just as peer educators.

Lauryn Hill's strong, raspy voice blared out of the speakers while Crys-tal stood motionless on stage. I held my breath wondering if she was ever going to move. It would not be too far out of character for Crystal to freeze up or decide to walk off stage, since she was unpredictable and had been the most inconsistent in rehearsal. When Crystal finally started to move, I hardly recognized the dance. She barely moved from her spot in the middle of the floor and was making up steps that I had never seen before. The look on her face, with furrowed brow and pursed lips, solidified her image as a tough girl and was in stark contrast to the feeling emanating from the music. I could feel the audience getting uncomfortable for her. From the back of the room, her mother, Gwen, shouted out "Okay, now!" Several people in the front of the room turned around to see who spoke, and then a male voice boomed out, "Do this, girl!" The audience members were soon engaged in call and response; one person would shout out words of support, and a few seconds later someone else would respond. Since the words seemed to have little effect on Crystal's abysmal performance, the audience seemed to be entertaining themselves, seeing who could come up with the most encouraging phrase. By the time Lauryn hit her last note, the audience was performing for themselves. I don't even remember how Crystal left the stage.

Rachel's biggest fear was that there might be some insensitive comments from the audience because of her size, even though the point of her performance was for Rachel to show that she was confident in her own skin. The music Rachel danced to was the sound of her voice reciting the poem she wrote, "Beautiful Women." The poem, inspired by Maya Angelou's "Phenomenal Woman," talks about the beauty in diverse bodies and ways of being and the life-affirming practice of learning how to become comfortable with who you are. Rachel owned the stage the moment she opened her mouth, her live voice in unison with her prerecorded track. She walked back and forth across the expanse of the room making eye contact and pointing at specific people as she spoke. Her minimal movements were confined primarily to her upper body, as she gracefully gestured with her arms to emphasize each phrase. Sounding like a congregation trying to impress the preacher on Sunday, the audience (warmed up by now, and having fun playing with each other and the performers) shouted out "Amen"s and told her to "Preach it!," perhaps too enthusiastically trying to prove that they were in support of this big girl on stage. I found it noteworthy that instead of the "girl" and "girlfriend" and "miss lady" used to call out to the other girls, for Rachel the audience called "Go, momma!" I'm sure her size had something to do with this unconscious shift: the audience saw this performer as more of a woman, a full-bodied nurturing mother whom they asked to "preach" and "speak that word." Rachel's focus on the spoken word made sense to her, not only because she was less confident in her ability to move well, but also because living in her body meant generally being seen and not heard. For a full-bodied young woman like Rachel, being heard is part of an important process of speaking herself into being in the way she chooses, to become more than just the body that others allow to visually overwhelm and solely define her existence.

Izetta was moving before her music came on. She wanted her piece to be the last one before the finale because at the end of the dance she choreographed a phrase for all of the girls to dance together. Izetta had two goals she hoped to accomplish: she wanted to show the audience what traditional Mexican dance looked like and to get all the other peer educators to feel what it feels like to move their bodies in that style. The look on Izetta's face as she danced was one of sheer joy. She shone brighter as each peer educator stepped back out on stage to join her in the group choreography she had created. At the end of the high-energy dance, the music stopped, but the performers kept moving as if they couldn't get enough of dancing together. Rachel then abruptly yelled "Stop!," and in a repetition of the opening sequence, the dancers froze in place. "Now," Rachel said, turning to speak to the audience, "let's see if by the time we come back from our break these girls can continue to dance together." During the intermission, I helped the girls change into their costumes for the final piece I choreographed. They were all excited about having finished their solos, which was undeniably the hard part, and were ready for the finale.

"Did you see the look on my boyfriend's face while I was dancing?" Sonya asked me, as I gelled her hair into a bun.

"Did I mess up? Was it okay?" Crystal seemed to know that she hadn't done her best but still didn't seem defeated. It was as if she just wanted reassurance that getting up on stage and trying was enough. I thought it was, so I told her that she looked great. We both knew I was lying.

"Y'all looked so good doing my dance!" Izetta was playing the proud teacher, walking around to hug each girl.

Rachel sat in a corner, still basking in the afterglow.

"Did you see my Momma? She is a trip. But, whatever, I worked it out, right?" Ashley was smiling as she said this, talking to no one in particular and not really looking for feedback.

Crystal was the inspiration for my piece. Out of all the physical movements, personal interactions, original creations, and unexpected incidents that occurred in the Move Experiment, what resonated with me the most was Crystal's attempts to release her anger. Her vulnerability in expressing the desire for other people to know that she is a caring person affected me deeply, especially coming from a young woman who had countless justifiable reasons to be angry and put up a self-protective façade. The relationships the other young women in the Move Experiment developed with Crystal kept her on task. They tried to understand her and meet her where she was, but they always let her know when they had had enough and needed her to make a change and meet them halfway. The dance was choreographed to John Coltrane's thirteen-minute piece "Africa," a rising and falling musical drama that fit the theme. I didn't want to make Crystal uncomfortable by pointing her out as the problem child in the group, so I explained the dance as a reflection of the relationships they had all developed with one another and the challenge of accepting each other's shortcomings while they all worked toward a common goal.

Even though Crystal was the initial inspiration, the dance (primarily because it was so long and due to the intense process of learning and executing the choreography) became the embodiment of our collective experience. We were learning each other and finding another layer of ourselves in the process. I have to admit that, although the impetus for the movement in this dance was tied to feeling and the expression of emotion, I couldn't help returning to the question of technique: I wanted the young women to look good *and* move the crowd. The dance was technically difficult, requiring that they dance together by supporting each other's weight, dancing in unison, and using each other's movements as a catalyst for their own. There were solos, duets, trios, and points where the entire group danced together. To my disappointment, there were no hoots or hollers from the audience. The only time they interacted with this piece was the moment when Rachel raised her hands above her head and slowly slid down into the Chinese splits.[14] This was a move that Rachel begged me to put in the dance because she wanted a chance to demonstrate her flexibility and show that even though she couldn't do all of the movements that the other dancers could, she still had exceptional technical skill. Even though the power of the performance the dancers had created up until this point was based on conversation with the audience, I was content to have them be passive observers as long as they "got it." The "it" was that these previously untrained young women looked like dancers after just a few short months of training. I took it for granted that this audience full of familiar faces would respond to each girl with love and encouragement; that the observers would feel something because they either knew the girls personally or knew them in the collective sense as a high-risk population working against the odds. My desire to see the audience wowed by the peer educators' technical skills came from my own egotistical desire to have my own professional skills recognized. I was happy that, in the end, they all looked like trained dancers to me. After this last piece, the dancers returned to the stage, greeted by raucous applause, for a brief Q-and-A session.

The entire performance was a collaborative creation between the peer educators and the audience, who like ethnographers, acted as participant observers. I knew that no matter how long a dancer practices, the actual performance may look very different from rehearsal. The Q-and-A session was an attempt by the peer educators to gain some control over the performance space. In case the audience missed the intended message embedded in the choreography or the poem, the session would allow the peer educators to present themselves as they had intended to do. Each dancer introduced herself and talked about why she had become a part of the Move Experiment and the meaning behind her solo piece. It was during this segment of the performance that the girls spoke directly to their mothers, babies' fathers, boyfriends, and family members, clarifying the messages that had gotten muddied up by the unpredictability of the performance. Louisa Schein offers this description of what occurs during a Miao dance performance: "It was, rather, a collective endeavor in which they [members of the audience], too, were participants. And for them culture was not an isolated object but something that their engaged spectatorship helped to constitute. Moreover, such engaged spectatorship became a social interaction, a personalized transaction between family and friends, all of whom derived pleasure from keeping the putative separation of stage and audience blurry" (1999, 380).

Although the audience's engagement in the show made for a joyful, celebratory space, this playfulness had the potential to undermine the seriousness of what the young women wanted to communicate. Thus, in her introduction, Ashley was able to tell her mother that her dance was a reflection of her independence, inner strength, and maturity—without being distracted by an unexpected slap on her backside. The other dancers also chose to use the session as a venue to re-present themselves and their creative works. Izetta talked about her Mexican American heritage and explained that having all of the girls dance together at the end symbolized the sense of community in her neighborhood. Izetta assumed that her friends and family members who lived in southwest Detroit could "feel her inspiration" and know where her dance was coming from, but she wanted to ensure that every person there was aware of her intention. Rachel, Sonya, and Crystal also talked about their choreographic process and the difference between rehearsals and what it felt like to dance on stage in front of an audience.

The distinction between the plan for the performance and the actual performance was the underlying theme of each girl's talk. In the case of Crystal and Ashley, it was used to apologize for the messiness of unintended behavior (freezing on stage and an overly interactive mother); for the other girls, it was a way to explain why their messages may not have been fully communicated in the way they were originally conceived. Realizing that it was impossible to maintain full control over how their dancing bodies were experienced by the audience, they instead tried to control how they were perceived as individual speaking bodies verbally filling in what they feared were the gaps left by their dance: the spoken word seemed potentially more reliable than the audience's readings of their bodies. The Move Experiment had become another type of home space for the peer educators in that it was a place where they could extend the tradition of public talk by working through their concerns and contemplating the choices they could make to address them. Although, as Paul Gilroy tells us, "it is nothing new to declare that music, gesture, and dance are forms of communication just as important as the gift of speech for black people" (1991, 113), the type of public talk within the Move Experiment (and seen operating in the shelter as a form of solidarity building and self-healing therapy) became a part of the postperformance discussion as a way to supplement the communicative power of music, gesture, and dance; the Q-and-A session became another way of establishing interactive performance.

BlackLight

Janice's participation in the Move Experiment was limited to being in the audience. She sat next to Gwen as the other young women performed and assisted with the sound system during the harried moments between the individual and group performances. It was now three months after the show. GGC was trying to locate funding to continue the project, and the Move Experiment was in an official hiatus. Rachel and Ashley had moved out of the shelter into their own apartments a month after the performance, and Sonya had discharged herself to move in with her boyfriend a few days after the show. She had returned to the shelter a month later, only to discharge herself again after a few days to move in with a new friend she had met working at the new Tigers' stadium. Izetta was kept busy with a densely packed school schedule and a host of after-school activities. Crystal was now a street-based peer educator in the Community

Outreach Program. I was no longer the shelter director, but I still spent a great deal of time at the agency assisting Camille and the shelter staff with the process of interviewing my replacement and developing a transition plan. By this time, Janice had been a Fresh Start resident for a little over two months after leaving the Job Corps.

Janice; her fifteen-year-old younger cousin, Bettina; her new best friend, Noni; and I had been meeting once a week for the past few weeks, mainly to take the dance classes I taught and to play around with choreography. Janice had met Noni in her music appreciation class at Wayne State University, where they bonded over the fact that the professor had mentioned Janice's uncles in class, and that they both seemed to appreciate music more than the professor. The young women spent most of their time off campus, at Noni's church on the east side of Detroit in Bible study, watching the toddlers during the weekday services, or facilitating one of the youth discussion groups. Their new task, once Janice mentioned that she loved to dance and had taken classes before, was to assist the youth praise dance team with new choreography.

"How did that go?" Bettina, Crystal's cousin, was offering her rendition of Crystal's solo. She kept her feet glued to the ground and put her arms out stiffly in front of her and moved her hips imperceptibly. Noni had not been at the performance, but she laughed with Janice anyway because Bettina looked so comical. Bettina took dance classes on a regular basis at school and was a talented dancer by any standard. She wasn't interested in choreographing but was eager to learn any new movement or sequence phrase we made up for her. Janice would mainly tell rather than show Bettina the most intricate shapes to make with her body, and we would all watch in amazement as she spun and wiggled and kicked her way through some of the most ridiculous requests.

"We should stop playing," Noni piped up in between Bettina and Janice's chuckles. "The praise team meets tomorrow and they expect us to have some new moves."

"Tired of trying to bring new steps." Janice was sober now. "It doesn't matter what you are doing if you can't dance from the heart. How you gonna be dancing for God and not feel something?"

"Come on, J," Noni said. "They young. They don't even know what they feel yet. It'll start to come through the dance once they understand what praise is."

Bettina took off the bandana tied around her head and started leaping through the air, waving the small square of fabric like a prayer cloth. She stopped in the middle of the room, put one hand on her hip and raised the other one with the bandana over her head, shaking her arm in rhythm with her bobbing head. Her body appeared to be convulsing as if waves of emotion were flowing from the ground through her feet and up through every part of her body. She shouted, "Yes, Jesus!," gave one last strong wave, and melted to the ground.

"Not funny. Like so not funny." Noni was visibly upset.

Janice tried to look serious as she tapped Bettina on the back with her foot. "Girl, get the hell up!"

"All I'm saying, Noni, is that I think that shit is backwards"—Janice caught herself—"I mean that stuff is backwards to me. You gotta know what you are trying to say before you say it. That's like getting into a fight and not knowing why you beating somebody's ass—I mean, you know— fighting battles with the wrong weapons or something like that." Janice's analogies were getting worse and frustrating Noni, who despised curse words and professed nonviolence. "I mean," Janice tried again, "the whole point of being an artist, whatever your art is, is to say something that you feel and make somebody else feel it, too."

Meeting over the next few weeks, we continued to dance and started to write, but mostly we talked about how we tried to both live in and understand the world. We disagreed a lot and used the luxury of the unfunded and, therefore, unpoliced space to revel in the process of creating without an expected output or outcome. Before one of our sessions, Janice bumped into her sister, Crystal, in the GGC lobby.

"Her attitude is so trifling. I don't understand why can't nobody in any of these programs help her with that. She horrible. Who she supposed to be reaching out to in street outreach and she that stank?" This interaction sparked a conversation among the four of us—Janice, Bettina, Noni, and me—about the purpose of what we were doing and why we were meeting. Was it just to see each other or get exercise? Was it really about finding new material for the praise team? Or was there a larger, more amorphous purpose? The goal, these young women decided, was to merge the creative activities of the Move Experiment with a political awareness that extends beyond the self. Our conversations since we had begun meeting informally covered themes that included creative expression, self-transformation, community accountability, and spirituality for starters, and Janice and Noni in particular wanted to lead a program of their own that encapsulated these concerns. Janice convinced a few of the shelter residents to join our conversation/dance/writing sessions.

And even though they were disgruntled at first when they realized that this was no longer the "dance classes that paid," we averaged three to four residents in addition to Janice every time we met.

"So, what should we call ourselves?" Janice stood over the seven young women who had gathered that day, as they sat around a piece of butcher paper the length and width of one of their bodies. Each person had a different color marker in her hand and was writing words to use in potential names of our group. I had stepped out of the circle a while ago, when my attempts at clever acronyms had been deemed too corny. *Girls, Women, Hot Hunnys, Fight the Power, Speak out, Hear Me, Listen Up, Shut Up! Dance This!, Dat Crew, God's Girls, Moving Thru, Move Somethin!, Lift, Ain't No Stopping Us, FLY, Fresh 2 Death, Flow, Magic Makers, Young Divas, Queens*, and other words and phrases that appeared to contradict or even cancel out each other covered the paper like pieces of bright, flavorful candy. Some of the young women stood up and started to walk along the perimeter of the banner-size paper, looking for something to stand out and draw them in.

Then from one end of the scroll a young woman called out, "Light! I like that. Whoever wrote that over here, I like that. We need that somewhere in the name."

"BlackLight," Janice said the name as if it had already been decided and stepped back to find a clean space to write. In bold block letters with a black Sharpie, she wrote BlackLight in a diagonal line in the middle of the paper in between the other colorful words. She capitalized both the B and the L and closed the space between them.

"BlackLight."

"Black Light?"

"Black . . . light . . . hmmm."

"BlackLight."

Every girl tried the name out in her own voice and own way. And then someone said, "We got it." That proclamation was followed by a surge of corroborating yeses.

The next task was to explain why those two words, *black* and *light*, resonated so strongly with every young woman in the room. After much editing and only a few arguments, they decided on this: "We are BlackLight. We take back the word *Black* and the way it has been used to describe all things bad, secret, broke-down, and ugly and combine it with *Light* to describe the reality of blackness as an illuminator. BlackLight is the truth that darkness reveals. Flippin' the script on who we are and what we can be. We are BlackLight."

Experiments in Space

Over the next two years, the number of participants in BlackLight would swell to as many as ten and shrink to as few as three. But Janice and Bettina were always involved. Unlike the Move Experiment, there was no formal audition process, employment agreement, financial compensation, or set of agreed-on goals that needed to be met by a certain grant period. The young women who flowed in and out of Blacklight collectively imagined and enacted their participation as if it were a project-by-project performance company. Although we held regular meeting times twice a week, our locations shifted from GGC to any free and safe space I could locate in the city. The Community Outreach Program secured funding to reinstate the Move Experiment as one of its core outreach programs and was able to begin paying young women as peer educators who used dance and other creative modalities to teach other young women about self-esteem, self-care, and healthy choices. Most of these young women were not shelter residents but lived in the community surrounding GGC and were younger (fifteen to seventeen) than the original Move Experiment members. Crystal told me that she felt as if the "new" Move Experiment was "a joke" because they weren't "really performing." However, Izetta came back to assist with training the new peer educators and felt that it was great that GGC was serious about maintaining a program that tried to "see young women as artists" and that "used the performing arts as a way to help girls live healthier lives." If this was the focus of the new Move Experiment, I wondered how Janice, Bettina, Noni, and the other young women who participated for as short a time as a week or as long as two years envisioned the scope of their unpaid work with BlackLight.

Kevin Young states that "like Negro heaven before it, the blackness of space, its vastness and unexplored quality, represents a powerful and intuitive critique of the earthbound, blues-based lives we live" (2012, 298) and sees the perpetual interaction between space and bodies as "experiment, recreation, and speculation" calling space "a series of fragmented selves, a place of possibilities and debris and explorations and atmosphere" (ibid.). Perhaps even more so than the Move Experiment, which included trial and error in its name, BlackLight was a testing of the boundaries of the body and the reciprocity between bodies and the spaces they move through, shift, and occupy. Expanding on the movement- and text-based work of the Move Experiment, the primary creative technique used in

Blacklight combined group discussions, choreography, fiction and nonfiction writing, and performance poetry.

A typical session began with an open discussion of the concerns and issues currently dominating each of the young women's lives. Robin, the discussion leader, would then tease out some of the common themes in the individual stories and facilitate a group dialogue that asked the young women to consider the ways in which their concerns might be linked to larger events in their local, and even global, communities. For example, Janice would discuss her difficulties focusing in class and completing her work when she had so many other familial and work obligations. Fatimah would express her fear that her older sister was going to lose her job because the commute from her house to work took close to two hours by bus, and that was only if the bus was operating according to schedule. Noni would talk about how great things were going for her in school now that she had found someone from the church who could watch her mother in the evenings, so that she could stay on campus and work on group projects and attend events. Bettina would mention still feeling unsafe making her way to BlackLight meetings from school and looking for yet another route to walk. Robin would take the reins and encourage the group to think about the factors that affected their ability to do the things that make them feel safe and happy. Structural realities such as the ineffective public transit system in the city and the lack of jobs close to where the young women and their families live in Detroit were presented as very real obstacles that influenced how they all thought about their ability to generate income and move freely through the city.

Robin would also challenge the group to think about the ways they had already started to create solutions and how they might identify other strategies for circumventing obstacles. Fatimah would point out that Noni's decision to ask for help through the relationships she developed in her church was an example of how essential networks are to working through difficulties. Their other challenges, everyone agreed, would require efforts beyond themselves and necessitate the mobilization of all Detroiters. After the group discussion, the participants would take time to write in response to the conversation. Their journal entries could take whatever form they liked and could raise additional questions related to the themes discussed, start mapping out a solution, or move to an entirely different issue.

Fatimah chose to write a poem about her sister's trials with the bus system and stood up to read it to the group.

Rain Wind Hot Sun and Snow
all the seasons pass by
and
She is still
HERE
On this spot
Waiting
Waiting
Waiting
but
her boss won't wait
and
by the time she arrives
it is always
too late
Turn right back around to go home again
But the No. 58 don't care about
your baby
your rent
or
you

Some of the other young women chose to share their writing, but others didn't. Those who preferred not to read started to clear the space for the movement portion of the session. This next phase could develop in multiple ways as the young women began to translate words (their own and each other's) into movement. On this particular day, Fatimah stood at the front of the room and read her poem again. Bettina closed her eyes and stood still the first time Fatimah read. She asked her to read again and this time began swaying to her words to find the embodied equivalences she was searching for in her arms, legs, feet, head, and torso. Janice started moving right away and seemed to be miming—looking for the exact expression in a word-to-gesture ratio. Robin, seated next to Fatimah with her notebook in hand, watched Bettina and Janice's movements before writing a new verse inspired by their movements, which, in turn, had been inspired by Fatimah's words. Robin then took Fatimah's place and read her prose, a fiery statement on the danger in public spaces for girls. Her minute-long monologue ended: "But we won't hide! But we can't hide!" She repeated the refrain several times, allowing her voice to rise and ride the swell of energy coming from the moving bodies of Bettina, Janice, and now Fatimah. Bettina dropped to the floor, covered her eyes, and rolled on her side. Janice, anticipating her movement, jumped over Bettina as she rolled toward her. Fatimah caught Janice from behind, wrapping her arms around Janice's waist as she completed her leap over Bettina. It was something to see. It was something to feel.

The layers upon layers of textual, verbal, and embodied translation continued like this for over an hour. I recorded as much of it as I could in my notebook, drawing stick figures when my words failed me in the moment. Winded and exhilarated, we made our way back into our circle to talk about what this process had exhumed. Bettina said that although moving to Robin's words made her feel fearless, she knew it was not going to be the case in a few days when she would have to face the reality of making the anxiety-producing walk from the bus stop again. Janice said that feeling Fatimah's arms around her after coming out of the leap she hadn't planned on taking until she was forced to by Bettina's moving body made her realize that there are some people who have her back, even if she doesn't always know they are there. She said something about how "feeling this in her body" made her less hesitant to ask her classmates and professors at Wayne State for help. This exercise did not improve the bus system in Detroit or bring more jobs to the center city. It did, however, provide an important experimental space for these young Black women to work through the ways in which they might take action and cultivate the sense of entitled worthiness that is part of their rights as residents of Detroit and citizens of the world.

As the young women in BlackLight and I started to make connections with other youth-serving organizations in Detroit engaged in innovative work with cultural production, arts practices, and social transformation, we gained access to additional venues to use this technique of embodied translation. We facilitated community workshops with participants from multiple generations on topics like the crisis in public education, corruption in city government, and the lack of safe public spaces in the city. The young women found that people do not need to define themselves as poets, writers, or dancers to employ creative strategies to confront persistent problems. They also found that, in fact, the process of allowing the body to respond to the words, ideas, and actions that take shape in space while generating new words, ideas, and actions may shift the very foundation of those spaces.

BlackLight shifted the body-in-space terms of the street itself and the bus stop in particular with a street theater exercise that Janice created. This was a riff on the performances that take place on subway platforms and sidewalks in cities like New York, Washington, and Chicago in which performers place hats or other receptacles in front of them to collect money while they sing, recite monologues, play the guitar, or impersonate Michael Jackson. The BlackLight performers made the bus stop their stage. Moving, singing, and performing their poetry, they would take over the canopied benches with their spectacle until they captured the attention of people waiting for the bus and passersby. At that point, one of the young women would give a signal and they would freeze in their tracks. One person in the small crowd would inevitably complain, request that the show go on, or at least ask what was happening while they were waiting for the bus. However, to see the rest of the performance, one of the audience members would have to reach into the hat placed in front of the stage. Instead of being empty and awaiting coins, the hat was filled with slips of paper covered with statistics on the current status of the city, quotes from elected officials, verses from poems about the city, and other information related to Detroit. Once the statement on the piece of paper was read aloud and the people gathered around responded to it, one of the Blacklight girls would facilitate a conversation between the Detroiters that replicated the work they accomplished in their Blacklight group sessions. The performance continued where it left off after the impromptu sidewalk symposium.

The Limits and Limitlessness of Shapeshifting, or How to Get Your Life!

Shapeshifters and *shapeshifting* are concepts typically employed in science fiction, folklore, fantasy, and even hip-hop imagery meant to refer to a generally involuntary altering or shifting of an individual physical body in reaction to an extreme or violent external force. Here we could imagine the comic-book character Luke Cage's transformation from a street kid, via an experimental procedure gone wrong while he was incarcerated for a crime he did not commit, to a being with superhuman strength and steel-like skin impervious to pain. Cage uses his new abilities to become a hero for hire, solving crimes and mysteries with the aid of his newly acquired mutant attributes. It is interesting to note here, and not at all disconnected from understanding how shapeshifting is used to contextualize the stories of the young women in this book, that Cage was one of the first African American characters who emerged during the 1970s blaxploitation trend in the comics, and that his character was controversial because of the perception by many in the Black community that he was intentionally presented as stereotypically thuggish in his comportment and speech. Although there are other examples of characters like Luke Cage in science fiction, as well as performers in other fantastical realms who embody shapeshifting, the example that resonated most with the young women in the Fresh Start shelter was Martha Washington.

During one of the BlackLight working sessions, the young women were, as usual, discussing the challenges, large and small, that they tackle on a daily basis. This somewhat mundane conversation moved into a hilarious, overtly competitive debate about their individual "powers" and the fact that they were indeed, in many ways, everyday superheroes. The lively dialogue inspired spontaneous online research on Black female superheroes. They were fueled by nervous excitement and the thought that it probably was not possible to find a Black woman superhero online and sought a representation of themselves that was otherworldly in ways that allowed them to courageously think beyond the confines of Fresh Start, educational programs, the love and troubles of their estranged families, and the daily judgments they encountered in all of these realms they were forced to ironically identify as safe or home spaces. Through their search they found Martha Washington, created by Frank Miller in 1990 in a series published by Dark Horse Comics.

Martha Washington—reared on the South Side of Chicago, brown-skinned, poor, and fearless because she had to be—became the Fresh Start residents' superlative version of themselves. Unlike traditional superheroes, Martha does not have extraordinary powers conferred by some mystical force, nor does she visually appear as anything other than a Black girl (and in later works in the series, a Black woman). In this Black girl who survived the Cabrini-Green housing project and all attempts on her life, the young women in BlackLight saw not only who they could be, but who they believed they already were. Self-knowledge, a keenly attuned barometer for justice, spot-on intuition, unconditional love for her community, and the fierce fighting spirit of the perpetual underdog are Martha's superpowers. She uses them to confront the conservative policies of the governing right-wing administration that has destroyed her family and threatens to make her low-income Black community disappear.

Martha Washington's resonance with the young women as a rare embodiment of superheroism in "everyday" Black femaleness is complicated by the circumstances of her production and commodification. Although the characteristics that define Martha are uncommon, and therefore noteworthy, in the hypermasculine, typically white world of comics, the progressive intent assumed in the young women's and even my own initial reading of Martha become challenged by her placement in a body of work by a comic-book creator known to include misogynistic, homophobic, and—more recently—anti-Islamic subtexts in his narratives.[15] Certainly, it is no surprise that Martha is appealing as a model of transformative possibilities in the context of BlackLight. Martha and the young women's response to her, in fact, inspired the concept of shapeshifting that is central to this ethnographic analysis. In the interest of engaging the potential of shapeshifting as theory and praxis, I find it helpful to consider shapeshifting through a comparison of Martha Washington and the writing of Octavia Butler.

Martha Washington is situated in a historical and geographic context that mimics the 1980s Reagan era of economic disinvestment and political disenfranchisement in overwhelmingly African American urban centers. Race, gender, and class are central to reading Martha as a phenomenal character in the context of the already fantastical realm of comic-book heroes. Even though in subsequent volumes in the series, Martha engages in warfare with aliens and is temporarily cognitively altered through computer technology, she is always Black and female. Her travels may be intergalactic, but her political battles remain entrenched in the oppressions and abuses of power formed in our global economy. Martha's battle begins in the south side of Chicago and eventually extends across imaginary planets and stratospheres that disrupt the concepts of space and time. Yet Martha is ultimately an economically challenged, politically savvy, Black woman born and reared in a poor, urban part of the United States, regardless of how many spaces she finds herself in to challenge readers' imaginative faculties.

Octavia Butler, an African American writer of science fiction and the recipient of a MacArthur Fellowship, wrote over a dozen novels in her lifetime investigating, among other things, the capacity to connect, build affective communities, and sustain love without the realism of our discernible borders around bodies, identities, and geographies. Through brilliantly articulated temporal and spatial reconfigurations, Butler renders race and gender, sexuality and desire, inherently mobile. In fact, within the continually shifting bodies of her characters and warped renditions of space and time, the notion of fixed identity becomes not only irrelevant but ludicrous. In order to enter Butler's texts, the reader is asked to grapple with questions of motivation, intention, character, spirit, and morality that shape what it means to be human. Race, power, gender, and capital are recurring themes across Butler's novels and short stories, but in the shapeshifting of the protagonists' bodies and the transcendence of identity markers related to space and time (the overriding of a fixed way of being or of geography) and their consequences are stripped down and made bare as definitively constructed through social and cultural processes. Women like Anyanwu, the protagonist in *Wild Seed* (1980), do not show up in a simple Google search for superheroes, yet they are true shapeshifters in that they move outside of their Black female bodies to take the shape of the human or animal form that will allow them to actualize their motivations and ensure their safety at any moment. Shifting from white male colonial landowner to dolphin, then to a soaring eagle and back to a young Black woman, Anyanwu transitions in her body, altering its shape, while immortally existing in these various forms.

Shapeshifting as it differently occurs in the Martha Washington series and in the work of Octavia Butler speaks, I believe, to the limits and limitlessness of performance. Shapeshifting here also speaks to the unpredictable but almost certain losses and failures that are just as central to the politics of the body and its attendant embodied theories and practices of resistance as the possibility of productive shifting. Outside of the worlds that Miller and Butler imagine in the space between their book covers and on cinematic screens, their image as public figures affects my reading of shapeshifting. Miller situates Martha in a comic-book world as well as in the context of his other work that, in itself, does not generally allow inclusion for her kind. What might it mean that a white, apparently politically conservative male writer envisions and subsequently brings Martha to life? What might Miller intend in Martha's resistance to political hegemony and capitalist greed? And in what ways might it ultimately matter if she is not only legible to, but seemingly emboldens, the young Black women residents of a homeless shelter in Detroit, Michigan? Both Miller and Butler demonstrate that practices of resistance are always tied to larger processes of capital and commodification and formed within spaces of contradiction that make easy evaluations of their success or failure nearly impossible.

The magical, malleable science fiction landscape Octavia Butler creates can never be realized, and therefore the impact of her brand of shape-shifting lies more in Butler's contributions as an artist creating against the norm in a genre that had no room for her vision. In answer to the question of why she started writing, Butler responded, "I wanted to write myself in."[16] It is this act of commanding space to shift, to open up in a response to a creative vision, that is aligned with the social choreography and performance arts practices of young Black women. Reading the social evaluations leveled at them through various public discourses and developing strategies that sustain their own visions of themselves are ways of writing themselves in.

The streets of Detroit provided a troubling and contradictory space for the young Black women in this book. As walkers and bus riders traversing neighborhoods often by themselves and at night, they found that the city streets were sites of potential danger and unpredictability. The challenge of moving around the city without a car, from home or shelter to job or school, added another layer of difficulty to achieving the goal of completing educational programs and holding down jobs. The young women in BlackLight repurposed the street and the possibilities for being in public through their bus stop performances as well as through the ways they created, performed, and encouraged others to perform community in public forums outside of GGC. The collective performance practices that young women like Janice, Robin, and Bettina shared with a willing public give testimony to Rosemary Roberts's assertion that "inequality/racism is not only encountered in linguistic forms or ideas and perception, it is also encountered intimately and provocatively in and through individuals as well as between bodies" (2013, 8). BlackLight was an intentional expansion of the Move Experiment's self-conscious focus on the body and its visual and representational excess. The Move Experiment peer educators located their expressive voices in the awareness of themselves and their bodies as both socially defined problem and self-defined solution, and their realization that the former made the latter nearly impossible. The tensions in the shelter around the Move Experiment's viability as a program came not just from a concern about the economic stability of the performance art model, but also from an overriding nervousness about what it might mean for young women to pay such close attention to themselves, their bodies, how they feel, what they desire, and the ways they can express all of these things and teach others to do the same. The Move Experiment felt too much like self-experimentation verging on self-love, and self-love in this sense called forth images of narcissism and selfishness among some of the Fresh Start staff members. There is a self-love, however, embedded in the theory and practice of Black feminist politics that reflects a more sincere version of this essential practice in the lives of the peer educators and, later more fully articulated, in the work of BlackLight.

Black feminists, particularly among what Jennifer Nash identifies as certain sectors of "second wave" Black feminism, advocated "love as a resistant ethic of self-care" (2011, 3). Scholar and artist activists like June Jordan, Chela Sandoval, bell hooks, Patricia Collins, and, perhaps most famously, Alice Walker have addressed self-love as a practice essential to collective liberation. This love is a self-love not to be confused with sentimentality, New Age philosophy, or "the end of political work, believing that once the self is taken care of the world will be too" (Wanzo 2005, 83). Self-love must first emerge from "a self that recognizes the limitations of selfhood, a self prepared for a certain kind of radical curiosity about the social world . . . an active working on the self, preparing it for the labor of social engagement, and for the task of advocating for the survival and wholeness of entire people" (Nash 2013, 10). The creative work that emerged from both the Move Experiment and BlackLight began with each young woman seeing herself (through multiple lenses), defining (and redefining) herself, and making the conscious effort to commit to the praxis of loving herself. Establishing self-love as the last goal in their eight-point plan for the Move Experiment meant that even if they fell short in their self-care practices, they were equipped with the tools to show others how to care for themselves. In this case, that meant leading meditation and self-care workshops for GGC staff members and participants and caring for Crystal even, or especially, when she was at her most intolerable. Self-love should not mean, as Ashley reminded us in her concluding remarks to the discussion following the meditation workshop, "holding it together" or thinking outside of yourself to the point of self-sacrifice. That is the superwoman dictate or Sojourner syndrome that Ashley defines as "that unhealthy shit." Martyrdom and self-love are not the same, and empathy and social transformation are not the same, because the ethic of self-love that ultimately engenders "political communities rooted in a radical ethic of care" (Nash 2013, 14) occurs through action.

In the brilliant essay "Apocalyptic Empathy," Rebecca Wanzo explores the ways in which Octavia Butler wrestles in *Parable of the Sower* with the relationship between empathy and political work through the character

Lauren Oya Olamina, who suffers from hyperempathy. Olamina and her community members are defined as outsiders and deviants, and although they are technically liberated, they labor in what is essentially slavery under structural conditions in which they are granted very little political power and are under constant threat of physical harm. Although Butler presents empathy as a positive and necessary attribute for transformative political work, she does not advance the idea that it is the end of political work. In fact, Olamina must ultimately learn how to "distance herself from feeling in order to survive and get political work done" (Wanzo 2005, 75). Empathy and connectivity through and across bodies and affects ground the embodied creative practices in BlackLight. This enables Fatimah's words to become Bettina's choreography, allows Janice to trust the hands that catch her, and compels the reaching out of the hands that grasp her before she realizes she might fall. This embodied and transferred empathy was also cultivated in the workshops BlackLight facilitated in the city and among the street theater audiences. As central as connections and relationships were to these young women, whether as fleeting as a touch or eye contact made during a workshop or as enduring as the love between sisters, the ever-present inquiry, "Do you *feel* me?" was meaningless if nothing productive was done with that feeling. Similar to Olamina, the young women of BlackLight found themselves embedded in sociopolitical contexts that highlighted the terms of their limited and conditional citizenship. They also worked through and beyond the space of empathy to do the shapeshifting political work of creating spaces to challenge these terms and imagine more life-affirming possibilities.

Katherine McKittrick writes: "It seems eerily natural that those rendered less than human are also deemed too destroyed or too subjugated, or too poor to write, imagine, want, or have a new lease on life" (2011, 955). When I was living in Detroit, and even now when I talk about the young women in this book, *possibilities, future, creation, love, care,* and *courage* are the words that I give the most space in my sentences. *Homelessness, poverty, violence, exploitation, danger,* and *racism* are the words that most people hear. Our failures to articulate and witness Black life—and, in particular, Black girlhood—as a dynamic, creative space continually being remade in the future tense have grave consequences. These failures prevent us from excavating the anticolonial practices that will rescue us from the life-snatching, capital-obsessed present and the human suffering it causes. Along with Henri Lefebvre (1974), Janice, Izetta, Noni, Bettina, Summer, and the many other young women who act as shapeshifters understand that space is organized through human activity, relational action, and the exercise of bodies. Thus, like the dances they choreograph, the institutional and social spaces they occupy are continually being remade through their activities. In the middle of choreographing a dance, Janice may pause to allow the flow of Bettina's words or the sound from the CD player to move her in a different direction than she anticipated. Where this improvisational interlude will lead her is unknown, but what is certain is that she will at least not remain in the same place.

The unknown and the unpredictable hold the potential for the esoteric work of soul fortifying and spirit lifting and their practical applications in transformative policies and legislation. But we have to imagine this as just the beginning. If we, like the Brown girls, want to map a different world, we have to use all our faculties to imagine life that is not beholden to the state and controlled through capitalism. As the shapeshifters create new publics and remap Detroit streets as sites for performance, networks of care, and spaces for open critique, they force a renegotiation of the "contract of citizenship," or what Mark Purcell explains as Lefebvre's belief in "the possibility of recapturing a revolutionary potential for the project of rights" (2014, 146). Through the contract of citizenship, rights are not abandoned but are conceptualized as the shifting and malleable outcomes of political struggle. And because rights are the result of struggle, they are "always subject to further struggle, to renewed political agitation" (ibid.). In this way, it may be appropriate to anticipate the demise of the narcoleptic struggly in favor of a struggle with the potential to continually rejuvenate and reorient itself to chart new alternatives. It is an optimistic goal. But shapeshifters are, by nature, optimists. Shapeshifters must always stay on the side of change, possibility, movement, and the future, or they would not be so adept at shifting the normative shapes and spaces that threaten their (and our) lives. Shapeshifters must be optimists, or they wouldn't be able to make themselves and others whole in the face of narratives and practices meant to fragment, disembody, scatter, and confuse them. Shapeshifters must be optimists, or they wouldn't be able to "get your life," as Bettina liked to call out when someone was dancing exceptionally well—meaning they were feeling it and unconcerned about how they looked. The cultural anthropologist and former dancer Jafari Allen defines getting your life in this way: "To get your life means to recover something that you profoundly need—perhaps parts of yourself, gathered together for once. All laid together side by side. To find a deep and authentic truth of existence. Getting your life means stepping outside of your current pretension to a life to see where yours may be hiding—what grace you might imagine, then help others to see" (2012, 252). When shapeshifters get their life, they remember the body and spirit of their seven-year-old selves fighting to be freed; they collect their too much, too loud, too visible selves and use this wonderful excess to claim more space, take up more room; they use their Blackness, recovered from bleach and renovations as the illuminator, "the truth that darkness reveals."

Epilogue

"So, what did you think?" I was sweating through my clothes, my mouth was dry from talking for over an hour, and I was anxious to hear what Janice thought of my presentation on Fresh Start and BlackLight. A small midwestern university had invited me to give a keynote lecture for a conference during Women's History Month, and the event organizer wondered if I was still in touch with any of the young women from Detroit who might be able to join me during the three days I would be in residence, visiting classes and giving talks about the implications of my research. Since Janice and I had worked closely on BlackLight in the years following my departure from the shelter and she had instituted her version of the project at her church, I asked if she was available. I was also eager to see her again in person and facilitate the BlackLight workshops with one of its founding members. In the years between the time we had spent at Fresh Start and this campus visit, we frequently talked about the shelter, our thoughts on the work that emerged there in the form of the Move Experiment and BlackLight, and the experiences that she and other young Black women continued to have in Detroit.

Janice read parts of the manuscript for this book and knew "the work" more intimately than I did because it is or was her life—or at least a version of her life seen through both of our lenses, which had become clouded by memory, love, regret, and a resounding desire to say something that mattered beyond ourselves, Fresh Start, and even Detroit.

Because of these factors, all mitigated by the fact that by now I considered Janice my sister, I hoped I hadn't gotten it wrong in her eyes during this first time she would hear me talk about BlackLight in front of a large audience of academics and undergraduate students. Although I was not talking specifically about the Brown family or Janice as my main interlocutor, I was giving voice and applying theory to the experiences we had shared. I thought this might also be complicated by the fact that Janice only stayed at Wayne State University for a semester, was now attending classes intermittently at Wayne County Community College, and expressed regrets about the fears that had prevented her from giving herself permission to succeed at a four-year university, which would have likely altered the trajectory of her life.

"What? Oh, my God!" Janice responded with more excitement than I had anticipated. "I was, like, sitting there like, 'Oh, that did happen!' and 'I forgot about that one time.' I was about to cry."

I can't say if I was seeking Janice's approval or critique or how I expected her, one of the young Black women I have written so extensively about, to respond to Black girlhood as a site of analysis. Samantha, the graduate student who was assisting me with the continuation of the BlackLight work in Newark, New Jersey, seemed surprised at her enthusiasm, since Janice maintained a confident cool for the majority of our time together on this unfamiliar, rural campus. I kept reminding myself that Janice and Samantha were the same age, twenty-three; Janice was, in fact, a few months older than Samantha. This trip provided the first opportunity for Janice to fly, and she worried about getting lost in the airport and not finding us in time to meet for our connecting flight. Although Janice and I were both excited about the campus visit and the chance to cofacilitate BlackLight workshops again in a new space, the event had different meanings and consequences for each of us.

Since the beginning of my time at Fresh Start, I knew that the success of this project would hinge on the willingness of the young Black women I encountered to let me share their lives and bear witness to their experiences, as well as to the ways in which they analyzed the intimate and broader implications of these experiences. Theorizing about young Black women while my primary source watched from the front row, however, highlighted the currency that can be accrued through Black girls' narratives even while the girls themselves are perpetually devalued. I fully realize that I owe my career to Janice, the Brown family, and all of the other young women at Fresh Start. This is an important point to make, I believe, as we (the researchers, practitioners, activists, and educators invested in the lives and livelihood of vulnerable young people of color) often build names and gain visibility from the cultural and intellectual labor of incredibly brave and incisive young people with the most to lose. I offer this observation not as a way to elicit guilt but as a segue into thinking about how the projects we try to get funded, the classes and workshops we run, the marches we organize, and the words we write might be more useful to the young people who are our subjects and whom we often assist in mobilizing as community leaders and visible political actors.

Soo Ah Kwon (2013) asks what it means to promote youth as political actors when they are not of voting age. This opens space for adults engaged in projects like BlackLight to think about the enduring positive outcomes of political work, even—or especially—in the cultural and creative realms, beyond the development of leadership skills or self-esteem. The young women involved in BlackLight's street theater events and workshops were establishing a new public where the most decentered Detroiters (those most likely to be at a bus stop, waiting for a bus that may not ever come) could cocraft dialogical spaces to address the points of stress that mark their relationship to one another and the city. These young Black women were also being asked, if only implicitly, to take responsibility for enacting community in the city spaces and with social actors who rarely prioritize their well-being and safety.

"What would you rather she be doing?" Lynnette asked me over the phone, after I gave her the latest update on Janice's life. It was less than a month before the final revisions of this manuscript were due, and I was giving Lynnette my regular update on the Brown girls. I had just told her that Janice was immersed in her church and still unemployed. She had not, in fact, held a traditional job since just before she made presentations at the midwestern university with me almost four years earlier. Janice was waiting for her pastor to sponsor her admission into a theological program affiliated with his church so that she would be allowed to minister. In the meantime, she was living with and helping care for Noni's partially blind mother, since Noni had recently married and was living with her husband on the other side of the city. Janice still maintained a Section 8 apartment near Give Girls a Chance but preferred to stay on the west side with Noni's mother, where there was "always some activity, kids around, and stuff to help out with."

"Well, she is almost finished with her American Sign Language classes and really excited about finding work as a translator," I told Lynnette. "She said signing feels like dancing. You, apparently, aren't doing it right unless your whole body is involved."

"Okay, so what's the problem?" Lynnette probed. "I hear it in your voice. Something you don't like about that?"

"No. I think the certification will be wonderful for her," I said. "I guess, on the real, and I don't mean this in a judgmental way, but how has she been unemployed for four years? I mean she is still eating and paying her cell phone bill the same way she was right after she left the shelter."

"Right," Lynnette said, "by doing hair, babysitting, and looking after adults with special needs. So, she makes money on her own while she's taking classes on something that feels creative to her and is exciting?"

"I know." I was less interested in proving a point than thinking through the nature of work and success with Lynnette, as I had always been since the time we first met thirteen years ago. "It just seems like precarious income, I guess."

"And these other nonexistent jobs out here are stable?" Lynnette made us both laugh at the seeming ridiculousness of my concern. "Dang, she sound like a social entrepreneur to me. I ain't at all mad at any of it." Lynnette was enrolled in a twelve-week social entrepreneur class where she was learning how to promote her package of self-love artifacts for women, which included the peace pictures she was still taking, her fashion line, and the latest iteration of her Inner Circle workshops. The classes were offered through one of many nonprofit entities that had coalesced around the possibility of the city's revitalization through homegrown talent. She had already produced several fashion shows around Detroit and returned to the shelter a few times since she resigned as a resident advisor to take photographs of the residents and staff.

"Oh, and she's working on two books," I was adding to the list of Janice's creative projects. "A coloring book where the main characters are crayons who teach children that no one can tell them who they are or what their purpose is in life. The main character is the color purple, who ultimately figures out that her purpose is to express royalty and offer praise."

"Well, all right now," Lynnette was amused and impressed. "What's the other book about?"

"It's an advice book for girls based on interviews she's conducting with older women," I said.

"Oh, wow, she didn't ask to interview me," Lynnette was performing offense. "Did she ask you?"

I was silenced for a second by the question. "No, as a matter of fact, she hasn't." We both laughed at our vanity before ending the conversation.

The week before I left Detroit for the East Coast, I was scrambling to help Janice's cousin, Bettina, obtain all of her high-school records and financial paperwork to determine if she might be eligible for the program at Wayne State in which Janice had briefly participated. It was late July, and Bettina, up until that point, had assumed that her high-school teachers had handled the massive amounts of paperwork required for the intensive application process on her behalf. She and I were both stunned to find out that she had no application on file and would not be attending school in the fall. Bettina, Janice, Noni, and I had been working together all summer on BlackLight, and it was becoming more evident by the day to all of us that Bettina was a stunning, exceptionally talented dancer with the potential to earn a professional dancing contract. Her plans to study at Wayne State also included auditioning for their prestigious dance program.

At the end of a long day of talking to the counselors and vice principal at Bettina's school and trying to locate documentation at both Bessie's and Donna's homes, I sat down to a glass of wine at the restaurant and bar in the building where I lived in the Cass Corridor, within walking distance from Wayne State. As I retold a friend the frustrating details of Bettina's apparently failed bid for college, I noticed the man seated behind her was paying unusually close attention to our conversation, particularly when I launched into the details of Bettina's talent as a dancer and choreographer.

"Excuse me, did you need something?" I was annoyed now as this stranger leaned in closer.

"Oh, no, I am sorry." He extended his hand. "It was hard not to hear what you were saying. I think I can help." The man introduced himself to me as the president of a very small liberal arts college in northern Detroit and said that if Bettina and I came by the next day he would do "everything possible" to make sure that she was admitted to the college. Bettina was accepted into the liberal arts institution and was the first in the Brown family to graduate from college. Janice told me she was frustrated that she was the only one in her family, including Bettina, who seemed to feel that this was a big deal.

Bettina was, by all unbiased accounts, one of the most actively recruited and most frequently featured dancers in the college's dance program. Her professors believed she had the discipline and the talent to dance with any contemporary dance company in the country. Unfortunately, discipline and talent rarely buy plane tickets; cover the rent in cities like New York, Chicago, or Los Angeles; or pay for clothing and food, so for now Bettina is teaching ballet and contemporary dance classes at a studio in the suburbs of Detroit. Neither I nor the president of Bettina's college can take credit for getting Bettina into college: she, in the spirit of Octavia Butler, wrote and danced herself in.

The type of capital that accrues in spaces like the upscale restaurant in my building allow for chance meetings; exceptional narratives that are overheard precisely because they emerge from what appear to be unexceptional bodies; and deal making that turns on empathy, access to resources, and perhaps even a bit of self-aggrandizing interest. These locations, like Fresh Start and the streets of Detroit, are social and political spaces that are continually constructed by the actors who exist within their boundaries, while they are also continually legitimized and valued by those who are excluded.

"You know my next project is to get my family to communicate." Janice is talking rapidly to me on her cell phone, and I struggle to hear her through the spotty service. "I told my mama the other day that I am going to do her like Fresh Start did with that money. Paying them to act right." Janice paused. "Do you remember that?"

I remembered all too well. "Would you believe," I told her, "I found some of those bills the other day?" I had been going through files that contained old grant reports and field notes and had found a fuschia $20 bill and an orange $1 bill stuck together by their laminated sides.

"Yep." Janice didn't seem to hear me. "Well, I told her and Karlyn and them that I am going to pay them every time I hear somebody say 'I love you' or every time I catch somebody giving a hug."

"That could get expensive," I said.

"I doubt it," Janice laughed, "at least not right away. But, just in case, I'mma start making up fake money like y'all did so I won't be out nothing."

Notes

Preface

1. I use the terms *Black girls* and *young Black women* interchangeably. *Black girls* is how the young women in this text referred to themselves and one another. *Black girl* is also a very evocative term that calls up popular cultural notions of girlhood and its supposed attendant attitudes and behaviors in ways that can be alternately empowering and degrading. The Fresh Start residents, however, use *Black*—not *African American* or *West Indian American*—as a term of collective pride and signification. And *girl*, as one sixteen-year-old shelter resident told me, just flows better than *young woman*. Saying *young women* suggests that you are trying to be polite and official, but it sounds like you have done something wrong or are in trouble with authority figures. I use *Black girls* to respect the young women's self-definition and because it does flow better, and *young Black women* because I think it more often accurately describes the age range of the residents.

2. See Imani Perry's discussion of the power of stories to convey deeper social truths (2010, introduction).

3. There are important organizations and individuals across the country working on behalf of Black youth, and Black girls specifically. Their services include information gathering and dissemination, support services, artistic engagement, and skill building. Please explore the work undertaken by Cathy Cohen's Black Youth Project; the Crunk Feminist Collective's workshops for Black girls; Black Girls Code; the *Feminist Wire*'s Elementary Feminisms; Aisha Turman's Black Girl Project; Brotherhood/Sistersol; Reina Jerman's Black Girl Everything Project; Alexis Pauline Gumb's Indigo Geniuses, which is part of her larger project, Eternal Summer of the Black Feminist Mind;

and Ruth Nicole Brown's Solhot Project. Brown has also mentored a cohort of graduate students at the University of Illinois at Urbana-Champaign who are working on courageously innovative projects related to Black girls. We should all familiarize ourselves with their groundbreaking work.

Introduction

1. All names except for those of public figures have been changed.
2. Melissa Harris-Perry discusses the ways in which Black women in America must battle derogatory assumptions about themselves as individuals and as a collective in ways that show up in small and large events during their everyday lives. She makes the claim, which I support here in this ethnography on Black girls, that "the internal, psychological, emotional, and personal experiences of Black women are inherently political" (2011, 5).
3. There are a few time periods that will be referred to throughout the ethnography in terms of my time in Detroit. In 2000 I started volunteering at Fresh Start. I was hired as the shelter's director in 2001, and I stayed in that role until 2004. From 2004 until 2008 I stayed connected to Fresh Start through a consultancy, where I ran an arts program called the Move Experiment (as discussed in chapter 5), served on the board of the Give Girls a Chance agency, and worked with the former members of the Move Experiment to start BlackLight, a politically engaged creative arts project in Detroit.
4. I am thinking here of Cheryl Clarke's essay, "Lesbianism," in which she affirms: "So all of us would do well to stop fighting each other for our space at the bottom because there ain't no more room. We have spent so much time hating ourselves. Time to love ourselves" (1996, 160).
5. On the web forum for the Social Science Research Council (hosted at http://ya.ssrc.org/african/Cohen [2006]), Cathy Cohen cites the following statistics from the Department of Justice, the Centers for Disease Control and Prevention, and the Census Bureau: Although only 16 percent of the adolescent population in the United States was African American in 2001, that group accounted for nearly 50 percent of adolescents arrested for murder and 40 percent of young people in public and private juvenile detention facilities. In the United States, 51 percent of people ages 13–19 newly diagnosed with AIDS from 1981 to 2001, and 61 percent of people newly diagnosed in 2001, were African Americans, even though they accounted for only 16 percent of all young people ages 13–19. Nearly 30 percent of African Americans ages 18–24 had not completed high school, compared to 18 percent of white youth. And in August 2003, 30 percent of African Americans ages 16–19 were unemployed, compared to only 15 percent of white youth.
6. For example, the murders of Trayvon Martin and Renisha McBride were received very differently by the public at large and within the Black community. There was an immediate outcry about the murder of seventeen-year-old Trayvon Martin by George Zimmerman in February 2012 and a series of

large-scale public protests and acts of civil disobedience in cities across the United States. Zimmerman's acquittal on charges of second-degree murder and manslaughter led to increased attention paid to the plight of young Black men, and recommendations for policy responses came from legislators, academics, activists, and community members of various ethnic groups and generations. Renisha McBride was nineteen years old when she was shot in the face by a man in Dearborn Heights, Michigan, after she approached his house looking for assistance following a car accident. Renisha's killer, Theodore Wafer, was convicted in August 2014 and sentenced in September 2014 to seventeen years. Although the outcome through the legal system was very different after Renisha's murder compared to Trayvon's, the attention paid to her case has been far less than that paid to the Trayvon Martin case, and the language used to talk about the vulnerabilities of young Black women is severely underdeveloped in comparison to the analyses and rhetoric that surround the plight of young Black men. An exception in the case of Renisha McBride is an important piece by Noliwe Rooks, who asks why Black women are "seen as more threatening, more masculine, and less in need of help," and who answers "because they are not seen as women at all" (http://ideas.time.com/2013/11/14/renisha-mcbride-and-black-female -stereotype/).

7. President Obama announced this initiative in March 2014. The website tied to My Brother's Keeper states its mission as creating opportunities for boys and young men of color. This mission is one that the website also tells us "doesn't only benefit our kids facing tough circumstances" (http://www .nytimes.com/roomfordebate/2014/03/12). Statistics on the low reading proficiency levels and high murder rates of black and Latino male youth are also provided as part of understanding the issues faced by young men of color that a collaboration of foundations and private businesses in coordination with the federal government will address.

8. Five academics and writers besides Case, along with a representative from the Rockefeller Foundation, participated in this debate hosted by the *New York Times* online Opinion Pages' Room for Debate on March 12, 2014 (www .nytimes.com/roomfordebate/2014/03/12). The question they were asked by the *Times* was: "Does the initiative offer hope for young men or reinforce harmful stereotypes?"

9. I find Ruth Nicole Brown's view of the utility of the term *Black girlhood* appropriate for this project. Brown says that she deploys "Black girlhood as a political articulation that intentionally points to Black girls, even as I mean for Black girlhood to direct our attention beyond those who identify and are identified as Black girls" (2013, 7). This definition is particularly appropriate as it relates to the young women who participated in the Move Experiment (see chapter 5).

10. This term was developed by Deborah King, who considers the "interactive oppressions that circumscribe" Black women's lives (1988, 42).

11. Janice was a resident of the shelter for six months, and at one point after her discharge from the shelter she led workshops in the Early Start program.

12. Generation Z is the generation of people living in Western or First World cultures that follows Generation Y. Opinions differ on when the first members of Generation Z were born, ranging from 1990 to 2001, though a majority of experts opt for about 1996. Several other names have been used to refer to this population group, including Generation V (for virtual), Generation C (for community or content), the New Silent Generation, the Internet Generation, the Homeland Generation, and even the Google Generation.

13. Prevailing, Westernized constructions of adulthood promote the idea of a productive man who labors in ways that are directly tied to maintaining capitalism. For women, the proper and compliant lady is an ideal that generally evades behavioral possibilities for young Black women who are most often ideally cast as resourceful, strong, and capable of overcoming economic constraints. These normative ideals are, however, always dependent on what is called for in the current historical moment.

14. The can-do girl is aligned in many ways with the girl power ethos that compels girls—primarily white and middle class—to be strong, independent, and leaders in their communities without much discussion of what the expectations should be from their communities and the state in terms of caring for and protecting girls.

15. For an in-depth discussion of controlling images and their material impact, see Collins 2000.

16. This is a point that was driven home in the Moynihan report and taken up in popular representations of Black women and Black families.

17. It could be argued that the complexity of Black girlhood has been most sensitively captured in fiction. Toni Morrison's *The Bluest Eye* (1972) and Alice Walker's *The Color Purple* (1982) are widely read novels that made Black girls legible as central protagonists. The beauty and sorrow the Black girls in Morrison's and Walker's work experienced as part of their quotidian existence are aligned with larger structures of power that form the basis of Black Feminist critique. Perhaps the weighty and untenable circumstances of real Black girls, especially those living in poverty, garner more sympathy and less incredulity when the accounts can be categorized as imaginary or fictionalized. Yet Black women and girls continue to write fiction that begs us to see and deal with Black girls in real time and space. See less well known but no less vital works such as Jordan 1971; Shange 1982; Silvera 1996; T. Jones 2002 and 2011; Bandele 2003; Evans 2010.

18. *Uninterrupted* means that the young woman has stayed for a consecutive length of time. Some young women are discharged or leave the shelter on their own and then return if they find themselves homeless again. Case management, counseling, and skill building services continue for up to eighteen months after a young woman leaves residential services. Even though the cutoff age for services is twenty-two years and six months, young

women in need are never turned away without some assistance or a referral to other, more appropriate services.

19. An article on the fast-food industry in *Detroit News* (Maldonado 2003) during the summer of 2004 highlighted the industry's high turnover rates in the city. Employees refused to become invested in an industry that historically was not invested in them—in effect, treating them as easily consumable and disposable as the food they sold. An owner of a Church's Chicken restaurant in the Detroit area stated that "18 employees leave for every 10 employees" (Maldonado 2003) the chain hired in a year, while the Detroit Regional Chamber of Commerce reported that fast-food businesses employed 22,998 people at 789 restaurants in the Detroit metropolitan area. Given the relatively large number of people employed through the fast food industry, it benefitted the leaders within the fast food industry to take steps to improve recruitment and retention. Around 2003, Church's Chicken, White Castle, McDonald's, and Burger King started using benefits, training programs, and opportunities for promotion to retain workers. In an interesting repetition of the history of youth employment in the inner city, the fast-food industry attempted to solidify its economic base by offering what looked like the potential for movement up the economic ladder through training and self-improvement. During the pro-business 1950s the individual worker became the site for addressing the problem of poverty, unemployment, and unequal opportunities. The individual worker, not the social realities, was confronted, redressed, and quietly revolutionized. Organizations like the Urban League took part in the remaking of poor Blacks by directing a good portion of their resources to programs that developed the personal skills and modified the behaviors of those labeled as unskilled, uneducated, and unacceptable. At the same time, well-educated and highly skilled Blacks were supported in attaining white-collar or break-through jobs formerly held only by white employees, which further widened the growing divide between middle- and lower-class Blacks in the United States.

20. Detroit's schools during the 1980s and 1990s were another system that posed an obstacle to low-income youth rather than allowing them to progress. In the 1980s the schools' drop-out rate was 41–57 percent and, based on ACT scores, those young people who did manage to graduate were ill-equipped to compete in the world (Snider 1989). Blacks made up 90 percent of the students in the Detroit public school system during the late 1980s and early 1990s, and the two-thirds of those Black students who lived below the poverty line were struggling in the educational system alongside disgruntled, underpaid teachers whose ability to access critical resources was just as constrained as their own (Lee, Croninger, and Smith 1994). Meanwhile, the city became the representation of blackness embodied by the dark-skinned person protesting against enslavement. Richard Marback asserts that "the city has become a spatialized simulacrum of an African-American body fighting against while living within embodiments of racialized injustice and

the geographic limitations of democracy" (1998, 88). Black bodies in Detroit, therefore, are intrinsic to the marking of urban space but also get read as dangerous as they move through these spaces—crossing and creating new boundaries through these movements and uses of the city landscape. The young women who were the reason why GGC was established in the 1980s started to move through the urban neighborhoods of southwest Detroit in ways that signified regressive change and structural deterioration for the adult residents attuned to the behavioral (bodily) ways that health and collective well-being were performed in their community.

21. The Move Experiment is discussed thoroughly in chapter 5, which explores the role of artistic creative productions in the process of young women's self-definition.

22. Patricia Collins (2000) offers a full engagement with the concept of standpoint theory and everyday Black women's theorizing.

23. The breadth and influence of these anthropologists' work are significant. For starters, see Mullings 1997 and 2005; Bolles 1996, 2009, and 2013; D. Davis 2004 and 2006.

24. Referring to Mayors Coleman Young and Kwame Kilpatrick, respectively.

25. I will take this point up in more detail in chapter 5.

26. Here Mark Purcell is summarizing the views on social space, utopia, and revolutionary society in his article "Possible Worlds."

27. Ailey II, formerly the Alvin Ailey Repertory Ensemble, is a professional touring and training company for younger dancers who generally move on to the Alvin Ailey American Dance Theater. Ailey II tours internationally and engages in extensive community outreach through teaching classes and lecture demonstrations.

28. Anthea Kraut (2006 and 2008) provocatively explores the way choreography and the title of *choreographer* have traditionally been infused with connotations of sole authorship, originality, and creative mastery that disallow Zora Neale Hurston's work with dancers performing the Bahamian Fire Dance in the 1930s to be seen as more than restaging. Hurston's positionality as a Black woman in that time and the collaborative nature of her engagement with the dancers meant that her creative work contradicted the assumed underlying masculinist and racist underpinnings of notions of who a choreographer could be. Within the dichotomies of authorship versus collaboration, choreography versus improvisation, creative artistry versus natural expression, and the known versus the unknown, Hurston's work was perceived to be in alignment with the latter aspect of each binary. Because of this, her creative labor and artistic innovation were denied. Like Hurston, Black girls are illegible as choreographers.

29. In "On Plantations, Prisons, and a Black Sense of Place" (2011), Katherine McKittrick provides an important discussion of the ways in which Ruth Wilson Gilmore's *Golden Gulag: Prisons, Surplus, Crisis, and Opposition in Globalizing California* (2007) centers those who were previously marginal-

ized in the prison system by attending to the ways in which people build and sustain community.

1. "We Came Here to Be Different"

1. I am interested in Judith Halberstam's conceptualization of "low theory" and working through what she calls "theoretical knowledge that works at many levels at once, as precisely one of the modes of transmission that revels in the detours, twists, and turns through knowing and confusion, and that seeks not to explain but involve" (2011, 15).

2. Hortense Spillers's brilliant "Mama's Baby, Papa's Maybe" (1987) is the foremother of this work. See also Giddings 1984; Jenkins 2007.

3. In addition to being the title of George Clinton's 1975 album, *chocolate city* is also a way that Black people in cities like Atlanta; Washington, DC; and Detroit and in Black communities in larger cities like New York, Chicago, and Los Angeles affectionately talk about their majority status.

4. The Pistons, as most hometown teams do, hold a special place in the minds of Detroiters but maintain an especially treasured space in the imagination of many of the young Black men and women I have come to know over the past six years. Although the Pistons ranked first in their division in 2004 and made it to the NBA finals two years in a row, they are still not given as much credit, television time, and endorsements as teams like the Los Angeles Lakers and the Miami Heat, who have big-name stars to go along with the glamorous image of their cities. The Pistons do not have any big-name headliners and are best known for their neighborhood court teamwork style of basketball. Their wins are collective achievements. Many Black Detroiters see the Pistons as showing what it is like to be Black in America.

5. This is how their style was described by blues enthusiasts in Detroit during the late 1980s, during the resurgence of the blues.

6. In the two decades prior to Bessie's migration, two-thirds of Detroit's Black population remained in unskilled work despite the increase in Blacks in managerial positions in service departments within the city government, such as sanitation, public works, and welfare, and in the public elementary schools (Sugrue 1996, 112).

7. In addition to the fast food industry, the "care deficit" has made low-wage work in child care and nursing homes an additional arena in the service industry that is dominated by low-income women of color. This plays out in the Brown family through the options made available to Janice's cousin, Anita, and her peers at the Job Corps, where young women are counseled to enter the health care field as certified nursing assistants to fulfill their expected roles as domestic workers in the new millennium. The policing of the boundaries of race in the home and at work, along with a politics of respectability that has worked to both disrupt and reinforce these boundaries,

contributes to reinforcing exclusions that make families like the Browns visible as social problems that institutions like GGC need to fix.

8. For a relevant discussion of homemaking and the related community-building work of Black women in Newark, New Jersey, see Isoke 2011.

9. These ideas are poetically argued by Rebecca Solnit (2007).

10. Thomas Sugrue (1996) has arguably produced the most eloquent and comprehensive history of Detroit's rise and deindustrial decline, as marked by shifting notions of race and class in America that are important for understanding what led to the riot of 1943 and what followed in terms of the political and economic trajectory of the city.

11. To this day, 8 Mile is the symbolic dividing line between Detroit and the suburbs. The white rapper and homeboy of Detroit, Eminem, used this symbol of race and class boundaries as the title of his semi-autobiographical movie about growing up poor in Detroit while contributing to the emerging hip-hop music scene.

12. Victoria Wolcott's research (2001) on African American women in Detroit during the interwar period and notions of respectable community identity reveals that the cultural expressions of working-class migrants were not only a source of release and freedom but also led to increased restrictions imposed on this community.

13. Darlene Hine notes that "the fundamental tension between Black women and the rest of society—referring specifically to white men, white women, and to a lesser extent Black men—involved a multifaceted struggle to determine who would control their productive and reproductive capacities and their sexuality. At stake for Black women caught up in this ever-evolving, constantly shifting, but relentless war was the acquisition of personal autonomy and economic liberation" (1989, 915). The question of bodily ownership and the right to subjecthood is directly linked to projects of care and the structuring of entitlement.

14. Even though Bessie imagined that the opportunities for self-making in the North would look different from those in the South, the similarities in her daily work in both places echo the question that Hine posed regarding Black migrant women: "One wonders why they bothered to move in the first place" (ibid., 913).

15. Janice's theory of entitlement echoes Robin D. G. Kelley's proclamation that "I am convinced that we need to get that sense of entitlement back" (1997, 81), which he made in response to the lack of outrage about the continual degradation of poor Blacks in sociological literature, policy mandates, reform efforts, and popular representations. Janice in some ways performs this outrage.

16. This statistic is from Axtell (2011). Seven years earlier, the Black Women's Health Imperative (2004) placed the rate of sexual abuse for Black women at 40 percent, which suggests that the problem is increasing. Although the Violence against Women Act was recently reauthorized through Congress

to continue to provide funding for the investigation and prosecution of violent crimes against women, many advocates for Black women assert that language needs to be added to the act that speaks directly to the needs and specific concerns of women of color and that recognizes "that sexual assault in the Black community is a growing epidemic that requires special attention and resources" (Starr 2011). It is important to note that in 2005, Representative John Conyers (D-MI) advocated strongly for race-specific language to be added to the act but was outvoted.

17. Janice sheds more light on this topic in chapter 5.

2. Renovations

1. The use of "Miss" by the residents appeared to me to be randomly assigned to adults in the shelter until I noticed a pattern. Miss was used before the names of women who were over the age of forty; administrators who were not direct service staff but who, like me, spent a good deal of time participating in the day to day routine of shelter life and gained a certain amount of respect from the residents for doing so; and women whom the residents felt were performing a type of middle-class status and respectability that seemed to be claiming a superior position to that occupied by the residents and RAs. I believe I likely fell into the latter two categories depending on the resident and the circumstances.

2. Some members of the board supported the idea that someone who did not have experience working directly with youth might be able to objectively assess programs and make decisions for the agency that were more cost-effective and produced better outcomes in terms of the goals outlined in the grant requirements of funders. For the shelter, these goals were often concrete, such as an increase in the number of young women served annually both as short-term residents and as graduates of the Transition to Independent Living Program. There were a slew of smaller foundation grants that required outcomes on less concrete goals—including an increase in amorphous life skills that could not really be fully tested within the institutional setting of the shelter, such as learning to stick to a budget and keep a clean home.

3. My own inclinations and presumptions about what it means to work productively and effectively were part of the neoliberal models I tried to resist, especially when Camille came on board. The dialogue and collective decision making that was an important part of how the leadership team functioned was beneficial for the overall morale in the agency as a democratic model that at least attempted to include as many voices as possible. Unsurprisingly, as a program coordinator in the Community Outreach Program, I appreciated this way of working. Once I became director of the shelter and my level of accountability to the board, funders, and the staff shifted, I felt the pressure to make decisions more quickly and decisively. Group processing and providing multiple

platforms meant that, inevitably, someone or some group felt slighted by whatever final decision was made. These were tensions that I was responsible for managing as a leader. Nonetheless, they point to how neoliberal practices thrive in the context of social service agencies whose ideas about success and positive outcomes compete with those of the entities that will ultimately evaluate the return on everyone's collective work.

4. The leadership team consisted of the directors of all three programs, the chief financial officer, the human resources manager, the volunteer coordinator, the development director, and the executive director.

5. Through the mid- to late 1990s, the changes in the welfare system brought about by the Personal Responsibility and Work Opportunity Reconciliation Act of 1996 made life more difficult for teen mothers attempting to earn wages, raise children, and continue or complete their education. This segment of the population, while being systematically erased socially and politically, was becoming all too prevalent and visible at GGC, where the number of pregnant and parenting young women seeking shelter and supportive services sharply increased. The GGC administration found itself butting heads with the board members who felt that pregnant and parenting young women had the power to undermine the process of retraining that needed to happen in the residential setting. The problem board members had with pregnant and parenting teens, the older women sex workers in the Community Outreach Program, and the nonheterosexual youth in the Free Project, stemmed from a belief that certain individuals are beyond help or unworthy of having the opportunity to experience transformation and to access care due to two key, interrelated factors: age and choice. There is an age-based cutoff at which people are thought to enter a zone of irreparability and after which sins are no longer forgiven and slates cannot be wiped clean. This cutoff is usually around the age of seventeen or eighteen, coinciding with legal distinctions between minors and adults. Beyond the late teens, life circumstances are generally attributed to personal choices and adult decisions. Board members framed these choices as unrelated to any mitigating political and economic factors. The perspective of the board members is not too far removed from the views expressed by social reformers working with working- and lower-class women and adolescents at the beginning of the twentieth century. Although the middle-class professional women such as Jane Addams, who founded Hull House in Chicago, were deeply entrenched in their own battles for gender equality, they actively policed the lives of working-class women. These women, who took progressive stances in their own lives, were unable to extend the same freedoms and rights to women further on the margins of society. All of the most contentious board members were women in their early sixties who at one time or another had held high-powered positions in the automotive and other industries. They had risen to the top in their careers in spite of overtly hostile sexism. Yet they did not apply the lessons of their individual battles to the lives of the young

women they chose to support at GGC. Most of these women made astute feminist analyses of the ways in which women were systematically marginalized and exploited in the automotive industry and larger society, but they did not understand how racism could operate along with sexism, misogyny, ageism, homophobia, and class biases in the lives of the GGC participants. The status of the Fresh Start residents—board members saw them as poor girls from broken homes—made it unlikely that they could be transformed into virtuous young women, although it was possible to retrain them to become productive workers.

6. Orna Sasson-Levy and Tamar Rapoport consider how "social institutions are reproduced through bodies and their techniques" (2003, 381) and how the female body in particular protests against its subjugation in institutions invested in the production of hegemonic identities. Camille's focus on the body as a vehicle for and of efficiency and production reflected the way in which she wanted the agency to function. The physical body and the body of the organization were intertwined, building on and creating one another. Thus, the prospect of transitioning young women out of homelessness at Fresh Start included not just moving their bodies through, out of, and into various geographic locations but working to have these bodies reflect the process of transitioning through these physical spaces. Transition was synonymous with self-improvement at Fresh Start, and the body was an outward sign of whether or not these goals were being met. However, as Sasson-Levy and Rapoport discuss, women—including the young women of Fresh Start—can use the very bodies that are constructed in institutions to protest and produce a "text of alternative and subversive knowledge" and "challenge deep social and cultural structures" (ibid., 399).

7. Fordism as characterized by mass production and mass consumption is relevant here for untangling how Camille envisioned the efficient management of the shelter. If we think of Ford and Fordism as symbolic of the transformation from an agricultural to an industrial economy, we can see that in Camille's mind the shelter was also in need of a transformation. She viewed the shelter's management as rudimentary and archaic, and she saw the entire GGC organization as overemphasizing emotionality, individualized care, and interactive group leadership. The new model for the organization would be more efficient and cost-effective in that it would follow some of the central tenets of Fordism, focusing on economies of scale and of scope. In economies of scale, costs are reduced by mandating strict regulations on expenses while requiring large volumes of output. Economies of scale exploit the division of labor by combining more than one function. In the shelter, this was represented through the laying off of staff members and the hiring of younger and less experienced employees who were willing to be paid less than more experienced workers, and the combining of more than one job description per role. For example, for nearly a year I fulfilled the role of the Fresh Start manager and director while also directing the Early Start Program.

During this time I also covered hourly shifts in the shelter. RAs' roles began to include duties that had typically been assigned to more experienced caseworkers and counselors, while counselors were given grant-writing and other duties that had typically been reserved for managers and directors.

8. Beauty and efficiency are often linked together as if they are mutually reinforcing. This is especially true in the case of architecture and design, where aesthetics and function are explicitly linked. Camille's connection of beauty and efficiency in the context of bodies reveals the ideal neoliberal body to be both physically normative, visually attractive, and productive.

9. In Black feminist literature, other mothers are introduced as figures in the lives of Black women. Not biological or legal mothers, other mothers may be considered as such because of their capacity to nurture and provide a space where Black women can find and/or develop a sense of community and safety. Historically, these other mothers could be identified in Black communities, where they provided additional guidance to, and structure in the lives of, their young neighbors. These women were respected because they held at the center of their value system the goal of promoting collective social mobility through individual well-being and personal accountability. The RAs are other mothers, a role not readily apparent to other employees or outlined in their job descriptions. Because other mothering is a cultural phenomenon formed out of the Black experience in the United States, it is not legible in certain contexts where Black culture is not the underlying force that guides institutional practices and organizational systems. Therefore, at GGC this significant component of the RAs' relationship to the residents and the critical value it added to the efficacy of the shelter program is dismissed primarily because it is not identifiable outside of the original cultural context. This does not mean that RAs are uniformly liked and respected, or that they all have healthy, nurturing relationships with the young women at Fresh Start. It does, however, demonstrate that inherent in the RA position is the potential for connecting with and influencing the young Black women who reside in the shelter in ways that other staff members are unable to do.

10. The concept of realness or authenticity is thoroughly and creatively interrogated in the work of John L. Jackson Jr. (2005). Realness and being real is also a pervasive theme in the conversations that marginalized young women have about who should be trusted and given respect in the shelter. Popular hip-hop culture and the media have capitalized on the concept of realness by creating a narrow vision of Black cultural authenticity that many people inside and outside of the imagined Black community respond and contribute to. "Keeping it real" has become the anthem of young Black urban youth and is used as a way of establishing the boundaries of Blackness.

11. The type of protection the RAs were expected to give was largely understood to be symbolic and was rooted in their physical presence as a deterrent rather than any weapon or even any special authority to truly protect the

residents. This is similar to the way unarmed security guards are exploited in many businesses and buildings in large cities. Their ability to protect is subsequently framed as comical in popular culture and the media.

12. For more on Temporary Assistance for Needy Families, welfare reform, and the nature of service work for low-income Black women, see Power and Rosenberg 1995; D. Davis 2004. To receive federal cash aid under TANF, a minor parent has to live with a responsible adult and participate in school or a training program. There were rarely teen parents at Fresh Start who were minors. Although one of the goals of TANF is to discourage teens from having children, the majority of teens on TANF don't have children and live in families receiving TANF. In 2003 (the year in which the employment program was initiated in the shelter), adults made up 26 percent of TANF recipients, teens 17 percent, and children 57 percent. Of the teens, 87 percent were not parents (Kaiser Foundation 2003).

13. The Target Store was essentially a room that held clothing and accessories donated to the shelter. Since the shelter also received a large quantity of toiletries from hotels, individual donors, and overstocked pharmacies and beauty supply stores, the Target Store also contained low- and high-end lotions, soaps, bath gels, loofahs, and hair products. No young woman was ever denied clothing or toiletries if she was in need; the store was a way to encourage the residents to take care of the items they "bought" from the store and to budget their Fresh Start "money."

14. The move to encourage longer-term stays also raised a problem with funders, since grant goals were based on serving a high number of unique residents per year.

15. Conditional stays are given in the shelter to residents who refuse to follow the program guidelines. They usually had a limited probationary time to improve their level of participation and avoid being discharged from the shelter.

16. Charlene had not been able to find consistent work since she left the agency.

17. Street behaviors are discussed in workplace and other business settings in the same way that anthropologists discuss the behavioral holdovers and cultural retentions from Africa in contemporary African American communities—especially in marginalized communities and usually in relation to artistic cultural productions such as music, dance, and the creative use of language. A concise fruitful discussion of this can be found in Anderson 2012 and Bowen 2005.

18. I do not mean to downplay the fact that Charlene needed an income.

19. To powerful effect, Rebecca Wanzo (2010) discusses the negative effects of the positive construction of African Americans. She demonstrates that the positive representations of African Americans suggest that civil rights–era policies have, essentially, done their work and that policies that are shaped by race are no longer relevant or needed. The positive representation of staff members such as myself at Fresh Start operated in a similar vein. The image

of mainstream success evidenced through degrees, familial structure, and ways of speaking and interacting among Black female staff members in the shelter was implicitly promoted during this time by Camille and some of the board members as a way to demonstrate that race was not a significant or defining factor in the lives of the residents or staff members, and that the programmatic goals need not directly address the challenges of racism, particularly in a majority Black city.

20. For a thorough discussion of the will to empower, see Cruikshank 1999.

3. Narratives of Protest and Play

1. The GGC mission statement was premised on the idea of girls' self-empowerment and ability to make their own decisions. Thus, GGC seems to stand in contrast to other social service organizations that view program participants as, in the famous words of Emma Lazarus's "The New Colossus": "tired, . . . poor, and . . . huddled masses yearning to breathe free." How the mission of the organization is actualized in interactions between staff members and young women does not, however, align with this ideal of self-empowerment.

2. The Sierra Club even has a separate sphere of work devoted to this cause, called Inner City Outings.

3. *Outside* has several connotations here. The young women are perceived to be outside of the socially constructed ideal for girls. The word also implies an inside that is an exclusive safe haven, defining all other spaces outside its boundaries. *Outside* is also an interesting inversion of the lack of safety experienced via homelessness, in this case being the normalized, seemingly healthy and nurturing space outside of reform institutions, while *inside* in this case would be the space that houses danger and dysfunction.

4. The idea of making a horse and telling a story about it seemed appropriate for a group of first graders, but the materials provided and the skills needed to construct the horse seemed like the final project for a professional course in advanced craft making.

5. The girls were parodying their own popular cultural styles along with the way they both identify with and are stigmatized by them.

6. Winning the Derby here is a euphemism for fulfilling the similarly staged (and often rigged) requirements for achieving social mobility in the United States.

7. Girls, Inc. is an organization whose mission is to make girls strong, smart, and bold. Its website features a diverse group of young women and proudly proclaims that 61 percent of the girls who participate in its programs are from "ethnic groups." A critical aspect of its mission is identified as helping young women combat "subtle societal messages" about who they are or should be. Clearly, Girls, Inc. does not intend to create the image that Janice has of it. Those subtle societal messages are difficult to control, especially in an agency charged with helping girls mediate them.

8. A November 1999 CBSNews article, "Detroit Battles Schoolgirl Rapes" (http://www.cbsnews.com/news/detroit-battles-schoolgirl-rapes), quotes this young woman and provides details on the town meetings Mayor Dennis Archer held. The students' critique of the city's slow and ineffective initial response can be found in the *Los Angeles Times* article, "Detroit Schoolgirl Rapes Test Nerves, City's Response" (December 8, 1999). This sixteen-year-old's statement shows the depth of frustration and betrayal felt by young women in particular, who didn't think they could even rely on their own parents to adequately protect them. The game of shifting blame and accountability played among community members, city officials, and parents leaves the young women, who should be the subjects of concern, feeling ignored and devalued.

9. Most of them were participants in my dance class.

10. Prior to the takeover and Camille's arrival, the GGC and the Fresh Start shelter in particular were known for providing employment training and personal development opportunities for the staff that mirrored the mission of offering a new range of choices.

11. Articulations of self-definition and reliance as defined by Patricia Collins (2004), along with practices of hiding and showing the self among the Black girls discussed in Signthia Fordham's work (1993), are only as effective as the performances through which they are expressed. Here, performance as a continual presentation of self in the sense used by Erving Goffman (1959) is essential to the process of Black girls' individual identity formation and external identifications placed on them by others. Since society has already established the roles that it expects Black girls to play, their performances and presentations of self are automatically limited by their social status and the bodily characteristics that mark their exclusion from normative standards of acceptability. Thus, working within the boundaries of silence and voicing, and of action and passivity, may be an unconscious way of imposing self-discipline and agency on the overly determined space of social interactions. To apply Goffman's theory of everyday performance to the experience of the young women and staff at GGC, it is helpful to also look at his concept of stigma to contextualize the need for strategic self-presentations in the first place. Goffman calls stigma a special type of relationship between attribute and stereotype and says this about the stigmatized individual: "The standards he had incorporated from the larger society equip him to be intimately alive to what others see as his failing, inevitably causing him, if only for moments, to agree that he does indeed fall short of what he ought to be. Shame becomes a central possibility" (1963, 7). Goffman's explanation of stigma, spoiled identities, and identity management also includes a discussion of repairing the stigma or achieving "a transformation of self from someone who had a particular blemish into someone with a record of having corrected a particular blemish" (ibid, 9). It is important to note that the repair of the stigma, or the self-improvement and transformation of the individual, does not, in Goffman's analysis, mean that "fully normal status" (ibid.)

is achieved. Melissa Harris-Perry applies the concept of stigma or shame directly to the status of Black women. She writes: "Black women in America have always had to wrestle with derogatory assumptions about their character and identity," and "these assumptions shape the social world that black women must accommodate or resist in an effort to preserve their authentic selves and to secure recognition as citizens" (2011, 5). Without the ability to control the naming of their attributes, socially produced stereotypes, or the continually shifting incongruence between the two, young Black women are always in the process of mediating the space between who they are and how they are seen, and between their theoretical rights as citizens and the reality of their exclusion from full recognition as citizens.

12. Sharita is the young woman in chapter 2 who expressed her willingness to assist the board with shelter renovations. Sharita's complicated relationship with Fresh Start shelter is explained later in this chapter.

13. Fresh Start is a voluntary program. Residents may discharge themselves or leave the program at any time. Residents may also be discharged by the staff for rule infractions or lack of progress in the program.

14. Give Girls a Chance's name and mission imply that opportunity, choice, and resources are what "high-risk" girls and young women most need to become independent and productive adults. The institution provides the site for change, but the responsibility for change and positive outcomes ultimately lies in the hands of the young women.

4. Sex, Gender, and Scripted Bodies

1. Booty clapping, also called twerking, is usually confined to the strip club or explicit music videos. The person performing the dance shakes her behind in such a way that the cheeks slap each other like hands clapping.

2. *Triflin'* can mean many things, including lazy, disrespectful, dirty, nasty, and sloppy. Here it is used to mean out of order and vulgar.

3. Lynnette is in her early fifties.

4. Mary Trautner's fieldwork (2005) in two strip clubs reveals the assumptions of club owners and dancers regarding how working- and middle-class sexuality should be expressed and shows how class differences get represented as sexual differences. In the working-class strip club the women presented diverse races, body types, and personalities on the stage, and their acts included simulated sex, interactions with the audience, and demonstrated pleasure from the performers. The women in this club danced energetically to routines they choreographed. The middle-class club, in contrast, hired mostly blonde women with thin, cosmetically enhanced bodies. A "voyeuristic sexuality" (ibid., 776) was highlighted in the performances in which the women stood on display, barely moving. Essentially, the strip club geared toward the middle-class spectator presented sex as a fantasy and the women in the clubs as a "delicate image of sexuality" (ibid., 781). However, the club

for working-class patrons represented sex as physical, interactive, and real (in the sense that the performers made sex with them seem like a plausible option for the patrons). At the Brown Bean, the sexuality performed by the majority of spoken-word artists was sweet, poetic, beautiful, and loving. LaT approached the boundary of acceptability in that context with one phrase— "He fucked me"—and completely crossed over it with her booty clap finale. Crystal was upset that LaT had performed something that Crystal felt should be confined to the sexualized space of the strip club, and—as LaT realized— was concerned with how LaT's actions made all of us appear to the rest of the audience. LaT claimed not to care what anyone thought because they were "fake" and "bourgie." Thus, LaT attached authenticity to class and race and confronted it with her sexuality. The Brown Bean café was the most appropriate space for LaT to demonstrate her contempt for the sanitized sexuality promoted by pretentious "Negroes."

5. I'm thinking here of welfare policies, sex education curricula, and even the schoolgirl rapes.

6. Not much anonymity is possible in a group of eighteen young women, most of whom the staff know extremely well. Not using names still left handwriting that could be identified and other clues that the staff tried to use to figure out who was saying what, which missed the whole point of protecting the safety and confidentiality of the workshop.

7. Meaning that the young woman finds her partner sexually satisfying.

8. GGC provides in-house counseling for these young women and also refers them to other agencies where they can get the assistance they need.

9. Cedar Point is an amusement park in Ohio.

10. Slang for being charming with women and being able to have many girlfriends at one time.

11. A male rapper with a very masculine image.

12. *Perp* is short for "perpetrate a fraud" or, in other words, to act like someone you are not.

13. Judith Butler writes that "gender is a performance and a stylized repetition of acts" (1990, 140). Current theories of gender performativity are derived from her work, including those of Betsy Lucal (1990) and Mary Trautner (2005). Erving Goffman (1959) also talks about gender as performance.

14. L. Susan Williams (2002) uses "trying on gender" instead of "doing gender" when she writes about the gendering processes of girls in the liminal stage of adolescence. For Williams, trying on gender implies the experimental, tentative, playful, and resistant nature of the trying-on process in comparison with "doing gender" found in the work of Candace West and Don Zimmerman (1987), which implies a "decisive, methodical, and recurring accomplishment."

15. The space to even begin these conversations is critically important to the well-being of young people, especially Black youth, as Cathy Cohen (2010) shows in her research.

5. The Move Experiment

1. Section 8 is federally funded housing that provides safe, clean, and afford-able housing to low-income families, the elderly, and people with disabilities.
2. Information regarding Erica's abduction can be found through several online sources. My summary here is largely based on Richard Jones's (2002) article published two days after Erica's abduction. Erica was also featured in *Time* as the magazine's person of the week (Coatney 2002). There were some contradictions in these stories, most notably in identifying whether Erica's sister or another young child was with Erica at the time of the abduction. I chose to use the narrative that gives the details of her sister's screams at the moment of Erica's abduction as the most credible story.
3. A safe streets campaign in Erica's neighborhood is discussed in R. Jones (2002).
4. None of these techniques can be considered pure or isolated forms. They are all in some way influenced by each other and, through their individual definitions, define and set boundaries for the others. For example, the diverse forms of movement categorized under the name *hip-hop* derive from the multiple strains of West African dance while also incorporating (in more recent incarnations) movements that would be identified as belonging to classical ballet and concert modern dance.
5. The Horton technique is a modern dance technique developed by Lester Horton. This is the primary movement method used in the choreography of Alvin Ailey and performed by the Alvin Ailey American Dance Theater. Along with ballet, pointe, Katherine Dunham's technique, and Martha Graham's technique, Horton was one of the required classes for students of the Ailey school when I attended as a scholarship student.
6. We received more funding in the middle of the project, which allowed peer educators who were willing and able to do so to work up to twenty hours a week.
7. Skin color has always been a central theme in discussions of Black women and beauty. Darkness and lightness have critical implications for how Black women are perceived and how they ultimately see themselves. Farah Jasmine Griffin (2000) talks about how even in the works of early Black authors, biracial main characters were prevalent because they represented mediation between Blackness and whiteness as well as being thought to convey intelligence, beauty, and worth in comparison to darker-skinned Blacks. Although dark skin has been thought to negatively affect self-esteem (M. Thompson and Keith Verna 2001), contemporary artists like India Arie sing about the beauty of brown skin and echo the sentiments of young Black women who challenge the association of dark skin with ugliness and badness and the association of light skin with beauty and goodness.
8. The portrayal of young Black women in the media is most prominent in rap and rhythm and blues music videos, in which the women are often depicted as overly sexualized bodies waiting either to be serviced by or to service the

male "artists" who play a part in shaping these images. The "video ho" was referred to by many of the young women I spoke with at GGC as the most infuriating and inaccurate representation of Black woman.

9. These founding members of the Move Experiment worked as a group with me for three months during the summer of 2004. After I left GGC, a coordinator was hired to continue the program, but only Izetta and Crystal continued as peer educators. Sonya, Ashley, and Rachel moved out of the shelter and found it difficult to remain committed to the project while also working and trying to get back into school. A few months after I left, Crystal was let go because of her "uncooperative attitude." The Move Experiment has now become a part of the street outreach program, and the focus has shifted to outreach workshops for young women as an intervention in high-risk behaviors. The performance component is no longer a part of the Move Experiment.

10. The shelter residents used the word *twisted* to mean drunk.

11. bell hooks devotes an entire book (1993) to the idea of the importance of Black women's self-care practices and how they affect the larger community.

12. Black girls' bodies are thought to be naturally larger than other girls' bodies, and fleshiness is more likely to be seen as the norm than as a problem in need of correction. See Bray 1992.

13. In *The Black Dancing Body*, Brenda Dixon-Gottschild outlines some of the key distinctions made between Africanist and European dance. In this impor-tant, innovative work, she discusses how in African-centered or emergent dance, energy determines form, and there is a "go for broke," "give it your all" (2003, 37) African American aesthetic that makes emotion rather than motion the primary means of expression. In the Move Experiment, emo-tional intensity and focused engagement in the dance was an important component of making the dance believable in the minds of the peer educa-tors. And all of the peer educators, including Sonya and Izetta who were not African American, were seen as having this emotional intensity by virtue of their experience in, what they called, "the struggle." Sonya's homeless status and experience growing up in a Black neighborhood meant that she was automatically included among the "struggly." Izetta's Mexican American-ness, residence in southwest Detroit, economic status, and identification as a "brown girl" meant that she was also a part of the struggle and carried the ability to convey this in her blood. As part of their Move Experiment training, the peer educators were learning ballet and modern dance along with some of the basic principles of yoga and Pilates. There was a difference in movement styles and the type of control needed over the body between, on the one hand, ballet and concert modern dance technique and, on the other hand, the West African dance, hip-hop, and freestyle improvisational movement that the dancers also experienced. In the European dance forms, the movement exists to produce the work and value is placed mostly on precision, unison, and symbols of good technique such as the ability to

make high extensions; long, elegant lines with the body; and multiple turns. Although there is a dichotomy in the dance world between European and African dance, movement categorized under either form has been inevitably influenced by the other. The Move Experiment dancers talked about the weaknesses in this dichotomy while upholding it at the same time. For the peer educators, all dance was about telling a story and using the body as the vehicle through which energy motivated by emotion could be channeled.

14. In the Chinese splits, your legs extend from the sides of your body rather than in front and behind like the traditional splits.

15. Frank Miller's *Sin City* (2005) is perhaps the most appropriate example of these tendencies. Many reactions to Miller's venomous commentary on the Occupy Wall Street protestors can be found online. I raise the complexity and possible contradictions in Miller's work to provoke dialogue about the potential seduction, appeal, dangers, and empowering spaces within mainstream and alternative images as they circulate among low-income Black girls.

16. This is from an interview on *Charlie Rose* (PBS), episode no. 9409, that aired June 1, 2000.

References

Additon, Henrietta Silvis. 1928. *City Planning for Girls*. Chicago: University of Chicago Press.

Alexander, M. Jaqui. 2005. *Pedagogies of Crossing: Meditations on Feminism, Sexual Politics, Memory, and the Sacred*. Durham: Duke University Press.

Alexander, M. Jaqui. 2007. "Danger and Desire: Crossings Are Never Undertaken All at Once or for All." *Small Axe* 24 (11): 154–66.

Allen, Jafari. 2009. "For 'the Children' Dancing the Beloved Community." *Souls* 11 (3): 311–26.

Allen, Jafari S. 2011. *¡Venceremos?: The Erotics of Black Self-making in Cuba*. Durham: Duke University Press.

Allen, Jafari S. 2012. "Black/Queer/Diaspora at the Current Conjuncture." *GLQ* 18 (2–3): 211–48.

Anderson, Elijah. 1990. *Streetwise: Race, Class, and Change in an Urban Community*. Chicago: University of Chicago Press.

Anderson, Elijah. 2012. "The Iconic Ghetto." *Annals of the American Academy of Political and Social Science* 642 (1): 8–24.

Anzaldúa, Gloria. 1996. "To Live in the Borderlands Means You." *Frontiers: A Journal of Women Studies* 17 (3): 4–5.

Axtell, Brooke. 2012. "Black Women, Sexual Assault, and the Art of Resistance." *Forbes.com*. N.p., April 25. Accessed August 17, 2013.

Beaubouf-Lafontant, Tamara. 2005. "Keeping Up Appearances, Getting Fed Up: The Embodiment of Strength among African American Women." *Meridians* 5 (2): 104–23.

Bergmann, Luke. 2008. *Getting Ghost: Two Young Lives and the Struggle for the Soul of an American City*. New York: New Press.

Bolles, A. Lynn. 1996. *Sister Jamaica: A Study of Women, Work, and Households in Kingston*. Lanham, MD: University Press of America.

Bolles, A. Lynn. 2009. "Forever Indebted to Women as They Carry the Burden of Globalization." *Caribbean Quarterly* 55 (1): 15–23.

Bolles, A. Lynn. 2013. "Telling the Story Straight: Black Feminist Intellectual Thought in Anthropology." *Transforming Anthropology* 21 (1): 57–71.

Bordo, Susan. 1993. *Unbearable Weight: Feminism, Western Culture, and the Body*. Berkeley: University of California Press.

Bourgois, Philippe I. 1996. *In Search of Respect: Selling Crack in El Barrio*. Cambridge: Cambridge University Press.

Bowen, Paulie. 2005. "Culture and Ghetto Related Behavior: Lessons Learned in the Bronx and the Bijlmer." *Sociologie* 1 (4): 357–81.

Bray, Rosemary. 1992. "Heavy Burden." *Essence*, January, 52–56.

Brook, Paul. 2013. "Emotional Labor and the Living Personality at Work: Labor Power, Materialist Subjectivity, and the Dialogical Self." *Culture and Organization* 19 (4): 332–52.

Brown, Ruth Nicole. 2009. *Black Girlhood Celebration: Toward a Hip-hop Feminist Pedagogy*. New York: Peter Lang.

Brown, Ruth Nicole. 2011. *Hear Our Truths: The Creative Potential of Black Girlhood*. Champaign: University of Illinois Press.

Butler, Judith. 1990. *Gender Trouble: Feminism and the Subversion of Identity*. New York: Routledge.

Butler, Octavia E. 1980. *Wild Seed*. New York: Warner.

Cacho, Lisa Marie. 2012. *Social Death: Racialized Rightlessness and the Criminalization of the Unprotected*. New York: New York University Press.

Carby, Hazel V. 1992. "Policing the Black Woman's Body in an Urban Context." *Critical Inquiry* 18 (4): 738–55.

Caron, Caroline. 2011. "Getting Girls and Teens into the Vocabularies of Citizenship." *Girlhood Studies* 4 (2): 70–91.

Carter, Prudence. 2005. *Keepin' It Real: School Success beyond Black and White*. New York: Oxford University Press.

Case, Mary A. 2014. "My Brother's Keeper Initiative Echoes of a Sexist History." *New York Times*, March 12. Accessed December 31, 2014.

Chin, Elizabeth. 2001. *Purchasing Power: Black Kids and American Consumer Culture*. Minneapolis: University of Minnesota Press.

Christian, Margena A. 2008. "Why African-American Teenage Girls Are Infected with STDs at Higher Rates." *Jet* 113 (14): 53–55.

Clark, Rodney. 2006. "Perceived Racism and Vascular Reactivity in Black College Women: Moderating Effects of Seeking Social Support." *Health Psychology* 25 (1): 20–25.

Clarke, Cheryl. 1996. "Lesbianism: An Act of Resistance." In *Feminism and Sexuality: A Reader*, edited by Stevi Jackson and Sue Scott, 155–61. New York: Columbia University Press.

Clifford, James. 1986. "On Ethnographic Allegory." In *Writing Culture: The Poetics and Politics of Ethnography*, edited by James Clifford and George Marcus, 98–121. Berkeley: University of California Press.

Coatney, Mark. 2002. "Person of the Week: Erica Pratt." *Time*, July 26. Accessed October 3, 2014. http://content.time.com/time/nation/article /0,8599,331695,00.html.

Cohen, Cathy J. 2004. "Deviance as Resistance: A New Research Agenda for the Study of Black Politics." *Du Bois Review* 1 (1): 27–45.

Cohen, Cathy. 2006. "African American Youth: Broadening Our Understanding of Politics, Civic Engagement and Activism." Social Science Research Council, June 7. Accessed December 29, 2014. http://ya.ssrc.org/african/Cohen.

Collins, Patricia Hill. 1998. "It's All in the Family: Intersections of Gender, Race, and Nation." *Hypatia* 13 (3): 62–82.

Collins, Patricia Hill. 2000. *Black Feminist Thought: Knowledge, Consciousness, and the Politics of Empowerment*. Rev. 10th anniversary ed. New York: Routledge.

Collins, Patricia Hill. 2000. "Gender, Black Feminism, and Black Political Economy." *Annals of the American Academy of Political and Social Science* 568: 451–53.

Collins, Patricia Hill. 2005. *Black Sexual Politics: African Americans, Gender, and the New Racism*. New York: Routledge.

Craven, Christa, and Dána-Ain Davis. 2013. "Introduction: Feminist Activist Ethnography." In *Feminist Activist Ethnography: Counterpoints to Neoliberalism in North America*, edited by Christa Craven and Dána-Ain Davis, 1–22. Lanham, MD: Lexington.

Crenshaw, Kimberle. 1991. "Mapping the Margins: Intersectionality, Identity Politics, and Violence against Women of Color." *Stanford Law Review* 43 (6): 1241–99.

Crouch, Stanley. 2001. *The Artificial White Man: Essays on Authenticity*. New York: Perennial.

Cruikshank, Barbara. 1999. *The Will to Empower: Democratic Citizens and Other Subjects*. Ithaca, NY: Cornell University Press.

Davila, Arlene. 2004. *Barrio Dreams: Puerto Ricans, Latinos, and the Neoliberal City*. Berkeley: University of California Press.

Davila, Arlene. 2012. *Culture Works: Space, Value, and Mobility across the Neoliberal Americas*. New York. New York University Press.

Davis, Angela Y. 1999. *Blues Legacies and Black Feminism*. New York: Vintage.

Davis, Dána-Ain. 2004. "Manufacturing Mammies: The Burdens of Service Work and Welfare Reform among Battered Black Women." *Anthropologica* 46 (2): 273–88.

Davis, Dána-Ain. 2006. *Battered Black Women and Welfare Reform: Between a Rock and a Hard Place*. Albany: State University of New York Press.

Davis, Lawrence. 1976. "Comments on Nozick's Entitlement Theory." *Journal of Philosophy* 73 (21): 836–44.

Dixon-Gottschild, Brenda. 2003. *The Black Dancing Body: A Geography from Coon to Cool*. New York: Palgrave Macmillan.

Drake, St. Clair, and Horace R. Cayton. 1945. *Black Metropolis: The Struggle of Negro Life in a Northern City*. Chicago: University of Chicago Press.

Du Bois, W. E. B. 1903. *The Souls of Black Folk*. Chicago: A. C. McClurg.

Durr, Marlese, and Adia Harvey. 2011. "Wingfield." *Critical Sociology* 37 (5): 557–71.

Education Week. 1988. "Detroit Casts a 'No' Vote on Direction of Schools." *Education Week*, October 16. Accessed December 31, 2014. http://www.edweek.org/ew/articles/1988/10/16/08070016.h08.html.

Emerson, Rana A. 2002. "'Where My Girls At?' Negotiating Black Womanhood in Music Videos." *Gender and Society* 16 (1): 115–35.

Evans, Danielle. 2010. *Before You Suffocate Your Own Fool Self*. New York: Riverhead.

Feldstein, Ruth. 2000. *Motherhood in Black and White: Race and Sex in American Liberalism 1930–1965*. Ithaca, NY: Cornell University Press.

Ferguson, Ann Arnett. 2000. *Bad Boys: Public Schools and the Making of Black Masculinity*. Ann Arbor: University of Michigan Press.

Ferguson, Roderick A. 2004. *Aberrations in Black: Toward a Queer of Color Critique*. Minneapolis: University of Minnesota Press.

Fine, Michelle. 1992. *Disruptive Voices: The Possibilities of Feminist Research*. Ann Arbor: University of Michigan Press.

Fine, Michelle. 1998. *The Unknown City: The Lives of Poor and Working-Class Young Adults*. Boston: Beacon.

Fleetwood, Nicole R. 2011. *Troubling Vision: Performance, Visuality, and Blackness*. Chicago: University of Chicago Press.

Fleetwood, Nicole R. 2012. "The Case of Rihanna: Erotic Violence and Black Female Desire." *African American Review* 45 (3): 419–35.

Fordham, Signithia. 1993. "'Those Loud Black Girls': (Black) Women, Silence, and Gender 'Passing' in the Academy." *Anthropology and Education Quarterly* 24 (1): 3–32.

Froyum, Carissa M. 2010. "Making 'Good Girls': Sexual Agency in the Sexuality Education of Low-Income Black Girls." *Culture, Health, and Sexuality* 12 (1): 59–72.

Giallombardo, Rose. 1974. *The Social World of Imprisoned Girls: A Comparative Study of Institutions for Juvenile Delinquents*. New York: John Wiley and Sons.

Giddings, Paula. 1984. *When and Where I Enter: The Impact of Black Women on Race and Sex in America*. New York: William Morrow.

Gilmore, Ruth Wilson. 2007. *Golden Gulag: Prisons, Surplus Crisis, and Opposition in Globalizing California*. Berkeley: University of California Press.

Gilroy, Paul. 1991. "Sounds Authentic: Black Music, Ethnicity and the Challenge of 'Changing' Same." *Black Music Research Journal* 11 (2): 111–36.

Goffman, Erving. 1959. *The Presentation of Self in Everyday Life*. New York: Doubleday.

Gregory, Steven. 1998. *Black Corona: Race and the Politics of Place in an Urban Community*. Princeton, NJ: Princeton University Press.

Griffin, Farah Jasmine. 2000. "Black Feminists and DuBois: Respectability, Protection and Beyond." *Annals of the American Academy of Political and Social Science* 568 (1): 28–40.

Halberstam, J. Jack. 2012. *Gaga Feminism: Sex, Gender, and the End of Normal*. Boston: Beacon Press.

Halberstam, Judith. 2011. *The Queer Art of Failure*. Durham, NC: Duke University Press.

Hall, Stanley. 1904. *Adolescence: Its Psychology and Its Relations to Physiology, Anthropology, Sociology, Sex, Crime, Religion, and Education*. New York: Appleton.

Hannerz, Ulf. 1969. *Soulside: Inquiries into Ghetto Culture and Community*. Stockholm: Almquizt and Wiksell.

Harrison, Faye V., ed. 1997. *Decolonizing Anthropology: Moving Further Toward an Anthropology of Liberation*. Washington, DC: American Anthropological Association.

Harris-Perry, Melissa V. 2011. *Sister-Citizen: Shame, Stereotypes, and Black Women in America*. New Haven, CT: Yale University Press.

Higginbotham, Evelyn Brooks. 1992. "African-American Women's History and the Metalanguage of Race." *Signs* 17 (2): 251–74.

Hine, Darlene Clark. 1989. "Rape and the Inner Lives of Black Women in the Middle West." *Signs* 14 (4): 912–20.

hooks, bell. 1992. *Black Looks: Race and Representation*. Boston: South End.

hooks, bell. 1993. *Sisters of the Yam: Black Women and Self-Recovery*. Boston: South End.

Hwa, M. Ang Chooi. 2012. "Emotional Labor and Emotional Exhaustion." *Journal of Management Research* 12 (3): 115–27.

Hyra, Derek S. 2008. *The Economic Transformation of Harlem and Bronzeville*. Chicago: University of Chicago Press.

Isoke, Zenzele. 2011. "The Politics of Homemaking." *Transforming Anthropology* 19 (2): 117–30.

Iton, Richard. 2010. *In Search of the Black Fantastic: Politics and Popular Culture in the Post-Civil Rights Era*. New York: Oxford University Press.

Jackson, John L., Jr. 2005. *Real Black: Adventures in Racial Sincerity*. Chicago: University of Chicago Press.

Jenkins, Candice. 2007. *Private Lives, Proper Relations: Regulating Black Intimacy*. Minneapolis: University of Minnesota Press.

Jones, Nikki. 2009. *Between Good and Ghetto: African American Girls and Inner City Violence*. New Brunswick, NJ: Rutgers University Press.

Jones, Nikki. 2009. "'I Was Aggressive for the Streets, Pretty for the Pictures': Gender Difference and the Inner City Girl." *Gender and Society* 23 (1): 89–93.

Jones, Richard Lezin. 2002. "7-Year-Old Philadelphia Girl, Abducted Monday, Breaks Free." *New York Times*, July 24.

Jones, Tayari. 2002. *Leaving Atlanta*. New York: Warner.

Jones, Tayari. 2011. *Silver Sparrow*. Chapel Hill, NC: Algonquin.

Jordan, June. 1971. *His Own Where*. New York: Feminist.

Jordan, June. 2002. *Some of Us Did Not Die: New and Selected Essays of June Jordan*. New York: Basic.

Kaiser Foundation. 2003. "Teens and TANF: How Adolescents Fare Under the Nation's Welfare Program." N.p. Accessed February 25, 2009. http://kff.org /hivaids/issue-brief/teens-and-tanf-how-adolescents-fare-under/.

Kelley, Robin D. G. 1994. *Race Rebels: Culture, Politics, and the Black Working Class*. New York: Free Press.

Kelley, Robin D. G. 1997. *Yo' Mama's Disfunktional!: Fighting the Culture Wars in Urban America*. Boston: Beacon.

King, Deborah. 1988. "Multiple Jeopardy, Multiple Consciousness: The Context of a Black Feminist Ideology." *Signs* 14 (1): 42–72.

Kraut, Anthea. 2008. *Choreographing the Folk: The Dance Stagings of Zora Neale Hurston*. Minneapolis: University of Minnesota Press.

Kyungwon, Grace, and Roderick A. Ferguson, eds. 2011. *Strange Affinities: The Gender and Sexual Politics of Comparative Racialization*. Durham: Duke University Press.

LaBennett, Oneka. 2011. *She's Mad Real: Popular Culture and West Indian Girls in Brooklyn*. New York: New York University Press.

Ladner, Joyce A. 1972. *Tomorrow's Tomorrow: The Black Woman*. New York: Anchor.

Leary, John P. 2011. "Detroitism." *Guernica: A Magazine of Art and Politics*. N.p., January 15. Accessed March 13, 2013. https://www.guernicamag.com/features /leary_1_15_11/.

Lee, Valerie E., Robert G. Croninger, and Julia B. Smith. 1994. "Parental Choice of Schools and Social Stratification in Education: The Paradox of Detroit." *Educational Evaluation and Policy Analysis* 16 (4): 434–57.

Lefebvre, Henri. 1974. *La production de l'espace*. Paris: Anthropos.

Lewis, Oscar. 1970. *Anthropological Essays*. New York: Random House.

Liebow, Elliot. 1967. *Tally's Corner: A Study of Negro Streetcorner Men*. Boston: Little Brown.

Lindsey, Treva B. 2013. "Complicated Crossroads: Black Feminisms, Sex Positivism, and Popular Culture." *African and Black Diaspora* 6 (1): 55–65.

Love, Bettina. 2012. *Hip Hop's Li'l Sistas Speak: Negotiating Hip Hop Identities and Politics in the New South*. New York: Peter Lang.

Love, Heather. 2011. "Queer Studies, Materialism, and Crisis: A Roundtable Discussion." *GLQ* 18 (1): 127–47.

Low, Setha, ed. 2002. *Theorizing the City: The New Urban Anthropology Reader*. New Brunswick, NJ: Rutgers University Press.

Lucal, Betsy. 1999. "What It Means to Be Gendered Me: Life on the Boundaries of a Dichotomous Gender System." *Gender and Society* 13 (6): 781–97.

Madison, D. Soyini. 2007. "Co-Performative Witnessing." *Cultural Studies* 21 (6): 826–31.

Marback, Richard. 1998. "Detroit and the Closed Fist: Toward a Theory of Material Rhetoric." *Rhetoric Review* 17 (1): 74–92.

McKittrick, Katherine. 2006. *Demonic Grounds: Black Women and the Cartographies of Struggle*. Minneapolis: University of Minnesota Press.

McKittrick, Katherine. 2011. "On Plantations, Prisons, and a Black Sense of Place." *Social and Cultural Geography* 12 (8): 947–63.

Miller, Frank. 2005. *Sin City*. Milwaukie, OR: Dark Horse.

Miller, Frank. 2009. *The Life and Times of Martha Washington in the Twenty-First Century*. Milwaukie, OR: Dark Horse.

Miller, Jody. 2008. *Getting Played: African American Girls, Urban Inequality, and Gendered Violence*. New York: New York University Press.

Mitchell, Katharyne. 2010. "Pre-Black Futures." *Antipode* 41 (s1): 239–61.

Morris, Rosalind C. 1995. "All Made Up: Performance Theory and the New Anthropology of Sex and Gender." *Annual Review of Anthropology* 24 (1): 567–92.

Morrison, Toni. 1972. *The Bluest Eye*. New York: Pocket.

Moynihan, Daniel Patrick. 1965. *The Negro Family: The Case for National Action*. Washington: Office of Policy Planning and Research, Department of Labor.

Mullings, Leith. 1997. *On Our Own Terms: Race, Class, and Gender in the Lives of African American Women*. New York: Routledge.

Mullings, Leith. 2000. "African-American Women Making Themselves: Notes on the Role of Black Feminist Research." *Souls: A Critical Journal of Black Politics, Culture, and Society* 2 (4): 18–29.

Mullings, Leith. 2005. "Resistance and Resilience: The Sojourner Syndrome and the Social Context of Reproduction in Central Harlem." *Transforming Anthropology* 13 (2): 79–91.

Muñoz, José Esteban. 1999. *Disidentifications: Queers of Color and the Performance of Politics*. Minneapolis: University of Minnesota Press.

Muñoz, José Esteban. 2009. *Cruising Utopia: The Then and There of Queer Futurity*. New York: New York University Press.

My Brother's Keeper Task Force. 2014. "Understanding the Problem." *My Brother's Keeper*, May 7. Accessed December 30, 2014. http://mbk.ed.gov.

Myerhoff, Barbara G. 1971. "The Revolution as a Trip: Symbol and Paradox." *Annals of the American Academy of Political and Social Science* 395 (1): 105–16.

Nash, Jennifer C. 2011. "Practicing Love: Black Feminism, Love-Politics, and Post-Intersectionality." *Meridians* 11 (2): 1–24.

Ness, Cindy D. 2010. *Why Girls Fight: Female Youth Violence in the Inner City*. New York: New York University Press.

Perry, Imani. 2010. *More Beautiful and More Terrible: The Embrace and Transcendence of Racial Inequality in the United States*. New York: New York University Press.

Phelan, Peggy. 1988. "Feminist Theory, Poststructuralism, and Performance." *TDR* 32 (1): 107–127.

Power, Marilyn, and Sam Rosenberg. 1995. "Race, Class, and Occupational Mobility: Black and White Women in Service Work in the United States." *Feminist Economics* 1 (3): 40–59.

Propper, Alice M. 1981. *Prison Homosexuality: Myth and Reality*. New York: Lexington.

Purcell, Mark. 2014. "Possible Worlds: Henri Lefebvre and the Right to the City." *Journal of Urban Affairs* 36 (1): 141–54.

Roberts, Rosemarie A. 2013. "With Social Ghosts: Performing Embodiments, Analyzing Critically." *Transforming Anthropology* 21 (1): 4–14.

Rooks, Noliwe. 2005. *Black Women's Studies: A Reader*. New York: ProQuest Publishing and the Schomburg Center for Research in African American Culture.

Rooks, Noliwe M. 2013. "Renisha McBride and Evolution of Black-Female Stereotype." *Time*, November 14. Accessed December 31, 2014. http://ideas.time.com/2013/11/14/renisha-mcbride-and-black-female-stereotype/.

Sasson-Levy, Orna, and Tamar Rapoport. 2003. "Body, Gender, and Knowledge in Protest Movements: The Israeli Case." *Gender and Society* 17 (3): 379–403.

Schein, Louisa. 1999. "Performing Modernity." *Cultural Anthropology* 14 (3): 361–95.

Schreiber, Katherine. 2012. "PT Puzzle: Shape Shifters Impossible Problem? Depends How You Look at It." *Psychology Today*, March 8. http://www.psychologytoday.com/articles/201204/pt-puzzle-shape-shifters.

Scott, James C. 1985. *Weapons of the Weak: Everyday Forms of Peasant Resistance*. New Haven: Yale University Press.

Shange, Ntozake. 1982. *Sassafrass, Cypress, and Indigo*. New York: St. Martin's.

Sharpley-Whiting, T. Denean. 2007. *Pimps Up, Ho's Down: Hip Hop's Hold on Young Black Women*. New York: New York University Press.

Simon, Stephanie. 1999. "Detroit Schoolgirl Rapes Test Nerves, City's Response." *Los Angeles Times*, December 8. Accessed January 12, 2005. http://articles.latimes.com/1999/dec/08/news/mn-41626.

Skelton, Tracey, Gill Valentine, and Deborah Chambers. 1998. "Cool Places: An Introduction to Youth and Youth Cultures." In *Cool Places: Geographies of Youth Cultures*, edited by Tracey Skelton and Gill Valentine, 1–34. London: Routledge.

Snider, William. 1989. "In Backing Tax Proposals, Voters Endorse Detroit School Reforms." *Education Week*, September 20. Accessed December 31, 2014. http://www.edweek.org/ew/articles/1989/09/20/09050008.h09.html.

Solnit, Rebecca. 2007. "Detroit Arcadia: Exploring the Post-American Landscape." *Harper's*, July, 65–73.

Soo, Ah Kwon. 2013. *Uncivil Youth: Race, Activism, and Affirmative Governmentality*. Durham: Duke University Press.

Spillers, Hortense. 1987. "Mama's Baby, Papa's Maybe: An American Grammar Book." *Diacritics* 17 (2): 65–81.

Stack, Carol. 1974. *All Our Kin: Strategies for Survival in a Black Community*. New York: Harper Row.

Star, Terrell Jermaine. 2011. "Study: More than Half of Black Girls Are Sexually Assaulted." *NewsOne for Black America*, December 2. Accessed August 18, 2013. http://newsone.com/1680915/half-of-black-girls-sexually-assaulted/.

Sugrue, Thomas J. 1996. *The Origins of the Urban Crisis: Race and Inequality in Postwar Detroit*. Princeton, NJ: Princeton University Press.

Susser, Ida. 2012. *Norman Street: Poverty and Politics in an Urban Neighborhood*. New York: Oxford University Press.

Thompson, Becky. 1994. "Food, Bodies, and Growing Up Female: Childhood Lessons about Culture, Race, and Class." In *Feminist Perspectives on Eating Disorders*, edited by Juliette Harris and Pamela Johnson, 355–78. New York: Guilford.

Thompson, Maxine S., and Verna M. Keith. 2001. "The Blacker the Berry: Gender, Skin Tone, Self-Esteem, and Self-Efficacy." *Gender and Society* 15 (3): 336–57.

Trautner, Mary Nell. 2005. "Doing Gender, Doing Class: The Performance of Sexuality in Exotic Dance Clubs." *Gender and Society* 19 (6): 771–88.

Ulysse, Gina A. 2007. *Downtown Ladies: Informal Commercial Importers, a Haitian Anthropologist, and Self-Making in Jamaica*. Chicago: University of Chicago Press.

Walker, Alice. 1982. *The Color Purple*. New York: Harcourt Brace Jovanovich.

Wanzo, Rebecca. 2005. "Apocalyptic Empathy: A Parable of Postmodern Sentimentality." *Obsidian III* 6–7 (2/1): 72–86.

Wanzo, Rebecca. 2009. *The Suffering Will Not Be Televised: African American Women and Sentimental Political Storytelling*. Albany: SUNY Press.

Wanzo, Rebecca. 2010. "Proms and Other Racial Ephemera: The Positive Social Construction of African Americans in the 'Post' Civil Rights Era." *Washington University Journal of Law* 33: 75–107.

Ward, Janie Victoria, and Beth Cooper Benjamin. 2004. "Women, Girls, and the Unfinished Work of Connection: A Critical Review of American Girls' Studies." In *All about the Girl: Culture, Power, and Identity*, edited by Anita Harris, 15–28. New York: Routledge.

Watkins-Hayes, Celeste. 2009. *The New Welfare Bureaucrats: Entanglements of Race, Class, and Policy Reform*. Chicago: University of Chicago Press.

West, Candace, and Don H. Zimmerman. 1987. "Doing Gender." *Gender and Society* 1 (2): 125–51.

West, Carolyn M., and Kamilah Johnson. 2013. "Sexual Violence in the Lives of African American Women." National Resource Center on Domestic Violence, April 16. Accessed August 18, 2013. http://www.vawnet.org/sexual-violence/print-document.php?doc_id=3556&find_type=web_desc_AR.

White, E. Frances. 2001. *Dark Continent of Our Bodies: Black Feminism and the Politics of Respectability*. Philadelphia: Temple University Press.

Whyte, William Foote. 1961. *Street Corner Society: The Structure of an Italian Slum*. Chicago: University of Chicago Press.

Williams, Patricia. 1998. "On Being the Object of Property." *Signs* 14 (1): 5–24.

Williams, L. Susan. 2002. "Trying on Gender, Gender Regimes and the Process of Becoming Women." *Gender and Society* 16 (1): 29–52.

Wilson, William J. 1987. *The Truly Disadvantaged: The Inner City, the Underclass, and Public Policy*. Chicago: University of Chicago Press.

Wilson, William J. 1996. *When Work Disappears: The World of New Urban Poor*. New York: Random House.

Wolcott, Victoria. 2001. *Remaking Respectability: African American Women in Interwar Detroit*. Chapel Hill: University of North Carolina Press.

Young, Alford A., Jr. 2004. *The Minds of Marginalized Black Men: Making Sense of Mobility, Opportunity, and Future Life Chances*. Princeton, NJ: Princeton University Press.

Young, Kevin. 2012. *The Grey Album: On the Blackness of Blackness*. Minneapolis: Greywolf Press.

Index

Black girls/women (*continued*)
245n10; narratives of, generally, 8;
organizations supporting, 243–44n3;
other mothers, 254n9; overeating
among, 206–7; politics of the body
established by, 27; research on, ix,
8, 243–44n3; resilience/strength
attributed to, 193–94; respectability
of, 43–44; self-care by, 206, 261n11;
sexual abuse of, 71–73, 86, 137, 169,
250–51n16, 257n8, 259n8; shapeshifting by, 25–26; teen mothers, 252n5;
in urban ethnography, 14–20; use of
term, 243n1. *See also* race
BlackLight, 37, 192, 195, 221–24, 229,
231–33, 237–39, 241, 244n3. *See also*
Move Experiment
Black matriarch, emasculating, 41, 63
Black Metropolis (Drake and Cayton),
14–17
blackout (Northeast U.S., 2003), 3–4
Black politics, 9, 232–33
Blacks: "difficult personalities" of, 113;
employment of, 249n6; middle- vs.
lower-class, 247n19; pathologization
of families, 41, 63; positive representations of, 255–56n19
Black Women's Health Imperative,
250n16
Black Women's Lament, 63
blaxploitation, 228
bleach baths, 188–89, 194–95
blues music, 46–47, 51–52, 67–68, 249n5
The Bluest Eye (Morrison), 246n17
body: ownership of, 68, 250n13; politics
of, 27; renovations of, 90–91, 143–44,
185; shape of, 89–90, 143–44, 206,
253n6, 261n12
Bolles, A. Lynn, 26
Bourgois, Philippe, 32
Bronzeville (Chicago), 14
Brown, Bessie (*pseudonym*), 46–52;
and artistic self-making, 66–68;
as caretaker/provider, 48–50, 68;
deindustrialization's impact on, 41;
on education, 58–59; employment
by, 48, 50, 72; home of, 44–46, 53;
on love, 78; men in her life, 49–51;

66–67; migration to Detroit, 35,
40–41, 250n14; on musicians in the
family, 47; rebellion's (1967) impact
on, 48–49, 61; on relying on men, 59;
on welfare, 50, 70
Brown, Johnny (*pseudonym*), 46
Brown, Ruth Nicole, 143, 243–44n3,
245n9
Brown Bean café, 156–57, 159–63, 259n4
Brown family (*pseudonym*), 38–60;
caregiving by/care for, 68–71, 76–78;
citizenship of, 41–42, 62–64, 68;
first college graduate from, 241–42;
generations of, 40–41, 55–56; home
life of, 45–46, 66, 71–72, 124; men in
the household, 72–73, 76–77; migration from the South, 44, 47–48, 61;
mothers and aunties, 52–55; outreach
staff's view of, 123–24; overview of,
35–36. *See also* Anita; Bip; Crystal;
Donna; Gina; Gwen; Janice; JoJo;
Karlyn; Mary; Phillip; Ruby; Samuel;
Simon
Brown Twins (*pseudonym*), 47, 49,
51–52, 66–67, 72
bullying, 13
Burger King, 102, 247n19
Butler, Judith, 182, 259n13
Butler, Octavia, 229–31; *Parable of the
Sower*, 232–33

Cage, Luke (fictional character),
227–28
Camille (*pseudonym*): corporate back-
ground/leadership style of, 87, 92,
94–95, 253–54nn7–8; as GGC interim
director, 36, 87–90, 251n3, 253n6;
relationship with staff/residents, 92,
119–21; role in Move Experiment,
191; role in renovating the shelter, 93
can-do/at-risk girls, 13–14, 16–17, 23–24,
246n14
Carby, Hazel, 25
care deficit, 249n7
Care project, 24
Caron, Caroline, 13
Carter, Prudence, 74–75
Case, Mary Anne, 7, 245n8

Lazarus, Emma, 256n1
Leary, John, 62–63
Lefebvre, Henri, 232–33
lesbians' experiences/relationships, 166–67, 184
libertarianism, 71
Liebow, Elliot, 18
Lindsey, Treva B., 162
literacy, 103–4
Little Sally Walker (game), 143
Lopez sisters (*pseudonym*), 196
Love, Heather, 158
loving as self-defining, 78
low theory, 249n1
Lucal, Betsy, 181–82
Lynnette (*pseudonym*), 161, 210–11, 239–41, 258n3; and Camille, 119–20; home of, 96; Inner Circle developed by, 114–16; on Janice, 239–41; in Move Experiment show, 210–11; as an RA, 94–98, 105, 156–57; social entrepreneurship of, 240

Madison, D. Soyini, 31–32
Marback, Richard, 247–48n20
Martha (*pseudonym*), 89–90, 92
Martin, Trayvon, 244–45n6
martyrdom, 232
Mary (*pseudonym*), 47–48, 50, 70
masculinity, performance of (gender display), 171–77, 181–83
McBride, Renisha, 244–45n6
McDonald's, 102, 247n19
McKittrick, Katherine, 26, 62, 233, 248–49n29
"mean girl" culture, 13
meditation workshops, 201–2, 232
Me Generation, 11
meritocracy, 16–17, 56–57
Miller, Frank, 228–30; *Sin City*, 262n15
minority students, research on, 74–75
Miriam (*pseudonym*), 82–83, 105, 119
missing the middle, 9–10, 245n10
Mitchell, Katharyne, 69
Monica (*pseudonym*), 126, 130–32, 134
Monroe High School (Detroit), 56–60, 74, 76
Morris, Rosalind, 182

Morrison, Toni: *The Bluest Eye*, 246n17
motherhood, 63–65, 68–70
motivations as informing acts, 76
Move Experiment, 191–232, 244n3, 245n9; components/goals of, 196, 199, 231–32, 261n9; establishment of, 191; funding for, 191–92, 195, 219, 223, 260n6; health problems addressed by, 206–7; movement techniques used in, 195, 260n4; overview of, 24, 37; peer educators for, 191–92, 195–205, 260n6, 261n9; self-love as a goal of, 231–32; and shelter goals, 205–6; the show, 210–19, 261–62n13. *See also* BlackLight
Moynihan, Daniel Patrick: *The Negro Family*, 17, 41, 63
Mullings, Leith, 26
music videos, 158, 200, 260–61n8
My Brother's Keeper initiative, 7, 245n7
Myerhoff, Barbara, 142

narratives, 122–51; on the Browns' porch, 122; camping story, 123–26, 135–36; dude ranch (Swoop's) story, 127–36, 141, 256nn4–5; oral history/storytelling tradition, 127, 136; overview of, 126–27, 147–48; for political mobilization, 147–48; of redemption/exception, 144–51; of the schoolgirl rapes, 136–37, 141–42, 257n8; of the shelter protest, 137–44
Nash, Jennifer, 232
The Negro Family (Moynihan), 17, 41, 63
neoliberalism, 70, 104, 251–52n3, 254n8
New York Times, 245n8
Nikki (*pseudonym*), 125–33
Noni (*pseudonym*), 220–21, 223–24, 239, 241

Obama, Barack, 5–7, 245n7
open heart chakra, 115–16
Outdoor Adventure Team, 124
outside vs. inside, 126, 256n3
overeating, 206–7

Pam (*pseudonym*), 124–25
Parable of the Sower (O. Butler), 232–33

Sharita (*pseudonym*), 32, 144–49
shelters. *See* Fresh Start Homeless Shelter
Sierra Club, 256n2
Simon (*pseudonym*), 47, 49, 66–67
Sin City (Miller), 262n15
Skelton, Tracey, 11–12
skin color and beauty, 260n7
Smart, Elizabeth, 192
Smith, Bessie, 67
social entrepreneurship, 240
Sojourner Truth projects (Detroit), 64–65
Sonya (*pseudonym*), 195–96, 198, 200–201, 203, 219, 261n9; in Move Experiment show, 210, 213–14, 216, 218, 261n13
Soo Ah Kwon, 239
soundscapes of power, 32–33
Stack, Carol, 18–19
stigma, 257–58n11
street behaviors, 113, 255n17
street outreach workers, 24
strip clubs, 258–59n4
"struggliness" concept, 55–60, 67, 73–74
student protest (Detroit, 1999), 136–37, 141–42, 257n8
Sugrue, Thomas, 250n10
Summer (*pseudonym*), 171–74, 182, 233–34

Temporary Assistance to Needy Families (TANF), 103, 255n12
Terri (*pseudonym*), 83–84, 87, 92–94, 105–8, 120, 144
theoretical knowledge, 249n1
Tina (*pseudonym*), 122–23, 125–26, 129–31, 133–35
Trautner, Mary, 258–59n4
triflin', meaning of, 160, 258n2
Turman, Aisha, 244n3

urban ethnography: Black girls' absence from, 14–20; on Black men as oppositional actors, 17–18; on culture's role in reshaping city spaces, 26; normative markers of success/respectability in, 16; observing participants in, 31–35
Urban League, 247n19

Valentine, Gill, 11–12
Van Dam, Danielle, 192
Violence against Women Act, 250–51n16

Wafer, Theodore, 245n6
Walker, Alice, 232; *The Color Purple*, 246n17
Wanzo, Rebecca, 147, 232–33, 255–56n19
Washington, Martha (fictional character), 228–30
Wayne State University, 100, 220, 226, 241
welfare, 50, 70, 103, 162, 252n5
West, Candace, 259n14
White Castle, 247n19
Williams, L. Susan, 259n14
Wolcott, Victoria, 250n12
women of color feminism, 19–20, 26
Works Progress Administration (WPA), 16

Yolanda (*pseudonym*), 188–89, 195
Young, Alford, 74–75
Young, Coleman, 60, 248n24
Young, Kevin, 127, 223
youth culture, vii–viii, 6–7, 11–14, 244–45n6

Zimmerman, Don, 259n14
Zimmerman, George, 244–45n6